Truth,
Love &
Clean
Cutlery

Truth, Love & Clean Cutlery

A guide to the truly good restaurants and food experiences of the

United Kingdom

———

Edited by

Giles Coren

Associate Editor Jules Mercer

Blackwell&Ruth.

Of all the qualities that distinguish a truly outstanding restaurant or food experience, perhaps truth, love and care are the most important. A passion for creating food that is so good that it will never be forgotten, an environment that makes that extraordinary food taste even better, and a care for the ground or water from which that food is derived and the community in which it is served.

Restaurants that care about these things aren't just good, they are exemplary. **Truth, Love & Clean Cutlery** was conceived to identify and shine a light on these inspiring exemplars so that the rest of us can find, support and enjoy them.

Geoff Blackwell and Ruth Hobday
Publishers

A note on navigation

We have tried to make this guide as simple
as possible to navigate. With this in mind,
the restaurants are listed first by country,
followed by region. Within each region, the
restaurants are listed first by major city, then
alphabetically by county, town or village.
We hope this enables readers to easily find
the wonderful restaurants near them, so that
they can celebrate sustainable, ethical, and
simply good food.

Contents

Introduction

Giles Coren

Editor

I remember it like it was yesterday, though a flick through my back catalogue online indicates that it happened in the summer of 2004. A beautiful old pub restaurant in Highgate had reopened under new ownership and people were raving about the food: the shellfish, the homemade pies, the wonderful desserts, but, most of all, the fish cakes.

Fish cakes. Soooo 2004. These were very fish-dense, people said. Lovely pink salmon, not too much potato, a little grated onion, nice and crisp, with excellent fries and a fresh green salad, sharply dressed. And it was only a couple of miles from my home. So off I went for lunch.

It was a lovely day, the pub garden was in fine fettle and the views over London pure poetry. I had a cool pint of whatever people drank before the hipster pale ale revolution (I truly can't remember) and my wife was tucking into a lemony New Zealand sauvignon.

"I'll have the fishcakes, please", I said to the eager young waiter. Recalling a recent conversation with an angler friend about the disastrous effects of salmon-farming off the coast of Scotland, I added: "Do you know where the salmon comes from?"

"The sea?" he replied.

"Yes", I laughed. "I imagine it does. But you get wild salmon and farmed salmon. Obviously this won't be wild, but I'm wondering where it is farmed and whether organically or non-organically. You do get levels of sustainability with fish farming and it does matter".

"I'll ask the chef", he said. And while he was gone I thought how impressive it would have been if he had known something about the provenance of the food he was serving – but that he was young, and probably new to the business, and running off to ask the chef was the next best thing. A minute or two later he returned, looking sheepish.

"The chef", he began shyly, "says, 'Who gives a f***?'"

"I beg your pardon", I said. Sniggering a little. Not really believing what I was hearing.

"I'm sorry", he said. "But that's what he said. He said, 'Who gives a f***?'"

And that was the moment my whole professional life changed. After ten years as a restaurant critic – for *Tatler* magazine, *The Independent on Sunday*, and, since 2002, *The Times* – I suddenly saw that the job of a restaurant critic in the twenty-first century was not to swagger into fancy joints and peer at dishes through one's monocle, show off how much one knew about classical French cuisine, and pick holes in the chef's technique before awarding a mark out of ten and swaggering out again. It was to hold these places to account for the way they treat not just their customers, but their meat and fish and the animals who provide them, their fruit and vegetables and the soil and water that grows them, the staff who work for them, and the community in which they ply their trade.

Passing the open kitchen later (for I stayed to eat my meal), I glanced in and saw the chef who didn't give a f*** tasting a sauce with a spoon, licking it clean and then sticking it in another sauce. Now, I knew this was a common (if regrettable) practice in UK restaurants, but to see this guy doing it was different. This guy didn't give a f*** about his fish, the sea, the seabed, sea lice, disease, germs, his customers, decent kitchen etiquette… what the hell did he give a f*** about?

So I gave his restaurant zero out of ten. It was the first time I had ever done that, and I think also the last. And a few months later, the pub closed. Not because of me, I should add. I take no pride in closing a business and would never set out to do so. It closed because he didn't care about anything. And I hope he learned his lesson.

After this experience I added an element to my already torturous scoring system in *The Times* that openly gave points for meat and fish provenance (making it as important as 'cooking', 'service', and 'atmosphere'). I asked rudimentary questions to arrive at my score. At first, I got a lot of "Er, it comes from the butcher", but gradually things began to change. People were proud to write 'organic', 'local', and 'seasonal' on their menus, and then to name the breeds, the farms, the farmers, the fishermen, and the hunters. Eventually also the foragers.

Suddenly information became the currency of restaurants, not just food and drink. Sometimes too much information, some thought. And indeed, it did occasionally go too far: I have more than once been told the name of the pig whose cured leg I am nibbling with my ice-cold Manzanilla En Rama – and I'm not sure even I want that.

But things have changed, and very much for the better. Restaurants have responded to the crisis facing our planet with a speed and agility of which the industry can be proud. In 2005, for example, I began penalising restaurants that offered bottled water before tap, and it is now almost unthinkable for free tap water (often filtered) not to be offered as soon as one sits down.

And so now the time has come for *Truth, Love & Clean Cutlery*, a new kind of restaurant guide for a new kind of restaurant world. In the year that Blue Planet II brought home the oceanic catastrophe wrought by single-use plastic and all but killed off the disposable drinking straw in a single evening, it is just not tenable to buy food and drink anywhere now without an assurance that every possible effort has been made to – in the words of the Hippocratic Oath – "do no harm".

Our first principle of selection for the guide was, of course, delicious food. No one crosses town for dinner because the restaurant recycles its grey water to feed the tomatoes on its roof, or makes its furniture from old plastic bottles, or teaches local kids to cook, or gives half its profits to a refuge for baby dolphins. We go for the crispy, gooey pizza, charred slightly at the edges and blobbed with *nduja* and sage, or the banana caramel ice cream with rum sauce (I made that up, but doesn't it sound good?), or just to get drunk and laugh, and maybe hook up. But, with that assured, don't we want to know that what they are doing in this place is 'good'?

So that is what we have made sure of for you. The selection here is not exhaustive or definitive. It is a first attempt for what is a first edition. My associate editor, Jules Mercer, and I have trawled the newspaper and magazine food pages, the critics and the recipe writers, the websites, the bloggers, the lists of award-winners, the guides, the bookshelves, and our own memories for places that are doing the right thing. And we have invited them to complete a survey about their practice in areas such as sourcing, recycling, energy use, employment, community … all that stuff. Where possible, we have double-checked their responses. We have visited most, but not all, of them ourselves. Some of the time, we have had to take their word. And if their word is not good, well, they won't be here next year.

We have had invaluable help in all this from our friends at the Sustainable Restaurant Association – both in compiling our list of restaurants and in arriving at our guidelines for inclusion – and we have arrived at what we think is a great starting point. There will be places missing and you will tell us, and they will tell us, and next year they may join our list. And there will be, I am sure, places that in the end are not as great as we thought they were. And they will have to go.

This is just a restaurant guide; not a manifesto for saving the world. It is a small start on a big deal. We all know that restaurants are a luxury. They are not a matter of life and death. If we fancy a meal out and can afford one, we go and have one. We keep that restaurant alive with our hunger and our money, and it is not unreasonable for us to expect something special from them.

By the same token, the restaurant business is a nice business to be in. It is hard work, but it beats going to the office. If you get things right, pay the right rent, employ the right people on the right terms, and find the right suppliers, there are good margins and a decent living to be made. So it is important to care about the world your restaurant serves, the people who work in it and live close to it, and the animals and plants and land and water and air that make it possible.

The restaurants you will find in *Truth, Love & Clean Cutlery* are the ones that do that. They are the ones, in short, that give a f***.

"Every place we list serves delicious food. That's a given. After that, our guiding principle has been the care taken by the people who run the restaurant. Care in sourcing the food and how it is produced; care in dealing with its staff, customers and community; and care for the environment, in terms of energy, waste, and water."

Jill Dupleix

Jill Dupleix

Truth, Love & Clean Cutlery is a new, kinder, dining guide designed to identify the restaurants and food experiences that go above and beyond great food and wine in the ethical and sustainable ways with which they run their business.

For the past decade, chefs and restaurateurs have been shifting their priorities to support sustainable and ethical practises by farmers, producers and wine-makers, placing a greater value on health, community, conscience and care. They are working harder than ever to cook with seasonal, locally sourced produce, reduce their carbon emissions and minimize their waste.

At the same time, more diners want their money to go to good restaurants with good food run by good people. This guide aims to bring everyone together at the table.

Every place we list serves delicious food. That's a given. After that, our guiding principle has been the care taken by the people who run the restaurant. Care in sourcing the food and how it is produced; care in dealing with its staff, customers and community, and care for the environment, in terms of energy, waste and water.

Establishing a clear criteria and rigorous auditing process hasn't been easy – and will never be flawless – but ultimately it comes down to everyone being open, transparent and respectful. Our editorial team is made up of some of the most experienced and talented food writers in the world. To assist them in their roles of identifying those restaurants most worthy of inclusion, each restaurant answers a rigorous survey – a self-audit if you will – citing examples of the sustainable practices and ethical principles that inform how they run their business.

This combination of experience, research and 'gut feel', validated by information from the restaurants themselves, can best be described as eighty per cent due diligence and twenty per cent leap of faith. It's a decision we have made to trust the process and trust the people.

We want to know if their seafood is sustainable, their waste minimized and their staff nurtured. We cover things like energy usage, community and collaboration, seasonality of ingredients, and respect for the local region and its people. We put a value on things like accepting imperfections in produce and in people,

"At last, the deeply
held beliefs of both
diners and chefs are
beginning to align
and reconnect."

producing one's own food, optimizing energy efficiency to reduce
carbon emissions, reducing chemical usage, encouraging a happy
and diverse workplace, working creatively to use what's readily
and immediately available, menus that provide alternatives to
meat, and owners who consider the health and well-being of their
diners. Being nice, tick. Being fair, also. Not being a bully, definitely.
It's basically 'best practice' for restaurants, encouraging change
towards a more ethical, sustainable food – and dining – system.

We want to eat where we can tick as many of these boxes as
possible: where the food is seasonal, which supports local farmers
and reduces waste; where there are healthy alternatives to red
meat, deep-fried stuff, and mayonnaise; where the fish and seafood
are as sustainable as possible.

We are deeply respectful of how hard it is to run a profitable and
sustainable business in the highly competitive world of hospitality,
and we are in awe of everyone who uses their business as a force
for good. That's why we want the world to know about them.

Truth, Love & Clean Cutlery is, we hope, a step in the
right direction, helping diners choose a place to eat based on
something beyond good food and wine. By choosing restaurants
that have a clear mission to improve their sourcing, seasonality
and sustainability, diners are endorsing ethical behaviour. By
encouraging diners to spend their money on people who are trying
to have a positive impact on the planet.

We value good food and good friends. We value time over
money, community over celebrity, and empathy over ego. We value
the seasons and the rhythm of nature, and people who work with
them rather than against them. And we value being able to dine
together and to work together to shape the world we live in.

The restaurants you will find in *Truth, Love & Clean Cutlery*
are ones we believe in; great places that are trying to do the right
thing; where the act of dining is joyful, and the enjoyment of good
food is amplified and intensified by the obvious care taken from
paddock to plate.

We live in a changing world, where our choices now dictate the
future. At last, the deeply held beliefs of both diners and chefs are
beginning to align and reconnect.

"These restaurants aren't just good … they're **good**."

21

England

Greater London

The 10 Cases

London

What
A simple bistro with a heavy focus on wine

Who
Ian Campbell & Will Palmer, owners

When
Lunch & dinner,
Monday to Saturday

Address
16–18 Endell Street, London, WC2H 9BD

+44 (0)20 7836 6801

10cases.co.uk

Bookings
opentable.com

Price guide

What they say
"We are all about serving wine that has soul and that respects the land it comes from, with selective seasonal tapas dishes to match. Our menu changes monthly to reflect availability and seasonality, so dishes change quite often. Our fish is responsibly sourced and we try to use less obvious or popular fish, such as dab, gurnard, etc. (same goes for meat – we use less popular cuts to showcase nose to tail).

"The core ethos of fine wine and food at great value in a fun, friendly, and dynamic space with knowledgeable and enthusiastic staff is what continues to drive the bistro."

Signature dishes
Green gazpacho; charred asparagus with UK-sourced goat's curd; and ox tongue and cress salad with horseradish.

What we say
Small producers are key when it comes to wine at The 10 Cases. They don't offer a completely "natural" list but most of the wines they list are from producers who understand that healthy vineyards are not ones that are repeatedly sprayed with chemicals to promote growth – they are ones in which wildlife is encouraged, something that comes at a financial cost but creates a sustainable environment and protects the ecosystem.

---

108 Garage

London

What
Critically acclaimed, award-winning gastronomic restaurant

Who
Luca Longobardi & Chris Denney, co-owners

When
Lunch & dinner,
Tuesday to Saturday

Address
108 Golborne Road, London, W10 5PS

+44 (0)20 8969 3769

108garage.com

Bookings
Phone, website, or email
bookings@108garage.com

Price guide

What they say
"The obvious go-to answer for us, when it comes to our greatest passion, would be 'produce'. And don't get us wrong, it's a close second, but in all honesty it's really our team. Mentoring, educating, research, and development sessions – we are a close team and all work together inside and outside the kitchen. As for produce, we are very passionate about using the best produce possible and then executing and delivering dishes without changing ingredients too much."

Signature dishes
Hogget with tongue, caper, and onion; salt-baked celeriac with sheep's yoghurt, apple and horseradish; and beef heart agnolotti with kombu dashi and pink onion.

What others say
"A delightfully blurry, multi-blended concoction of modernity and classicism."

London Eater

What we say
Chris Denney has worked for many of the best and most innovative chefs in London – Phil Howard, Éric Chavot, Nuno Mendes – and he has been paying attention, not just checking names for his CV. His cooking is tightly controlled, clear, original, and incredibly ballsy. It is at the cutting edge of produce-driven cookery – every leaf, seed, and animal part appears at the very top of its form – without being fanciful half-foraged hipster rubbish of the kind that so often passes for hip in this town. Located in what used to be a garage, this restaurant just happens to be serving some of the best food in West London. Which is exactly what it is.

A Wong

London

What
An innovative take on traditional Chinese cuisine showcasing the diversity of China's food culture

Who
Andrew Wong, chef/owner

When
Dinner Monday, lunch & dinner, Tuesday to Saturday

Address
70 Wilton Road,
London, SW1V 1DE

+44 (0)20 7828 8931

awong.co.uk

Bookings
Phone or website

Price guide

What they say
"I want to make people happy and make sure everyone in my restaurant is having a good time. On top of that, if I can get people to try new things and perhaps look at Chinese cuisine differently, I consider that a success. Chinese food is naturally low in waste and is known for utilizing all parts of the produce, for instance chicken feet or blood. We use a lot of dried ingredients, too, as well as pickles and ferments so next to nothing gets thrown away."

Signature dishes
Shanghai steamed dumpling; egg custard bun; and soy chicken.

What we say
The first truly modern British Chinese restaurant, this place sources top-quality sustainable produce from local and British suppliers – almost unheard of in the genre. A Wong makes provenance a high priority with a strong understanding of sustainability in seafood and informs customers of this on menus. Most importantly, this is a secret favourite of the best restaurant critics and is where they go on their own money.

Andina

London

What
An award-winning restaurant serving fresh, colourful food inspired by the Peruvian Andes

Who
Martin Morales, owner

When
Breakfast, lunch & dinner, daily

Address
1 Redchurch Street, London, E2 7DJ

+44 (0)20 7920 6499

andinarestaurants.com

Bookings
Website

Price guide

What they say
"We're open from breakfast through to dinner. Drop by for a quick healthy bite to eat, a perfect Peruvian coffee, a nutritious smoothie, a heavenly pisco cocktail, or a mouthwatering meal. Our menu pairs the best British ingredients with an authentic touch of contemporary Peruvian creativity. We've been inspired by Picanterias – family-run restaurants in the Peruvian Andes. These have resisted the lure of too much modernisation; they remain hubs of culture and tradition, which spills over into their unique cooking. It's this cuisine that we celebrate at Andina."

Signature dishes
Corn tamale with seabass ceviche and pork shambar; and tacu tacu Quechu.

What others say
"Andina is hands down the best Peruvian breakfast we've tasted in London."

Refinery29

What we say
Andina is one of the most exciting restaurants to have opened in London in this decade. It comes on like a sexy hipster all-night bar, with storming music, full of people, great vibes, awesome cocktails... and then you start to eat and suddenly you are riding the crest of the great Peruvian food wave now washing deliciously over the city. The flavours are crisp, the colours are bright, the presentation is playful. And we LOVE how are they are doing such authentic Peruvian stuff with almost exclusively British ingredients. Martin Morales, you are the king!

Anglo

London

What
A modern British dining room, with an emphasis on simple, refined dishes

Who
Mark Jarvis, owner

When
Dinner Monday, lunch & dinner, Tuesday to Saturday

Address
30 St Cross Street, London, EC1N 8UH

+44 (0)20 7430 1503

anglorestaurant.com

Bookings
Website

Price guide

What they say
"We work with farmers and suppliers that we have known for years, who work in the right way using sustainable sources and treat their cattle with the utmost respect. We use vegetables that are the best seasonally possible, which does mean our menu moves around a lot, but it's the way we like to work."

Signature dishes
One-and-two-day aged sourdough with yeasted butter and smoked oil; hand-dived scallops with white asparagus and Parmesan; and Cornish line-caught pollack with broccoli Jersey Royal tartare.

What others say
"This is Noma if Noma was born and raised in Norwich."

–Grace Dent, *London Evening Standard*

What we say
In a warren of moody Farringdon back streets, a spare and hard-surfaced, linenless but nicely lit space, with a small kitchen visible at the back, four or five men in whites in there, moving sparely around, sending out, or bringing out (in the modern Nordic manner) dishes of rare refinement: small portions of perfect protein attended by vegetables in the best imaginable condition. Clearly thought-out menus; directional, ambitious but without pretension. Seven courses rendered a pleasure rather than a chore. The wine pairings are perfect but unshowy, and anyone who can bring down the house with a dish as folksy as cheese and onion on malt loaf, as Jarvis does (it is a thing of sublime originality, savour, and wit), deserves all the accolades that are heaped upon him.

The Barbary

London

What
Food from countries from the Atlantic Coast through to the Mediterranean Sea leading to Israel

Who
Zoë & Layo Paskin, founders

When
Lunch & dinner, daily

Address
16 Neal's Yard, London, WC2H 9DP

thebarbary.co.uk

Bookings
Website

Price guide

What they say
"We aim to create places that we would like to go. We strive to make both the staff and the customers feel special, a place that is relaxed, comfortable, and welcoming but with very careful attention to detail. It is the confluence of the design, the feel of the place, of course all we serve, and to do this time and again to the highest standard. Seeing people within the teams grow, diners from babies to great grandmothers from every corner of the globe. Our suppliers are aware that using local and seasonal ingredients is very important to us, and so they keep us in the loop about when certain ingredients are at their best so that we can make informed decisions about what to include in our menu. These small restaurants are a wonderful whirl of life."

Signature dishes
Naan e barbari; Jerusalem bagel; and *msabacha* chickpeas.

What others say
"Seductive kitchen wizardry."

–Grace Dent, *London Evening Standard*

What we say
We actually queued for this place. We do not often do that. But we'd had such good times at their first restaurant, Palomar, that we wanted to see if they could nail it again. And they did. Wonderful atmosphere at the eating bar, terrific smells, beautiful service, some of the best bread you will ever eat, and some wonderful stuff to slather all over it. The group does wonderful things for charity and of course supports #CookForSYRIA.

Bean & Wheat

London

What
Bean & Wheat is a zero waste café & bottle shop using locally sourced, artisanal ingredients

Who
Adam Handling, chef/owner

When
Dinner Monday to Friday

Address
45–47 Hoxton Square, London, N1 6PD

beanandwheat.co.uk

Bookings
No bookings taken

Price guide

What they say
"Food wastage is an issue that's increasingly important in our industry, and one that's particularly close to my heart. Restaurants tend to waste so much food on a day-to-day basis, and we are trying to tackle this – in the next few years we hope to reach zero waste status."

Signature dishes
Kilner jars of sweet and savoury fillings; seasonal, off-cut salads; and "Black and White" juice.

What we say
Adam opened Bean & Wheat to provide delicious and innovative food-to-go while also helping to create a zero waste cycle for his restaurant group. The menu at Bean & Wheat changes daily, to support the zero waste approach, as the café makes use of daily off-cuts and by-products from Adam's two London restaurants.

Better Health Bakery

London

What
A social enterprise producing sourdough, supporting well-being & recovery from mental ill-health

Who
The Centre for Better Health

When
Breakfast & lunch, Tuesday to Sunday

Address
13 Stean Street, London, E8 4ED

+44 (0)20 3479 7006

betterhealthbakery.org.uk

Bookings
No bookings taken

Price guide

What they say
"The aim of Better Health Bakery is to support individuals distanced from the employment market through mental ill-health, and the bakery provides an activity that is therapeutic and supportive in nature. All the things that might have been lost through ill-health and which need to be regained before an individual might be able to return to employment. Baking and bread are the interesting and therapeutic mechanism to facilitate this. Our sourdough is central to what we do. It is made in the traditional way by using only natural sourdough starter and takes time to develop flavour and character. The activity of working around a table, shaping and scaling dough, represents the teamwork involved in what we do, the normalization of the experience, the individuals, and their contribution to the production of a delicious product. Our sourdough loaf represents all of this, and the determination, effort, and patience of many hands."

Signature dishes
Sourdough bread; freshly baked pastries; and sourdough pizza.

What we say
Man cannot live by bread alone. To use it as a way to preserve the mental health of one's fellow humans is the very essence of Truth and Love. The way Better Health Bakery distribute their surplus loaves to the needy is reminiscent of the Feeding of the 5,000. And they really do give people their daily bread. Sorry for getting all New Testament, but this kind of thing makes us come over all religious.

Bistrotheque

London

What
Restaurant, bar & private dining room

Who
Pablo Flack & David Waddington, founders

When
Dinner, daily, weekend brunch

Address
23–27 Wadeson Street, London, E2 9DR

+44 (0)20 8983 7900

bistrotheque.com

Bookings
Website

Price guide

What they say
"We offer good food and drink using common sense and good taste, delivering it with charm and precision. Much of our menu is seasonal and evolving but it's also anchored by a few familiar classics, which we've been serving since day one. We aim to work mainly with suppliers of sustainable products, such as Martin Denny (forager and unfarmed produce), James Knight, and Henderson Seafood."

Signature dishes
Steak tartare with asparagus, *ajo blanco* and almonds; and strawberries and rice custard, made from rice slow-cooked in soy milk.

What we say
"Ho ho ho, Bethnal Green!" people thought when Bistrotheque opened in the heart of old cockles-and-jellied-eels East London back in 2004. But they blinked and the world moved to Hackney, and Bethnal Green was the centre of the universe, and Bistrotheque was the centre of Bethnal Green. White-clothed tables in an old warehouse are what people came (and come) for, as well as the French bistro cooking and weekend brunches accompanied by live piano.

Black Axe Mangal

London

What
Concentrates on quality-produce, high-impact, original dishes in a playful environment

Who
Lee Tiernan, chef/owner, & Kate Tiernan, owner

When
Dinner Monday to Saturday, weekend brunch

Address
156 Canonbury Road, London, N1 2UP

blackaxemangal.com

Bookings
opentable.com

Price guide

What they say
"We thrive on creativity, being genuine, and our eclectic, evolving menu. We serve bold, high-impact flavours and strive to be as original as possible. One of our aims is establishing an accessible and alternative environment in which to dine. We feel this helps us celebrate London's multiculturalism and diversity.

"Sourcing-wise, we buy from suppliers that use traditional, low-impact farming methods, which we believe gives us the best possible product. We are continually learning from suppliers and peers about sustainability and ethically sourced produce."

Signature dishes
Squid ink flatbread and smoked cod's roe (signature smoked potato flatbread with whipped smoked cod's roe, egg yolk, and seaweed powder and glitter); foie gras and cherry doughnut (poached foie gras, morello cherry jelly, salted trifle almonds in a brûléed cinnamon doughnut); and grilled hispi cabbage and katsuobushi butter (cabbage with butter blended with fermented shrimp paste and katsuobushi, served with deep-fried baby shrimp and katsuobushi flakes).

What others say
"Quietly, [Tiernan] is creating something astonishing."

–Tim Hayward, *Financial Times*

What we say
Black Axe Mangal first came to our attention as the best kebab shop in the world, serving perfectly constructed, postmodern kebabs to a belting death metal soundtrack hard by the Arsenal stadium. They have changed the offering now, branching out, playing with other kinds of food. But with the brilliant Lee Tiernan in the small open kitchen and Kate Tiernan running the floor it remains as unique and exciting as ever.

Blanchette

London

What

Parisian-style bistro with trompe l'œil murals, serving French sharing plates with a modern twist

Who

Alary Brothers & Tam Storrar, chefs/directors

When

Lunch & dinner, daily

Address

9 D'Arblay Street, London, W1F 8DR

+44 (0)20 7439 8100

blanchettelondon.co.uk

Bookings

Phone or email

info@blanchettesoho.co.uk

Price guide

What they say

"We love to make tasty dishes that people want to eat again and again. We're also passionate about keeping it sustainable and work with Vertical Future, who deliver their brilliant produce by electric bike – delicious, organic micro herbs grown in London. As part of our community, at our Brick Lane restaurant we make pancakes for the local primary school for pancake day and prepare sandwiches for the homeless."

Signature dishes

Braised lamb shoulder with anchovy, rosemary, and soubise sauce; confit duck leg with swede, chestnuts, and truffle butter; and passion fruit Vacherin.

What others say

"Blanchette in Soho knows exactly what it's doing."

–Jay Rayner, *The Guardian*

What we say

Blanchette pulls off the wonderful trick of being incredibly French and incredibly "new Soho". You sit up at the bar on an architectural stool, looking at tiled scenes of rural Southern France while sexy young kids with big hair and fashion spectacles, narrow black jeans and vintage Nikes, play edgy tunes and flick you a menu of cheeses and charcuterie followed by a tight little set of dishes for sharing. There are frogs' legs and *chou farci* but different, modern; and then maybe a sharp-as-hell lemon tart with a gin and parsley sorbet, a couple of tuile biscuits, and a perfect espresso. Just dreamy.

Bobo Social

What
Restaurant & cocktail bar

Who
Michael Benson, founder

When
Lunch & dinner, Monday
to Saturday

Address
95 Charlotte Street, London,
W1T 4PZ

+44 (0)20 7636 9310

bobosocial.com

Bookings
Website

Price guide

What they say
"Provenance, quality, and consistency of ingredients in a friendly and relaxed dining environment. Seasonal produce is reflected in our small plates menu and we source locally when possible. Cobble Lane, a really great British charcuterie supplier, uses the highest welfare British meats, which we love to support on our menus. Our products are all cut, cured, smoked, and hung by us, at our butchery in Islington, North London."

Signature dishes
Watermelon and heritage tomato salad with crumbled British feta and basil oil; Islington saucisson and Parmesan chunks with British free-range pork; and "The Debauchery Burger" with Wagyu beef and rare-breed beef, Ogleshield cheese, confit shiitake mushrooms, onions, shaved truffle, and a buttermilk bun.

What others say
"There's a lot to love here."

–Grace Dent, *London Evening Standard*

What we say
This place launched in the autumn of 2014 at what we can now see was the moment of "peak burger" and went out of its way to do everything just that little bit better. When we went, we were tickled to find not just "today's beef", which was Dexter, but "today's wood", which was silver birch. Yes. Truly. They were telling us the flavour of the wood they would be burning under our lunch. Although obviously we would have been able to tell that just from the flavour of the char lines on the burger. We jest. We love that they take their work so seriously. So do we.

The Breakfast Club

What
A family caf business serving cracking food & drink offerings

Who
Jonathan Arana-Morton, co-founder

When
Breakfast, lunch & dinner, daily

Address
11 Southwark Street, London, SE1 1RQ, plus other locations – see website

+44 (0)20 7078 9634

thebreakfastclubcafes.com

Bookings
Website

Price guide

What they say
"'Do well by doing good' (wise words once said by Benjamin Franklin) lies at the heart of The Breakfast Club. It's the framework by which we live. It can be broken down into three key areas: good at what we do, good to our people, and good to our world. You can't have one without the other. We're proud to serve bacon butties under giant disco balls with a drag queen dancing at you (good at what we do) but a business can't truly be a success unless it makes a positive impact on its local communities (good to our world). Our people are the reason for our success, they are the ones who interact with our customers and come up with good ideas to help our world and what we do so we need to be good to them. By doing all three we are determining the type of business we are and, by making it a cornerstone of who we are, it will determine the business we will be in the future."

Signature dishes
"Butternut Bubble"; "The All American" (comfort food at its best); and Korean chicken pancakes.

What others say
"This was the twelve inch remix of an English breakfast."

London Review of Breakfasts

What we say
From small beginnings, these lovely people have gone on to change the way thousands of us breakfast. And if you're going to do good things, you need to start the day properly, don't you?

The Breakfast Club (p. 30)

Brawn

London

What
Daily menu of seasonal, produce-driven dishes reflecting a love of cultural European cooking

Who
Ed Wilson, chef

When
Dinner Monday to Saturday, lunch Tuesday to Sunday

Address
49 Columbia Road, London, E2 7RG

+44 (0)20 7729 5692

brawn.co

Bookings
Phone, website, or opentable.com

Price guide

What they say
"We are seriously enthusiastic about the highest quality seasonal produce, with dishes that reflect a love of cultural European cooking alongside a love for wines that reflect the quality of both the produce and the cooking. Working closely with small and trusted local suppliers, who in turn promote the finest quality ethically sourced ingredients, is part of our philosophy. From E5 Bakehouse, Androuet, Ham and Cheese Co, Natoora, Keats Farm, to Kernel Brewery. Welcoming people into Brawn is akin to welcoming them into our home, and we love to share this passion with them."

Signature dishes
Cantabrian anchovies and rosemary oil; raw scallop with Marinda tomato, olives, and Colatura di Alici; and lamb sweetbreads with vignarola.

What we say
There's a cool, bright, pleasantly schoolroomy feel to this corner space at one end of fashionable Columbia road. From the moment we walked in, early in its life at the beginning of 2011, we knew Brawn was going to be serious about its work in ways that we hadn't seen before. Serious about outstanding natural wines matched to densely flavoured European dishes made from produce of impeccable provenance, and messed about with as little as possible, served by staff who know and care about the industry in which they work. Truth and love, guys. Truth and love.

The Bull & Last

London

What
A pub & restaurant in North London

Who
Ollie Pudney & Joe Swiers, owners

When
Lunch & dinner, daily, weekend breakfast

Address
168 Highgate Road, London, NW5 1QS

+44 (0)20 7267 3641

thebullandlast.co.uk

Bookings
Phone, website, or opentable.com

Price guide

What they say
"Now in our tenth year of operation, we run with the same passion as we did on day one. We use the best ingredients we can get our hands on throughout the year and produce a menu that resounds with integrity. The aim is to support almost exclusively small-production farmers, breweries, and winemakers who share our passion for not just delicious produce, but artisanal values and natural processes, too."

Signature dishes
English asparagus with crispy hen's egg, Parmesan custard and sorrel; charcuterie board (duck prosciutto, ham hock terrine, chicken liver parfait, rabbit rillettes, pig's head, pickles, and toast); and Yorkshire Belted Galloway steak with triple-cooked chips, mixed leaf salad and Béarnaise.

What we say
With its position adjacent to Hampstead Heath, its vibrant kitchen under the stewardship of Ollie Pudney – whose way with pies and game is as deft as his touch with salads and delicate spring vegetables – and the smooth-running of staff under the management of the ever-smiling Joe Swiers, it is not surprising so many people in the know call this place "The Best Food Pub in London".

Burro e Salvia

London

What
A traditional artisan *pastificio* and trattoria with a focus on fresh pasta, handmade daily

Who
Gaia Enria, founder/ head pasta maker

When
Lunch, daily, dinner Thursday to Saturday

Address
52 Redchurch Street, London, E2 7DP

+44 (0)20 7739 4429

burroesalvia.co.uk

Bookings
Phone or email
shoreditch@burroesalvia.co.uk

Price guide

What they say
"A *pastificio* is one of the most traditional trades in Italy. Bringing it to life by sharing the stories and recipes with the unique audience of London is energizing. Based on traditional Italian recipes, we source local produce every time if possible. We found beautiful eggs in Cornwall to make the pasta dough. We work with an Italian butcher based in London who only uses British pork breeds to make his sausages. We only use seasonal ingredients, so if pumpkin pasta is one of the most successful dishes, we still only make it for the autumn/winter season when the product is ready."

Signature dishes
Signature pasta: agnolotti Cavour; *strozzapreti* with Sicilian pesto; and tortellini with ricotta.

What others say
"Beautifully cooked fresh pasta really is a thing of beauty. It doesn't need fancy garnishes or sauces, and this is what Burro e Salvia demonstrates so perfectly. I don't think I've had such good pasta outside of Italy before."

–Fiona Barrow, *The Very Hungry Londoner*

What we say
They have run an educational programme of one or two pasta-making workshops per week, passing on the tricks of the trade and delivering a wider message about taking the time to learn new skills and what it means to make your own food rather than buying ready meals. Give a man a bowl of pasta and you feed him for a day, but give him a pasta workshop and...

Cafe Murano

London

What
Northern Italian·restaurants from Angela Hartnett in St James & Covent Garden

Who
Angela Hartnett, chef/owner

When
Lunch & dinner, Monday to Saturday, lunch Sunday

Address
33 St James's Street, London, SW1A 1HD, plus other locations – see website

+44 (0)20 3371 5559

cafemurano.co.uk

Bookings
Phone or website

Price guide

What they say
"Cafe Murano champions quality, integrity, and authenticity. We love to work directly with farmers, fishermen, and growers to source the best produce perfectly in season. By cutting out the middleman, our chefs get to learn firsthand when seasonal produce is ready to put on our menus. A great example is Greg from Forge Farms, who will directly liaise with us every year about when our signature dish of pumpkin tortelli will feature on our menus. The wine list at Cafe Murano focuses on 100 per cent Italian small producers who grow organically and biodynamically. Our restaurants use water filter systems with recyclable bottles rather than purchasing bottled mineral water. We believe in treating our staff, guests, and suppliers with equal respect!"

Signature dishes
Vitello tonnato; orecchiette with broccoli, radicchio, and pine nuts; and mackerel with spring slaw, pickled red onions, and golden raisins.

What others say
"I don't want to review my spinach and ricotta tortelli as much as compose a hymn to it."

–Andy Lynes, *Metro*

What we say
The brilliance, warmth, generosity, and pure fun-loving spirit of Angela Hartnett is woven into the very DNA of these two wonderful cafés. She calls them cafés but the level of attention to detail, the skill in the cooking, the beauty of the presentation, and the professionalism of the staff bespeak far higher things – but without all the tosspottery of fine dining. Cafe Murano is *Truth, Love & Clean Cutlery* to the max!

Cafe Murano (p. 36)

Caravan King's Cross

London

What
Fresh produce & bold flavours: this food is well travelled

Who
Laura Harper-Hinton, Miles Kirby & Chris Ammermann, owners

When
Breakfast, daily, lunch & dinner, Monday to Saturday

Address
1 Granary Square, London, N1C 4AA

+44 (0)20 7101 7661

caravanrestaurants.co.uk

Bookings
Walk-ins or phone

Price guide

What they say
"ENERGY! The great thing about all-day dining establishments is that from morning to night there is a constant flow of energy and positive spirit in the dining rooms. Our spaces are filled with coffee drinkers, paper readers, professionals, meetings, parents, laptop workers, creatives and students, evening diners and cocktail swillers – some stay quite literally all day! All our meat is locally sourced from reputable farms and we are committed to evaluating the impact of our personal and professional carbon shadow. Lowering carbon emissions, reducing food and product waste, offering reusable solutions to our takeout customers. All add to the energy and the buzz, and it's the thing we love the most about what we have created."

Signature dishes
Cornbread with chipotle butter, coriander, spring onions, and lime; kimchi pancake with slow-cooked pork belly and fried duck egg; and chicken and rice.

What we say
There is no getting away from the exuberant Kiwi vibes at Caravan, with its stripped-back dining room and terrace spilling out onto Granary Square with its choreographed fountains and cavorting students. Sharing plates of great dishes from all over the world and small batches of interesting coffee beans roasted daily make for a scene that would have been unimaginable in this once benighted district behind King's Cross station until, well, until Caravan rolled into town.

Caravan Kings Cross (p. 40)

Ceremony

What
A modern vegetarian restaurant with equal focus on food & drink

Who
Ali Dedianko & Joe Stokoe, co-owners

When
Dinner Tuesday to Saturday, lunch & dinner, Sunday

Address
131 Fortess Rd, London, NW5 2HR

+44 (0)20 3302 4242

ceremonyrestaurant.london

Bookings
Website

Price guide

What they say
"Rather than being a vegetarian restaurant, Ceremony is a restaurant that just happens to be vegetarian. We place equal importance on great food and drinks, including an inventive cocktail menu plus thoughtfully curated wine list. While we are certainly passionate about vegetables, we are also passionate about flavour, and treat our produce with the same reverence a chef would meat. Most of our sustainable practices are tied in with our other practices: using veg from our garden, seasonal produce, reducing single-use plastic, composting, and working with local suppliers to reduce our carbon footprint."

Signature dishes
Crispy duck egg with shaved hard cheese, asparagus and truffle; linguine with pesto of wild garlic, rocket, cashew and goat's curd; Eton mess with strawberry meringue, Chantilly cream and lemon balm.

What we say
You would never know this was a vegetarian restaurant if nobody told you. The vibes are so lively, the cocktails so beautiful, the menu so gutsy and wide-ranging, and the dishes so deep and hefty, that it just wouldn't occur to you. Eggs and dairy feature heavily to create backgrounds against which the vegetables can really sing. Ali and Joe come from a booze background – she is the queen of the London beer scene, he is probably the best young cocktail maker in England – and they just went at this place hammer and tongs from the outset. Ceremony is a shining beacon of joy in once-drab Tufnell Park.

Canteen No 4

What
Pop-up dinners that share information on environmental issues through great food & good times

Who
Zoe Reed, founder

When
Dinner, hours change seasonally

Address
Multiple locations – see website

canteenno4.com

Bookings
Website

Price guide

What they say
"Canteen No 4 is all about natural, delicious seasonal produce and skilled artisan producers. We try to create an experience that encourages people living in the city to reconnect with where their food comes from and to empower people with the knowledge and inspiration to build their own food ethos."

Signature dishes
Waste bread and goat's whey butter; croissant scraps *pisladier* (scraps of leftover croissant dough covered in slowly stewed onions and baked in a hot oven, served with fresh thyme and a tonnato sauce made with anchovies and tuna trim); and whole cage barbecued Lyme Bay brill with brown butter and sherry vinegar.

What we say
A philosophical salon rather than a caterer, per se, Canteen No 4 aims to share factual information on environmental issues along the food chain. They do this by hosting themed pop-up dinners on such subjects as food waste and sustainable fishing, exploring each topic while eating food that exemplifies it. They collaborate with emerging and innovative designers, artists, and artisans, shedding light on contentious environmental issues and highlighting ways to deliver change.

Ceviche

What
Blends bustling Lima with the creativity of London through exquisite dishes, drinks & music

Who
Martin Morales, owner

When
Lunch & dinner, daily

Address
17 Frith Street, London, W1D 4RG

+44 (0)20 7292 2040

cevicherestaurants.com

Bookings
Website

Price guide

What they say
"With a focus on Peru's Criollo, Nikkei, Chifa and Afro-Peruvian cuisines, Ceviche Soho kick-started the Peruvian food revolution as the first Peruvian restaurant of its kind in the UK. Bringing together elements of fine dining, casual eating, and street food through our small sharing plates and innovative pisco cocktails, Ceviche Soho was inspired by our founder Chef Martin Morales' childhood in Peru and by the cooking of his great aunts Carmela and Otilia. Ceviche takes its inspiration from the unique flavours of Peru's coast and the hip urban culture of Lima, Peru's capital city."

Signature dishes
Classic and don ceviche; steak *lomo saltado* and chips; and *picarones*.

What we say
One of the eating and drinking bars that kick-started the current Soho food revolution, Ceviche is also responsible for guiding modern British tastes towards this famous Peruvian fish dish and demonstrating how important the finest, freshest ingredients are when all the "cooking" that goes on is a bracing little dunk in citrus juices. But, oh, that heavenly tiger's milk of pungent liquid that you drink down off the saucers when the plate is empty – truly, the literal milk of that ferocious predator could not be more potent or life-affirming. Sitting up at the bar at Ceviche with a pisco sour, watching the world go by, is one of the great pleasures of modern urban life.

by CHLOE.

What
A fast-casual, plant-based restaurant

Who
Samantha Wasser, founder

When
Lunch & dinner, daily, weekend brunch

Address
Drury House, 34–43 Russell Street, London WC2B 5HA, plus other locations – see website

eatbychloe.com

Bookings
No bookings taken

Price guide

What they say
"We owe so much to the support and loyalty of our fans and customers, and love seeing their experiences on social media from NYC to London. One thing that really sets by CHLOE. apart is the accessibility of our food and that everything is made from scratch, from our burger patties to our sauces and nut cheeses. It took us almost two years to finalize our recipes before we even opened our first store! As a plant-based restaurant, we proudly offer a full menu of items that our guests can feel good about eating – ingredients that your body will naturally recognize."

Signature dishes
Guac burger with house-made patty topped with corn salsa, onion, guacamole, tortilla strips, and chipotle aïoli on wholegrain bun; mac 't' cheese with shiitake bacon, almond parm; and fish 't' chips with crispy tofu with chips, mushy peas, and vegan tartare sauce.

What we say
We we were so excited about the arrival of this super-slick New York vegan restaurant in Covent Garden that we rolled along on its opening night to soak up the beautiful hipster crowd, the witty throwback design, and simply the best vegan burger in town and the most authentic-tasting fake fish and chips (made with battered tofu and sweet potato). A fast-food venue that kills nothing and makes everything fresh on site deserves to go nationwide and SOON.

Cinnamon Club

London

What
London's original fine dining modern Indian restaurant

Who
Vivek Singh, owner

When
Breakfast, lunch & dinner, daily

Address
30–32 Great Smith Street, London, SW1P 3BU

+44 (0)20 7222 2555

cinnamonclub.com

Bookings
Phone or website

Price guide

What they say
"Cinnamon Club is devoted to providing sustainable, delicious, modern Indian food in a unique London setting. Amongst the many projects within the restaurant, we've teamed up with Igor Vaintraub from Indie Ecology to promote farming in the food waste that we have generated in the kitchen. We take care with provenance, choosing local ingredients like free-range chicken from Norfolk and MSC-certified fish from Peterhead Market in Scotland. Our menu features many vegan and vegetarian dishes, including our vegetarian tasting menu."

Signature dishes
Smoked Herdwick lamb fillet and *galouti* kebab millefeuille; wild Spencer Gulf king prawns with mango coriander sauce and rice vermicelli; and Balmoral Estate tandoori venison loin with black stone flower reduction and fenugreek potatoes.

What we say
When the great chef Vivek Singh met the visionary PR guru Iqbal Wahhab at a wedding reception in Jaipur towards the end of the last century and hatched a plan for a new business, they changed the way we think of Indian restaurants in this country forever. Cinnamon Club opened in the old Westminster Library, in the shadow of Westminster Abbey, in March 2001 and has been wowing guests with its magnificent architecture, flawless service, and delicate, progressive but intensely flavour-packed Indian cooking ever since. I don't think we had ever seen breeds and farms mentioned in a South Asian restaurant before. I mean, Balmoral Estate tandoori venison? It's pure genius!

Claw

London

What
A casual seafood restaurant

Who
Fabian Clark, owner

When
Lunch & dinner, daily

Address
21 Kingly Street, London, W1B 5QA

+44 (0)20 7287 5742

claw.co.uk

Bookings
Website

Price guide

What they say
"At Claw, we are passionate about serving approachable dishes highlighting sustainable seafood. We take extra special care in our sourcing. Our seafood is almost entirely from UK waters (striving always to use healthy stocks), our oysters hail from Colchester Oyster Fishery, delicious British trout from a family fishery in Hampshire, and, of course, crab from Salcombe. Crab is our main focus, which is naturally incredibly sustainable. We also have a strict no-single-use-plastic policy and continually aim to reduce waste."

Signature dishes
Poke trout; crab mac and cheese; and grilled oysters.

What we say
When Fabian Clark learned that eighty per cent of all Britain's crab gets shipped off to Europe and Asia, he was appalled. But instead of ranting and raving he decided to champion the cause for seafood self-sufficiency – starting with a beast that is in itself already so sustainable. First came a Hackney pub residency, that became a takeaway site in Liverpool Street, and now it's a restaurant on Carnaby Street, the first really exciting thing to happen there since the 1960s.

Whole crabs to crack and devour is the star attraction, naturally, but the crab beignets – bundles of choux pastry made with the brown meat and served with a chunky crab mayonnaise – are becoming legendary. As is the giant crab mac and cheese, made with raclette and a splash of pale ale.

The Clink at HMP Highdown

What
Group of fine dining restaurants in a unique prison setting

Who
The Clink Charity

When
Lunch, Monday to Friday

Address
High Down Lane, Sutton, London, SM2 5PJ

+44 (0)20 8678 9007

theclinkcharity.org

Bookings
Phone or website

Price guide

What they say
"As a training restaurant within a prison, The Clink's aim is to reduce reoffending rates of ex-offenders. We work in partnership with Her Majesty's Prison Service to run fine dining restaurants that train and give practical skills to prisoners to aid their rehabilitation. This allows prisoners to learn, engage with the public, and take their first steps towards a new life. Using locally sourced ingredients including vegetables from HMP Send gardens, we provide a varied menu including vegetarian and vegan options."

Signature dishes
Shallot tarte Tatin with crispy leeks, sprouting spring salad and beetroot purée; pan-fried lamb rump with slow-cooked lamb shoulder croquettes, sweet potato fondant, spring greens, and salsa verde; and rhubarb trifle with elderflower-soaked sponge, stewed rhubarb, custard ice cream, rhubarb jelly, rose-infused cream, and mixed nut crumble.

What we say
Eating at The Clink is a restaurant visit like no other: the razor wire, the holding rooms, the security checks, the frisks and scanners, the surrendering of all electronic equipment including phones (no Instagramming photo merchants here)... and then the food, which is pretty damned good, considering. Charmingly served and cooked by the prisoners themselves, it is well-balanced, prettily presented, and nutritious. And at times, excellent. After good arancini and chicken bourguinon, we were served a pecan nut steamed pudding with crushed caramel and vanilla pod ice cream that was simply unimpeachable. A project to feed the soul as much as the belly.

Clipstone

What
All-day neighbourhood restaurant

Who
Stuart Andrew, head chef

When
Lunch & dinner, Monday to Saturday

Address
5 Clipstone Street, London, W1W 6BB

+44 (0)20 7637 0871

clipstonerestaurant.co.uk

Bookings
Phone, website, or email

Price guide

What they say
"We aim to be everything a modern bistro should be, with a focus on high-quality cooking, wine, and service in an informal setting. Our food is seasonal, imaginative, familiar, and nourishing. Our menu is focused on English produce as much as possible – suppliers such as Flying Fish Seafoods, who fish in the Cornish waters and buy only from dayboats run by responsible fishermen. We ferment, pickle, and make vinegar from produce that might ordinarily go to waste. Historically, a well-run bistro kitchen would waste very little. Zero waste is not a new principle but in fact a very old one, and one that we subscribe to passionately."

Signature dishes
Crudo of sea trout with sorrel, buttermilk, celery, and dulse; grilled green asparagus with hazelnut miso and egg yolk; and fermented mushroom ravioli with wild garlic pistou and Parmesan.

What others say
"This is the most compelling menu I've seen for a long time."

–A. A. Gill, *The Sunday Times*

What we say
There is street corner hustle and bustle at Clipstone – a real urgency from the open kitchen, and dazzling excitement in the slick list of sharing plates. Best of all, serving a lot of wine on tap instead of in bottles reduces emissions, energy, and waste – so we can booze our way to a healthier planet.

Cub

What
Comfortable & fun;
sustainability can be easy
& delicious

Who
Mr. Lyan & Doug McMaster,
partners

When
Dinner Thursday to Saturday

Address
153 Hoxton Street, London,
N1 6PJ

+44 (0)20 3693 3202

lyancub.com

Bookings
Website or email
reservations@mrlyan.com

Price guide

What they say
"We want you to enjoy a space that
feels comfortable and honest and
let you have a great time, but also
highlight how modern sustainability
can be delicious, luxurious, and not
about sacrifice. We love the people
behind great food, and we want to
champion them and how they've
helped us create something fun and
different. In essence, aiming to not
just have a considered impact, but to
have a very positive one."

Signature dishes
Jersey Royals with blood orange and
turbo whey; beeswax old fashioned;
and rhubarb with parfait, miso caramel
(made from Scottish barley), and
toasted British quinoa.

What we say
From a team with previous experience
mainly in bars, this brilliant little
restaurant took East London by
surprise when it opened late in 2017.
£55 buys you a no-choice tasting
menu of crazy-fantastic platefuls
matched to wonderful cocktails, of
which you get about four or five
and then lose count. A lot of the
ingredients are potential waste items,
you eat off tables made from recycled
yoghurt pots, and the vibe is a level
on from mere supper club or pop-up:
this is a freaking house party! It's all so
beautiful, we could just cry.

Cub (p. 50)

The Clove Club

London

What
A modern restaurant

Who
Daniel Willis & Johnny Smith, owners & Isaac McHale, chef

When
Dinner Monday, lunch & dinner, Tuesday to Saturday

Address
380 Old Street, London, EC1V 9LT

+44 (0)20 7729 6496

thecloveclub.com

Bookings
Website

Price guide

What they say
"Here at The Clove Club, we pride ourselves on creating an amazing experience, a meal our guests will hopefully remember for a long time. McHale has described his menu as, 'just simple food, which brings vegetables to the fore. Rather than veg being the foil to a lovely bit of protein, we're interested in making it the star of the show.' We have our own small farm/allotment growing vegetables in the Lea Valley."

Signature dishes
Raw Orkney scallop with clementine, hazelnut, and Périgord truffle; dry aged Aylesbury duck with fermented red cabbage; and blackcurrant and pheasant with morel and ginger consommé, and hundred-year-old Boal Madeira.

What we say
We first ate these guys' cooking during the Young Turks residency at The Ten Bells back in 2012, when hipsters were a newish thing on the food scene, checked shirts were not an embarrassment, cathedral beards were a novelty, and Hoxton was still almost cool. The food was edgy, challenging, and great maybe three-out-of-five dishes. It's now more like five out of five and the experience of eating in this divine, light, airy, high-ceilinged old building is one of the great pleasures of East London life.

Cook For Syria

London

What
A global movement celebrating Syrian cuisine & raising funds for Unicef's Children of Syria Appeal

Who
Unicef NEXTGeneration, partner

When
Pop-ups

Address
1 Westfield Avenue, Stratford, London, E20 1GL

cookforsyria.com

Bookings
Website

Price guide

What they say
"#CookForSYRIA is a global fundraising initiative curated by Clerkenwell Boy, Serena Guen of *SUITCASE Magazine*, and Gemma Bell in partnership with Unicef NEXTGeneration London. It first started as a simple supper club, where a group of foodie friends came together to celebrate Syrian cuisine and raise money to help Unicef protect Syrian children. Now it's a global movement, with regular events in the UK, France, USA, and Australia, and everybody is invited to the table. From cookbooks to supper clubs, #CookForSYRIA is raising vital funds for Unicef with support from the world's top chefs, restaurants, and volunteers. We're continuing to raise as much money as possible."

Signature dishes
Harak osbao, donated by Yotam Ottolenghi and Sami Tamimi at Ottolenghi; "bird's nest", donated by Imad Alarnab of Imad's Syrian Kitchen; and *laham bahine*, donated by Pizza Pilgrims.

What we say
#CookForSYRIA has helped to create a global community, united in their efforts to raise funds for the children of Syria: from the chefs who have donated dishes for the cookbooks, restaurants who have raised funds, home-cooks who have hosted supper clubs, and everyone who has supported the initiative. The easiest way to support them from your armchair would be to buy their second cookbook, #BakeForSYRIA, published in collaboration with London baker Lily Vanilli.

Craft

London

What
Restaurant, café, cocktail bar & shop

Who
Stevie Parle & Tom Dixon, owners

When
Dinner Tuesday to Friday, lunch & dinner, Saturday

Address
Peninsula Square, London, SE10 0SQ

+44 (0)20 8465 5910

craft-london.co.uk

Bookings
Website

Price guide

What they say
"Craft London is a new British restaurant, café, cocktail bar, and shop. We focus on quality in production by collaborating with modern experts, fanatics, and obsessives to craft world-class products through the roasting of coffee, smoking of fish, beekeeping, meat curing, fermentation of vegetables, and the creation of a contemporary kitchen garden. Both the restaurant dishes and the products are created using almost exclusively British produce bought from farmers we know well and always handled with a light, modern touch. The interior is crammed with the best of Britain from Scottish tweed to British limestone and London-designed furniture and lighting."

Signature dishes
Wild herb dumplings with mushroom tea, foraged greens and elderberry capers; kid goat with turnips, tarragon, and pumpkin seed pesto; and pollack with leek, wild cabbage, smoked cod's roe, and dulse.

What we say
In the chain-heavy environment of the O2 Centre, where you can't move for dopey old burger chains and awful pizza joints, it is extraordinary to find this oasis of deep thought, love, care, and attention to detail. By day, it looks like a posh new restaurant somewhat out of place in the gastro desert, but at night, as lit-up London sparkles in the darkness and the turquoise, mauve, sapphire, and copper of the ravishing colour scheme take hold, Craft shows itself for the temple to good taste that it is. And that's before you get on to the wood-fired ovens, curing rooms, fermenting cellar...

The Culpeper

London

What
Seasonal, nose-to-tail restaurant & pub with a rooftop

Who
Antonio Santos da Mota, head chef

When
Lunch & dinner, daily

Address
40 Commercial Street, London, E16 6LP

+44 (0)20 7247 5371

theculpeper.com

Bookings
Phone, website, or opentable.com

Price guide

What they say
"The Culpeper was designed to honour the history of the building it sits on, adding some modern touches but always preserving the original aesthetics. Our pub is named after Nicholas Culpeper, the great sixteenth-century herbalist, botanist, and astrologer, who spent his days cataloguing hundreds of medicinal herbs and whose pharmacy was in Spitalfields. It is in his honour that we grow medicinal and edible produce on our rooftop. We practice nose-to-tail cuisine, doing our best to waste as little or as close to nothing as possible when it comes to animals. We also have a composter up on our rooftop where we take our raw food waste, and then use this in our planter borders where we grow our produce/herbs."

Signature dishes
Yorkshire pork chop, olive oil mash, romane courgette, and pipérade; beer-battered haddock, chips, crushed peas, and tartare sauce; and caponata with pine nuts, and house ricotta.

What we say
This summer they redesigned their rooftop and renamed it PICULPEPER to make preservation the theme of the season. With the sunshine helping the cucumbers to grow abundantly on the roof, they served up the big ones fresh, preserving the little ones in brine to bring joy to the winter months. Across cocktails, dishes, and workshops, the modest pickle was elevated to a new height. What a way to foreground the importance of fresh, local produce and the power of preserving.

Cornerstone

What
A casual, fine dining restaurant aiming to offer the best seafood of the day in sharing plates

Who
Tom Brown, director/chef

When
Lunch & dinner, Tuesday to Sunday

Address
3 Prince Edward Road, London, E9 5LX

+44 (0)20 8986 3922

cornerstonehackney.com

Bookings
Phone or website

Price guide

What they say
"We aim to work with suppliers who are fanatical about the quality and sustainability of their products. This applies to our food, wine, and even our soaps! Our menu changes daily based on the best fish our fisherman can provide. Local artists' work from Hackney Wick adorns our walls to help promote our creative community, which is supported by the Hackney Wick Cultural Interest Group, whose code of conduct we work to, taking part in events and initiatives that aim to improve and support the Hackney Wick community. We also aim to hire locally with the majority of our staff living in the local area."

Signature dishes
Pickled oysters with horseradish and dill; raw scallops with green sauce and hazelnuts; and roast hake with Café de Paris hollandaise.

What we say
One of the most exciting new restaurants we visited this year. A big, no-messing-around boxy grey space with square tables and smiling, charming staff. Manager Holly is a pocket rocket, server Dominique is loveliness personified, and Tom Brown is a nailed-on genius. With his burly band of tattooed buddies in the open kitchen, he knocks out dish after dish of spectacular control and power. Those pickled oysters! That lime pickle cured monkfish! The potted shrimp crumpet! The cider-braised cuttlefish! We were in heaven. And all without financial backing, just a small inheritance from his nan. Go, Tom!

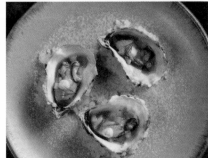

Cornerstone (p. 56)

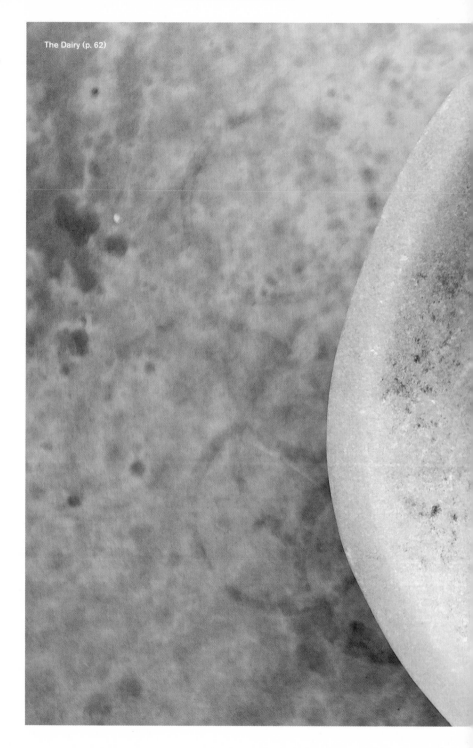

The Dairy (p. 62)

The Dairy

What
A London restaurant with a coastline farmhouse kitchen feel

Who
Robin Gill, chef/owner & Sarah Gill, owner

When
Lunch & dinner, Tuesday to Sunday, weekend brunch

Address
15 The Pavement, London, SW4 0HY

+44 (0)20 7622 4165

the-dairy.co.uk

Bookings
Phone or website

Price guide

What they say
"The entire experience is important: the playlist, atmosphere, food, interaction with the team – all play an equal part in our guests' experience. We've had a garden on the rooftop at The Dairy since opening in 2013. Here we grow our own salads and herbs, which get used across the menus. The roof is also home to the bees who produce our rooftop honey, a staple in so many of our dishes."

Signature dishes
Warm sourdough with charcuterie and ferments, chicken liver mousse, and smoked bone marrow butter; Lady Hamilton pollock with monk's beard, leafy lemon, and applewood-smoked eel tart; and Yorkshire lamb, peas and broad beans cooked over fire with lamb bacon, merguez, and roasting juices.

What we say
The Dairy works with Tom at Full Circle Farms, who takes their food waste and uses a Japanese method known as *bokashi* – using a type of fermented molasses and naturally occurring micro-organisms – to turn it into an almost black, nutrient-rich compost. Tom has a farm in Sussex and regularly consults with The Dairy on what they would like to grow, then The Dairy buys the seeds and the rest is left to Tom and nature. They get deliveries twice a week and the menu works around what is produced. It's plate to farm and back to plate again.

Darwin and Wallace

London

What
A unique collection of independent neighbourhood bars, more home than high street

Who
Mel Marriott, managing director

When
Breakfast, lunch, & dinner, daily

Address
No 29 Power Station West, 29 Circus West, Battersea Power Station, London, SW8 4NN, plus other locations – see website

+44 (0)20 3857 9872

no29powerstationwest.co.uk

Bookings
Email reservations@ no29powerstationwest.co.uk

Price guide

What they say
"Independent in spirit and rich in design. A name indicative of a private address; spaces that feel home-from-home. Handpicked (rather than off-the-shelf) interiors, tailored to the habits and tastes of locals. A welcoming bar with delightful drinks from morning coffee to nightcaps (and everything in-between). This is how we're redefining what a pub can be... Our philosophy is to create interesting, tasty, and virtuous dishes that can be enjoyed by everybody. Great value, genuinely inspiring dishes are made with locally sourced, sustainable produce, scratch-cooked on site and made with love."

Signature dishes
House salad with warm quinoa, edamame, thyme-baked squash, roast beets, broccoli, sesame wakame, and miso dressing; British grilled sea bass and chips with pea hummus, watercress, and crème fraîche tartare; and roast butternut squash curry with sticky short-grain brown rice, coriander, and toasted coconut.

What we say
If you're fed up with identikit faux-distressed, mock-Victorian, hipster-driven gastropubs (and we're not saying we are) then these wonderfully original, bright, breezy, modern, beautifully designed, and independent bars will come as a blessed relief. As will the way they put sustainability at the heart of everything they do. They are SRA three-star rated and we have always been especially impressed by the way they rejected all packaging from day one and insisted on deliveries arriving in returnable or recyclable containers.

Darwin and Wallace (p. 63)

Drake & Morgan

London

What
A collection of bars & restaurants offering an everyday escape from the ordinary

Who
Jillian Maclean, owner

When
Breakfast, lunch & dinner, daily

Address
6 Pancras Square, London, N1C 4AG, plus other locations – see website

+44 (0)84 5468 0107

drakeandmorgan.co.uk

Bookings
Website, opentable.com, or bookatable.co.uk

Price guide

What they say
"We're most excited about giving people an experience of great seasonal food, drink, and service rather than simply filling a need. Being accessible to all is one of our key philosophies. We have worked to ensure that all areas of our menu have options for vegans and vegetarians as well as customers with intolerances or allergies. We change our menus twice a year so that we can make sure we are using seasonal ingredients where possible. All our fish is sustainably sourced, all our meat is from local butchers who only use British farmers, and our vegetables are all from farmers in Kent. We have restaurants across London, as well as in Manchester and Edinburgh, and at each site we ensure we use suppliers local to them, rather than a central distribution centre."

Signature dishes
Avocado hummus flatbread; lamb rump with samphire; and cauliflower fettucini.

What we say
A really thoughtful mini chain that has recently upped its vegetarian and vegan range massively as well as keeping a varied range of vegetable side dishes and salads. Children's dishes all come with vegetables and they offer drinks that are under fifty calories. Devotees rave up the evening cocktails, but then whoever didn't enjoy a cocktail?

The Dysart Petersham

London

What
Informal fine dining restaurant overlooking Richmond Park

Who
The Taylors, owners & Kenneth Culhane, head chef

When
Lunch Wednesday to Sunday, dinner Wednesday to Saturday

Address
135 Petersham Road, Richmond, London, TW10 7AA

+44 (0)20 8940 8005

thedysartpetersham.co.uk

Bookings
Phone or website

Price guide

What they say
"People, food, wine, and music: all these important parts of the restaurant are crucial. Our chef uses his extensive knowledge and curiosity searching for better ingredients, grown locally by our own gardener, or from a little further afield. Our menus tell the stories of our suppliers – from tomatoes bicycled to our restaurant from the farm to wild foraged coastal herbs."

Signature dishes
Petersham tomato salad with lovage, olive oil jam and blackberry vinaigrette; Wiltshire beef with confit heritage carrots and miso mustard sauce; and skrei cod with cockles, mussels, leek, potato, coastal herbs.

What others say
"Culhane's food plays with classic French technique and outré Japanese flavours. Here are hand-dived scallops, caramelised outside and opalescent within, in a crystal-clear broth scented with fennel and the savoury thrum of wakame; so far, so conventional(ish). Then you discern a fleeting note of popcorn in the hot liquid. Or mackerel, energised by its thorough charring, daikon braised in kombu dashi, ginger and, er, champagne. There's always a welcome little jolt of surprise."

–Marina O'Loughlin, *The Guardian*

What we say
Rarely is such technical skill and high gastronomic ambition married to such an all-pervading commitment to sustainability. But here are fresh garden produce, foraged herbs and flowers, a dedicated recycling team on top of all aspects of waste management, English wines and beers, beetroots roasted in coffee grounds, bread made with carrot peelings – and the product on the plate is world class. Simply magical.

E5 Bakehouse

What
An East London artisan bakery, café, shop, & mill

Who
Ben Mackinnon, founder

When
Breakfast & lunch, daily

Address
395 Mentmore Terrace, London, E8 3PH

+44 (0)20 8525 2890

e5bakehouse.com

Bookings
No bookings taken

Price guide

What they say
"We're passionate about artisan methods, ethical sourcing, sustainable farming, and delicious food. Our bakery is home to a small, committed group of bakers, chefs, and baristas, and we do our best to support the local creative industries, for example by supporting the work of local artists and entrepreneurs. Sustainability runs through all our sourcing decisions; all of the vegetables, fruit, meat, and dairy we use are organic, seasonal, and supplied by producers we know and trust. All our sourdough bread represents our philosophy and is handcrafted using a long fermentation method. Our flour is organic, using UK-grown grain and milled fresh on-site where possible. It is our belief that to bake beautiful and nutritious sourdough loaves requires a clear conscience and a great deal of respect and care for our leaven – the life of our sourdough."

Signature dishes
Hand-crafted sourdough bread.

What we say
Since 2015, E5 Bakehouse have been running a training programme for refugee women, in collaboration with the Refugee Council, to help refugees and asylum seekers integrate and grow in confidence, as well as learn employability skills for working in the UK food industry. In September 2017, they opened a new café called E5 Roasthouse at the Poplar Union community arts centre, with the aim of providing employment for women who have taken part in the bread training, as well as providing a stepping stone into employment for other vulnerable communities. This is truly the bread of heaven.

Ekte Nordic Kitchen

What
Nordic tradition using local, seasonal & sustainable produce where possible

Who
Soren Jessen, owner & Bjorn Freeman, head chef

When
Breakfast & lunch, daily, dinner Monday to Saturday

Address
2-8 Bloomberg Arcade, London, EC4N 8AR

+44 (0)20 3814 8330

ektelondon.co.uk

Bookings
Website or opentable.com

Price guide

What they say
"True to Scandinavian tradition, the roots of our establishment are steeped in sustainability. It comes naturally to Nordic cuisine – source what you have locally, forage to create different and exciting flavour profiles, support your producers, and create the best experience you can with that beautiful plate of inspiration. We love our customers feeling welcomed and spoilt, enjoying our simple but delicious produce and food that is made with love."

Signature dishes
Pickled fried herring *smørrebrød*; fresh tomato herring with onion and cress *smørrebrød*; and *gravad var* salmon, mustard and dill sauce, and rye crumbs.

What we say
Based in the most sustainable office building in the UK, Norman Foster's Bloomberg HQ with a 98.5 per cent BREEAM rating, Ekte employs unimpeachable UK sourcing techniques to provide the best you can get of the Nordic kitchen in London. The herring here is spectacular – more than enough to convert the sceptics. Which has to be done if the British are to start looking lower down the food chain for their fish than the cod, haddock, and halibut on which we so often insist.

El Pastor

London

What
Mexican taqueria serving tacos with homemade tortillas

Who
Sam, Eddie & James Hart & Crispin Somerville, owners/directors

When
Dinner Monday to Saturday, lunch, daily

Address
7A Stoney Street, London, SE1 9AA

tacoselpastor.co.uk

Bookings
No bookings taken

Price guide

What they say
"We aim to consistently produce delicious, authentic Mexican food in a fun environment. Ingredients are top priority: Mexican-style cheese from Gringa Dairy in Peckham; pork, chicken, and beef are British, certified free-range; fish is sustainably sourced. All tortillas are made using heirloom corn sourced with partners Tamoa in Mexico. Tamoa seeks out the few farmers preserving and cultivating native Mexican corn, linking them with restaurants in Mexico and beyond, ensuring they are compensated fairly for protecting the country's biocultural heritage. El Pastor believes strongly that this native corn is on a far superior level in flavour and nutrition and that the resulting tortillas are profoundly different."

Signature dishes
Taco al Pastór; sesame tuna tostada; and short rib.

What we say
Like all projects by the brothers Sam, James and Eddie Hart, El Pastor simply screams "authenticity". They know Mexican food like nobody outside Mexico and the colour and fun they bring to this big space under the railway arches makes it seem a portal to another world. The tacos are light, powerful, and gleaming with flavour, and the range of mescals and tequilas on offer is mind-boggling. El Pastor was close to the scene of a terror attack in 2017 and the way staff protected their beloved customers that night and then bounced back afterwards is testimony to just what a special place this is.

Ethos

London

What
Specializing in deliciously different meat-free cuisine

Who
Sundip Bhundia, director, Kashif Akram, managing director & Guilerme Pina, head chef

When
Lunch & dinner, daily, breakfast Monday to Friday

Address
48 Eastcastle Street, London, W1W 8DX

+44 (0)20 3581 1538

ethosfoods.com

Bookings
Phone or website

Price guide

What they say
"Ethos is dedicated to serving delicious and creative meat-free cuisine that appeals to a large number of people. Our menu is rich with options for those with special dietary requirements such as vegan, gluten-free, dairy-free, and refined-sugar-free. We focus on four basics: amazing food, exceeding expectations, investing in our team, and no wastage."

Signature dishes
Veggie scotch egg filled with smoked aubergine; good green salad with chickpeas, green beans, sugar snaps.

What we say
Oh, just feel the health in here as you take in the Nordic blue and white of the colour scheme, the sexy shafts of silver birch, and the way in which, having loaded up with healthy vegetarian goodies from the dishes arranged sexily on white podiums, you are invited to pay for your food by weight – a practice common in Spain and Latin America but less familiar in Teutonic climes. How could you not take that little bit less food when the world is going to see the scales yodelling out "THREE KILOS!" as you hoist your giant platter aboard? After the ravages wreaked upon us in terms both of our own health and egregious food waste by years of all-you-can-eat buffets, this is a welcome corrective. And the food is good, healthy, and pretty cheap.

Farmacy

What
Plant-based & organic all-day restaurant & bar

Who
Camilla Fayed, owner

When
Breakfast, lunch & dinner, daily

Address
74 Westbourne Grove, London, W2 5SH

+44 (0)20 7221 0705

farmacylondon.com

Bookings
Phone, website, or opentable.com

Price guide

What they say
"The aim of Farmacy is to make healthy eating fun in a beautiful setting that welcomes everyone – and this is a cause the whole team are dedicated to and passionate about. As a team, we are passionate about not only serving delicious and nutritious food and creating a great atmosphere for our diners, but also using education and information to create conversations on wellness, conscious eating, responsible food-growing practice, biodynamic farming, and sustainability. We chose the name Farmacy as it incorporates our belief that food is medicine (to paraphrase Hippocrates), as well as emphasizing our obsession with the provenance of food and organic farming."

Signature dishes
Nice cream brownie sundae; high tea; and macro bowl.

What others say
"... undoubtedly one of the best health-food restaurants in the capital."

–Samuel Muston, *MR PORTER*

What we say
It is not just plastic straws that are eschewed at Farmacy; they try to avoid using any plastics at all. By using suppliers such as Vegware to source plant-based packaging alternatives, they have been able to ensure that all of their packaging is not only 100 per cent recyclable, but in many cases compostable, too.

Foxlow

What
A casual-dining, family-friendly group of restaurants with a strong focus on British produce

Who
Will Becket & Huw Gott, founders

When
Breakfast, lunch, & dinner, daily

Address
8–10 Lower James Street, London, W1F 9EL, plus other locations – see website

+44 (0)20 7680 2710

foxlow.co.uk

Bookings
Phone, website, or email soho@foxlow.co.uk

Price guide

What they say
"At Foxlow we are most devoted to our food, the experience, and our people. We take great pride in ensuring that all our teams are happy and enjoy their job. Our passion for sustainable produce sourced from British suppliers is evident in our dishes and we strive to maintain that relaxed, informal atmosphere that makes our customers as comfortable as possible. We work very closely with the charity Magic Breakfast, who run breakfast clubs in schools where a majority of the pupils arrive at school too hungry to learn."

Signature dishes
Spice-roasted cauliflower, chickpeas, wilted spinach, and curried aubergine sauce; chicken burger and fries with fried chicken breast and Kewpie mayonnaise; and rare-breed spare ribs, slow-cooked with green slaw.

What others say
"We left Foxlow in a rosy glow – it's hats-in-the-air good."

–Tracey MacLeod, *The Independent*

What we say
This is a small friendly chain from the guys who founded the altogether more ball-breaking Hawksmoor outfit. There is a good balance between healthy and heftier dishes, generally terrific beer, wine, and cocktails, light and airy design, and a nice, family-oriented, high-street vibe to set off some really top-class modern brasserie standards.

Franzina Trattoria

What
Sicilian trattoria

Who
Pietro Franz, chef, & Stefi Taormina, co-owner

When
Lunch & dinner, daily

Address
Pop Brixton, 49 Brixton Station Road, London, SW9 8PQ

+44 (0)78 6482 5980

franzinatrattoria.com

Bookings
Website or email
info@franzinatrattoria.com

Price guide

What they say
"In the buzz of Pop Brixton, we conjure up traditional Sicilian recipes combining the best of local produce and hospitality. By getting to know our local suppliers in Brixton Market, we have been able to find great ingredients at good prices. When unavoidable, we import produce from Sicily, direct from producers we have personally met and checked. Vegetables and oily fish are our staples, together with fresh herbs and olive oil. Our pasta flour comes from Molini del Ponte, Castelvetrano, Sicily. They pioneer the cultivation of non-hybrid, traditional durum wheat with a low gluten content, which also happens to be organic."

What others say
"Franzina's springy, sinuous tagliatelle is the best I have tasted in London…"

–Bill Knott, *Financial Times*

Signature dishes
Cornish sardines with orange zest, pine nuts, raisins, and toasted breadcrumbs; Braised Cornish octopus with lemon, salt, and pepper; and cinnamon *sfingette* (baby doughnuts), with sweetened sheep's ricotta and bitter chocolate drops.

What we say
Stefi Taormina is one of the most passionate and dedicated people we have encountered in putting this guide together. A brilliant short-term pop-up in the crazy higgle-piggle of shipping containers that is Pop Brixton, Franzina Trattoria somehow seems to distil all the excitement and honesty of plain Sicilian peasant food into affordable plates of unbelievably delicious plates of pasta that are accessible to almost everyone.

Franklins

London

What
Seasonal British food

Who
Tim Sheehan & Rod Franklin, owners

When
Lunch & dinner, daily

Address
157 Lordship Lane, London, SE22 8HX

+44 (0)20 8299 9598

franklinsrestaurant.com

Bookings
Phone or website

Price guide

What they say
"Franklins prides itself on quality British ingredients, perfectly cooked. Our menu is simple and solid, with fish from British waters, Kent farm vegetables, and rare-breed British meats. Our provenance is sustainable and traceable. The restaurant's work in the community reaches from local schools to local beekeeping. We began Franklins in the nineties and have kept the same strong ethos and principles pretty much to this day, standing the test of time as a neighbourhood favourite."

Signature dishes
Devilled kidneys; calves faggots and mash; and Barnsley chop, cauliflower, and anchovy.

What we say
Franklins is a great local asset that stood up for fresh, local food at a time when it wasn't especially fashionable and neither was Lordship Lane. Both world and neighbourhood have caught up now, and Franklins is as strong as ever, with a relaxed atmosphere round its open kitchen, friendly staff, buzzing bar area, outdoor seating when the sun shines on East Dulwich, and their own farm shop just down the street, full of predominantly Kentish produce.

Frog by Adam Handling

London

What
Adam Handling's flagship restaurant in Covent Garden

Who
Adam Handling, chef/owner

When
Lunch & dinner, Monday to Saturday

Address
34–35 Southampton Street, London, WC2E 7HG

+44 (0)20 7199 8370

frogbyadamhandling.com

Bookings
Phone or email
info@frogbyadamhandling

Price guide

What they say
"This restaurant is a very personal thing for me – it's a showcase of me and my life on the plate and everything I love, from the artwork on the walls to the cutlery. I love collaborating with producers, suppliers, designers, and artists and seeing everything coming together to create something special that we can share with our guests. I also feel very strongly about reducing the almost 200,000 tons of food waste that's produced by the UK restaurant industry each year. We grow much of our own produce for the restaurant, and any food waste or surplus food is used – either as compost or at my sustainable deli, Bean & Wheat. We need to see more chefs speaking out against food waste, encouraging and educating people on how we can all do our part to make eating out more sustainable."

Signature dishes
Posh potato; chicken butter; and salt-baked celeriac (a dish inspired by Handling's vegetarian mother that showcases all five flavour profiles – sweet, salty, umami, sour, bitter).

What we say
Ever so slightly more formal than its sister restaurant, The Frog Hoxton, Adam's flagship site in Covent Garden is a real smash hit. Wonderfully assured cocktails get you in the mood, deft and unusual mouthfuls begin to pluck at your gut-strings, Handling's naturally inquisitive and outgoing personality get you in their grip, and you're on a roller-coaster ride of a dinner that is unlike anything else around.

The Gallery Café

What
Award-winning vegan community café that hosts an exciting programme of live events & art exhibitions

Who
St. Margaret's House

When
Breakfast, lunch & dinner, daily

Address
21 Old Ford Road, London, E2 9PL

+44 (0)20 8980 2092

stmargaretshouse.org.uk

Bookings
No bookings taken

Price guide

What they say
"Our goal is to empower our community to lead a healthy and environmentally conscious lifestyle. We are not only passionate about the impact that veganism has on animal welfare but also the huge environmental benefits that come from following a vegan lifestyle. That's why we like to try and boost our credentials even further by constantly making and effort to reduce our carbon footprint. Not only have we won many awards, but all profits generated by The Gallery Café go straight back into St. Margaret's House, so by hanging with us, you'll not only enjoy award-winning food, drinks, and good vibes, you'll also be helping to support the local community."

Signature dishes
Superfood breakfast bowl; "The Gallery Burger"; and full English breakfast.

What we say
St Margaret's House has been doing good work in Bethnal Green since the days of Jack the Ripper and Sherlock Holmes. One hundred and thirty years later, they are still working to promote positive social change by bringing people together to play a more active part in their community, providing spaces for residents to shop, learn, create, and enjoy a diverse cultural programme. And, of course, to eat in a café as passionately loved by its regulars as it is garlanded with awards for its sympathetically priced, ethically sourced meat-free food, from avocado on sourdough toast to a full English with vegan sausage and scrambled tofu to quesadillas filled with refried beans, vegan cheese, tomato, and wilted spinach.

The Gate Hammersmith

What
Celebrating great vegan & vegetarian cuisine since 1989

Who
Michael Daniel, owner/director

When
Lunch & dinner, daily

Address
51A Queen Caroline Street, London, W6 9QL, plus other locations – see website

+44 (0)20 8748 6932

thegaterestaurants.com

Bookings
Website

Price guide

What they say
"It's always been about the food. From the day we started The Gate in 1989, we've been passionate about how food is made and how we can communicate our passion and educate the public about healthy-eating and using more vegetable-based dishes. We're also interested in the evolution of veganism. We started out as vegetarian in Hammersmith and now we have three restaurants in London and our menus are ninety per cent vegan. Our owner is also passionate about foraging and this is reflected on our menu."

Signature dishes
Wild mushroom *rotolo*; aubergine schnitzel; and miso-glazed aubergine.

What others say
"It's hard to choose from their tempting menu, which includes spinach, feta and artichoke tart, but I particularly like their crispy-coated aubergine – it's delicious."

–Rose Elliot, *The Telegraph*

What we say
Leading the way since 1989 with their deep and meaningful commitment to vegetarianism and veganism, The Gate has taken caring to another level now with their work alongside Ambitious about Autism. They are supporting and training children with autism by making them more self-sufficient, for instance teaching them how to produce chocolate, pack it, sell it, and market it. But most impressive is the way staff are trained to spot and give the right kind of service to customers with autism, explaining menus in an accessible way, recognizing the different needs of their customers, and providing a quiet space for anyone experiencing stress in what can be a challenging environment. An example to us all.

Gourmet Goat

London

What
Eastern-Mediterranean dishes using sustainable British ingredients

Who
Nick & Nadia Stokes, founders/owners

When
Lunch Monday to Saturday

Address
Borough Market, Rochester Walk, London, SE1 9AF

+44 (0)20 8050 1973

gourmetgoat.co.uk

Bookings
No bookings taken

Price guide

What they say
"Nadia was born and lived the majority of her life in rural Cyprus. Her village background has influenced our ethos: delicious and sustainable eating with respect for the environment. In relation to meat, we only use byproducts of the British dairy industry, so free-range kid goat and rose veal and underused meat such as mutton that is free-range and organic. We work directly with farmers to ensure our meat meets our exact standards. We have minimal waste, all of our packaging is compostable, we use eco-friendly products for cleaning, and we have a three-star rating from the SRA for all of our efforts on sustainability, which includes environmental impact."

Signature dishes
Baharat-spiced and pomegranate molasses slow-roasted rose veal; kid goat kofta; and North London handmade mature halloumi.

What we say
A small stall at the back of Borough Market where long queues snake around the block as local workers slaver for their lunchtime fix of dairy-industry byproduct slapped into hot flatbread. Generally three young women working the place: one on the grill, one on salads, and one telling people, "Sorry, no, we don't sell water in single-use disposable bottles anymore, instead we sell our own reusable bottles for two pounds, which you can fill up at that fountain over there". Carb-dodgers can skip the bread if they like and get their unforgettable kid goat kofta and slaw served in a biodegradable bowl.

Great Queen Street

London

What
Seasonal European menu, using the best ingredients cooked simply

Who
Robert Webster-Shaw, owner

When
Dinner Monday to Saturday, lunch daily

Address
32 Great Queen Street, London, WC2B 5AA

+44 (0)20 7242 0622

greatqueenstreetrestaurant.co.uk

Bookings
Phone or website

Price guide

What they say
"Situated in the heart of London, at Great Queen Street we're mad about hospitality and service. We create delicious dishes from seasonal and mostly organic produce, and have a wide range of natural wine on the list. All our fish is from dayboats and sustainably caught, and we support non-intensive farming. We support local, small scale, and native but as much for the quality as for anything else. It's all naturally part of our thinking to be as environmentally sound as we can, and we make sure our staff meet gender equality and non-discriminatory employment policies."

Signature dishes
Lamb sweetbreads with pea purée and mint; pot roast beef shin with chips and horseradish for two; and roast suckling pig shoulder with choucroute and horseradish for three.

What we say
This wonderful, cosy, vibrant restaurant emerged in 2007 out of The Anchor and Hope, with its giant sharing pots, hearty English style, no-reservations policy, and messianic approach to great food. Covent Garden was a gastronomic wasteland then, but GQS started the ball rolling – for which we can all be grateful. The cooking is ballsy and heroic, the atmosphere is upbeat late-Victorian (think Dr. Watson on his night off, tucking into a rib of beef and a flagon of claret with some old med-school pals), and the location is second to none.

The Green Clerkenwell

London

What
Pub & dining room serving British bistro-style food

Who
Sandy Jarvis, head chef

When
Lunch & dinner, daily

Address
29 Clerkenwell Green, London, EC1R 0DU

+44 (0)20 7490 1258

thegreenclerkenwell.com

Bookings
Phone or website

Price guide

What they say
"We create a relaxed environment where people can enjoy each other's company while having good food and drinks. We work closely with the SRA to improve all aspects of sustainability. We are passionate about developing and investing time in a team of enthusiastic people wanting to progress in this industry."

Signature dishes
Asparagus with broad bean, pea, and pearl barley risotto; beer-battered haddock with chips, peas and tartare sauce (using MCS-rated-one haddock); and beef Wellington (using native-breed cows).

What we say
A really good-looking old-fashioned gastropub, a proper boozer but light and hairy, boldly coloured, high-ceilinged, with a nice Georgian feel to the dining room, battered leather club chairs, school-room furniture, and then bright, ballsy food presented without fuss, so good at times that devotees taste echoes of the great pioneers: The Eagle, The Peasant, The Lansdowne, and even St John.

Honest Burgers

London

What
Great British burgers & rosemary salted chips

Who
Tom Barton, Phil Eeles, & Dorian Waite, founders

When
Lunch & dinner, daily

Address
31 Paddington Street, London, W1U 4HD, plus other locations – see website

+44 (0)20 3019 6566

honestburgers.co.uk

Bookings
No bookings taken

Price guide

What they say
"We opened the first Honest Burgers in Brixton Village with an ambition to make the best British burgers on any menu. That meant great cuts from great butchers who source the best beef from native British breeds. Seven years on and we've now opened our own butchery so we can make the burgers we've always dreamed of, from scratch. That homemade passion extends to everything we do – veggie fritters, iced tea, lemonade, pickles, relish, and Honest sauces. And, of course, our chips, too. We season them with rosemary salt then serve them with the burger for free – just because we think that all burgers should come with chips."

Signature dishes
Rosemary salted chips fried and seasoned with rosemary, salt, and lemon zest; and "The Honest Burger": Honest Butcher's patty with homemade red onion relish, smoked bacon, cheddar, pickled cucumber, and lettuce.

What we say
With so many outlets now, it is wonderful to see Honest Burgers running regular Honesty Box Days, when the community around each restaurant nominates local charities to support, and then pay what they like – all sales from that day being donated to the chosen charities. Their most recent event in Chiswick raised over £2,200 for Ealing Samaritans, St. Mary Abbots Rehabilitation and Training (a local mental health charity), and Bishop Creighton House (supporting elderly people in the community). An example to us all.

Greenberry Café

London

What
All-day dining in the heart of Primrose Hill

Who
Morfudd Richards, owner & Dan Hesketh, chef

When
Breakfast & lunch, daily, dinner Tuesday to Saturday

Address
101 Regent's Park Road, London, NW1 8UR

+44 (0)20 7483 3765

greenberrycafe.co.uk

Bookings
Website or email reservations@greenberrycafe.co.uk

Price guide

What they say
"We are a small, lively restaurant in the heart of Primrose Hill dedicated to cooking delicious food. Our chefs are an enthusiastic, enquiring bunch and love to cook with seasonal produce and quality ingredients. They believe that less is more and that the best ingredients should be allowed to speak for themselves, so are always on the lookout for great produce, a sourdough, perfectly roasted coffee beans, Spanish hams from acorn-fed pigs, or wild garlic from the Afon Dwyfor in Wales."

Signature dishes
Waffle, maple-glazed bacon, poached eggs, and Hass avocado; wild rice, quinoa, butternut squash, goat's cheese, spring onion, rocket, mint, and pomegranate salad; and soba noodles with shiitake and wakame, soy, and sake broth.

What we say
Greenberry Café is a bright-and-bustling, on-trend, exposed-brick, eclectic-menu, all-day-dining sort of a place, where well-heeled locals squeeze into small tables in the shimmering skylit back room for impeccable, healthy little platefuls and excellent wine by the glass. All their electricity comes from renewables and they use no gas at all. Whether or not the area's new population of international hedge fund managers, Filipina nannies, and assorted semi-disguised celebrities care about all that stuff is a mystery. But we certainly do.

The Harwood Arms

London

What
Game-focused, hearty food with real ales & a great wine list

Who
Sally Abe, head chef

When
Lunch & dinner, daily

Address
Walham Grove, London, SW6 1QP

+44 (0)20 7386 1847

harwoodarms.com

Bookings
Phone, website, or email admin@harwoodarms.com

Price guide

What they say
"The only Michelin-starred pub in London, we love creating an experience for each and every guest to pass through our doors. Our rooftop garden provides us with our homegrown produce, and we love sourcing wild food from our trusted farms (you'll find more Lake District deer and game on our menu than beef, for example). All of our food is sourced from the UK, and transformed into impressive plates by our incredible team. We nurture a healthy and happy working environment, and have become a great local restaurant for our community."

Signature dishes
Wild garlic soup with brandade and crispy hake collar; haunch of sika deer with beetroot, bone marrow, and walnut; and English strawberry and elderflower trifle.

What we say
Unquestionably one of the best gastropubs in the country with that famous star for a certain delicacy of presentation and service. At a cute little butcher's trolley in the corner a woman cuts fresh, warm ciabatta and a dark brown, malty soda bread type of loaf, serving it in the upturned linen bonnet of a seventeenth-century Dutch milkmaid. The same fabric, with a twist of brown raffia, wraps the cutlery. Food is served on dainty wooden pallets... and simply glows: grilled lamb chops from the Hampshire Downs with haggis croquettes, green sauce, and capers was simply stellar and the schnitzel of longhorn English rose veal with broken eggs, raw cauliflower, and wild celery is a dish for the ages.

Hood

London

What
Modern British bistro-style restaurant

Who
Melanie & Robin Frean, co-founders & Mike Brown, head chef

When
Lunch & dinner, Tuesday to Saturday, weekend brunch

Address
67 Streatham Hill, London, SW2 4TX

+44 (0)20 3601 3320

hoodrestaurants.com

Bookings
resdiary.com

Price guide

What they say
"We're all about good food, great drink, provenance, and community here at Hood. We work closely with our veg supplier partners to keep us up to date with seasonal produce, we forage wild garlic and fennel from parks close to us, and local residents (like Paul Riley) often donate local honey to the restaurant. All the bread that we serve in the restaurant is baked about 100 metres away at our local Turkish high-street bakery – zero food miles, 100 per cent freshness. We hire from within our community, so we have a hugely diverse team working with us who represent many backgrounds, cultures, languages, and orientations and we are very proud of that diversity."

Signature dishes
Laverstock Farm buffalo mozzarella panzanella with Nutbourne tomatoes; buttered Evesham asparagus, poached egg; and slow-roast pork belly, bubble and squeak, and apple jus.

What we say
This brother and sister from Sussex and their Caprice-trained chef have brought a real buzz of excitement to jaded Streatham over the past couple of years. Having crowdsourced £11,000 for finishing touches, they erected a blackboard "thank you wall" to commemorate donors of more than £50 and it lends a real sense of community while adding to a quirky look along with the multicoloured chairs and restored dumb waiter that is wonderfully different from the usual postindustrial or bleak minimalist choice. Great cooking, too, and a sense of countryside bounty on a South London high street.

Ikoyi

London

What
Combining bold heat & umami with the highest quality products in a warm environment

Who
Iré Hassan-Odukale & Jeremy Chan, co-founders

When
Lunch & dinner, Monday to Saturday

Address
1 St. James's Market, London, SW1Y 4AH

+44 (0)20 3583 4660

ikoyilondon.com

Bookings
Website

Price guide

What they say
"We are a restaurant about optimized quality and ingredients, therefore we hunt for the best, but where we can we champion farmers from the British Isles to bring the best quality new growth and seasoned vegetables as well as the freshest fish possible from Scotland, Cornwall, and Orkney. We have root-to-stem and nose-to-tail policies with our ingredients, maximizing and finding new ways to create flavour with products otherwise used for waste, and we source our wines from biodynamic sustainable vineyards. Ikoyi is the name of our locality and it is simply the originating point from which we look outwards while interpreting the ingredients of its surrounding region."

Signature dishes
Buttermilk plantain and smoked scotch bonnet; smoked crab jollof rice; and duck, *uda*, candied bacon, and bitter leaf.

What we say
The neo-Nigerian menu here is one of the most original you will see anywhere. Nothing is familiar; everything is brilliant. Grilled rib of Manx Loaghtan sheep marinated in roasted kelp and a play on calf's foot soup stand out, but the crowning glory is the jollof rice, roasted and smoked and cooked in a dense stock of shellfish and chicken, served with a split roasted marrowbone on top, to be emptied and stirred in. Creamy, roasty, popping with wit and history, not traditional jollof rice but a riff on it, livelier, more modern, the seasoning more insistent and deliberate, just comforting and wholesome and moreish.

Jamie's Italian

London

What
Classic Italian food with a Jamie twist from celebrity chef Jamie Oliver

Who
Jamie Oliver, founder

When
Lunch & dinner, daily

Address
17–19 Denman Street, London, W1D 7HW, plus other locations – see website

+44 (0)20 3376 3391

jamiesitalian.com

Bookings
Phone, website, or bookatable.co.uk

Price guide

What they say
"At Jamie's Italian we fully support Jamie's fight for better food worldwide, and his mission to make good food accessible for everyone. That's why we're passionate about disrupting the high street with affordable, fresh plates of food made with incredible quality ingredients. Everything we use in our kitchens is carefully selected and traceable, and supports local supply chains, farmers, and producers wherever possible, setting us apart from our competitors. We put a lot of love, time, and effort into sourcing our ingredients so we can always guarantee freshness, top-notch welfare standards, and no nasties. Although our menu is rooted in Italy, we also use lots of great British produce to recreate the flavours of the Mediterranean."

Signature dishes
Chicken *al mattone*; seafood linguine; and pepperoni pizza.

What we say
Jamie Oliver has never taken a penny in salary or dividends from ANY of his restaurants. Did you know that? At Fifteen in London and Cornwall he has devoted fifteen years to the preferment of young cooks from disadvantaged backgrounds. On television, he has campaigned for better food in schools, better information on nutrition, action on obesity... and at Jamie's Italian he has been giving the closest thing to genuine rustic Italian vibes you are ever going to see on the high street. He does not compromise on ingredients, only organic meat and dairy are used, every kid's meal contains two of their five-a-day... Jamie is our food Superman and we LOVE him!

Kricket

London

What
Modern Indian plates made with British ingredients, with the authentic flavours of India

Who
Rik Campbell, owner & Will Bowlby, owner/chef

When
Lunch & dinner, Monday to Saturday

Address
12 Denman Street, London, W1D 7HH, plus other locations – see website

+44 (0)20 7734 5612

kricket.co.uk

Bookings
Website or resdiary.com

Price guide

What they say
"Our main prerogative is to exceed any expectations that people have coming through the door. Sustainable is a big focus for us: from rib bones from the breast that we turn into soup, baby carrot tops that would usually be discarded we turn into chutney, and smoked monkfish bones are turned into delicious broth."

Signature dishes
Samphire pakoras, date and tamarind chutney, and chilli garlic mayonnaise; Lasooni scallop, wild garlic, Goan sausage, puffed *poha*, and seaweed; and Kashmiri lamb ribs, jaggery and pomegranate vinegar glaze with wild garlic raita.

What we say
In its first incarnation, in a shipping container at Pop Brixton, we were blown away by the quality of Indian food on offer from these two white guys. We recall especially a blood orange gin and tonic and then joyous bhelpuri (puffed rice) with yoghurt and tamarind sauce; a lush, charred sweet potato with black garlic over a blob of tangy labneh; creamy, hot, smoky Hyderabad baby aubergine with flaked coconut and curry leaf, the butt end and tail of the vegetable nuzzling down into the baba ganoush-like mess; a kind of lentil kedgeree called *khichri*, full of smoked haddock and pickled cauliflower; and most wondrously of all, a piece of roasted, shimmering hake in malai sauce (a kind of korma-like, butterfat gravy) with crunchy monk's beard. A historic meal. It was great to see them win a Michelin Bib Gourmand within a year of opening in Soho.

Lamberts

London

What
Seasonal British restaurant

Who
Joe Lambert, owner/chef

When
Dinner Tuesday to Saturday, weekend lunch

Address
2 Station Parade, London, SW12 9AZ

+44 (0)20 8675 2233

lambertsrestaurant.com

Bookings
Phone, website, or email bookings@lambertsrestaurants.com

Price guide

What they say
"Everything on our menu, with a couple of very minor exceptions, comes from the land or sea around Britain. By using small independent suppliers we have found the quality of the produce is far superior – larger companies and corporations do it for the money and it's all about margins, small suppliers do it for the passion, and that comes through in the produce. Lamberts is very much part of the community here in Balham. We donate to all the local state schools' summer and winter fairs, along with various other local charities – Ickle Pickles is one of our most supported charities, started by local regulars."

Signature dishes
Heritage tomatoes with sourdough croutons, charred spring onions, and lovage (Isle of Wight tomatoes, croutons from homemade sourdough); chargrilled High Hall Farm asparagus with hollandaise and spicy crumb; and sea trout with Jersey Royals, slow-roasted cherry tomatoes, and wild garlic pesto.

What we say
A high-quality, small, independent, ethically-minded restaurant that has been quietly selling amazing seasonal British food to the good people of south-west London for over a decade – without getting anything like the recognition it deserves from the critics, obsessed as they are with all that is brand new, hip, and attention-seeking. Scandalous!

Lardo

London

What
A local neighbourhood restaurant, an Italian eatery at its very best, classic yet innovative

Who
Eliza Flanagan & Hugh Thorn, owners & Matt Cranston, head chef

When
Lunch & dinner, daily

Address
197-201 Richmond Road, London, E8 3NJ

+44 (0)20 8985 2683

lardo.co.uk

Bookings
Phone or designmynight.com

Price guide

What they say
"Provenance of carefully selected produce, quality of preparation in the kitchen, an informal environment, and attentive, friendly service are all key to our success. This is a destination restaurant, one not to be overlooked. We pride ourselves on great quality food with incredible service from happy people. Our wine list works with old-world winemakers, ideally organic and biodynamic. We love working with charities such as Pink Plates, Shelter, and StreetSmart."

Signature dishes
Nettle *gnudi* with sage butter; summer tomato tonnato; and homemade *casarrece* with Romano courgettes and pistachio pesto.

What others say
"... have just eaten the best pizza in London in living memory. It's the spicy seafood pizza @lardolondon – ordered without the mozzarella. I suggest you do likewise."

–Nigella Lawson, @nigellalawson

What we say
We went when this place first opened and were dazzled by the superb quality of the pizzas from the super-sexy pizza oven, the aroma and heft of their homemade charcuterie, the glorious lobster salad, and the best arancini we had ever eaten. But when we gently enquired about their recycling policy, they admitted they didn't have one. We were aghast!

But that was 2012 – less enlightened times, even in Hackney – and all that has changed. Now they ensure that all their paper and glass waste is recycled. All takeaway containers are recycled cardboard, cutlery is from recycled plastics, and they use only paper straws and bags. Welcome to the fold.

Leroy

London

What
Wine bar & bistro, sharing plates with low intervention & classic wines

Who
Ed Thaw & Jack Lewens, owners & Sam Kamienko, chef

When
Dinner Monday, lunch & dinner, Tuesday to Saturday

Address
18 Phipp Street, London, EC2A 4NU

+44 (0)20 7739 4443

leroyshoreditch.com

Bookings
Phone, website, or resy.com

Price guide

What they say
"We favour simple but thoughtful food. We're not into food that is more about technique than heart. When we get a dish right it's surprising but also satisfying. Something that makes you think but also something that you want more of. We look for wines with identity. We're not dogmatic about natural wines but if you get something well-made with less stuff in it then that makes us really happy. We're not into funky, farmyardy shit. We are also really passionate about music. We try and work with suppliers who are at the forefront of what is happening sustainably in the UK. Whether that is Swaledale in Yorkshire, who are reviving rare breeds, or Flourish, who are doing amazing things with vegetables in East Anglia."

Signature dishes
Leroy salad (ewe's milk cheese, Chardonnay vinegar, olive oil, bitter leaves, croutons); whipped cod's roe and crisps; and veal sweetbread with broad beans, courgette, and basil.

What others say
"Both in the glass and on the plate, Leroy pursues the path of righteousness and significance."

–David Sexton, *London Evening Standard*

What we say
This barnstorming triangular cake slice of a restaurant was formerly a French wine bar and still has some of that feel, with bistro chairs and a marble bar overlooking the kitchen. Windows on all (three) sides give wonderful natural light in the daytime and something reverberative for the vinyl music on which they pride themselves to bounce off in the evenings.

Leroy (p. 82)

Le Bab

London

What
Contemporary kebab house with a strict focus on provenance, inspired by classic kebab cultures

Who
Ed Brunet & Stephen Tozer, co-founders

When
Lunch & dinner, daily

Address
Kingly Court (Second Floor), Carnaby Street, London, W1B 5PW

+44 (0)77 4078 1090

eatlebab.com

Bookings
Email info@eatlebab.com

Price guide

What they say
"At Le Bab we aim to serve totally delicious and innovative food, that challenges preconceptions about a misunderstood but beloved dish – the kebab. Our suppliers are our heroes, there are so many incredible people that we source from to find the best British produce we can. All of our meat is British, and the majority of our veg. The majority of our fish is bought directly from fishing boats through the amazing FoodChain App (an incredibly innovative and effective app that connects restaurants directly to producers)."

Signature dishes
Barbecue paneer kebab with beetroot and coconut purée, pickled rainbow chard stalks, curry mayo, and crispy shallots; pork shawarma with charred and pickled hispi cabbage, chermoula mayo, and crackling; and fondue fries, double cooked with a molten cheddar sauce.

What we say
All the splatter and fizz of a tangy, mouth-whacking doner but backed up with a concern for provenance that the purveyors of such morsels can rarely afford, and all the perfectionist skill of haute cuisine from the guys' impressive past track record. Wahoo! They are extremely seasonal with their dishes, rotating the menu regularly (bar some staples such as fondue fries). Kebab garnishes change to suit the season so that the pickle on the pork shawarma changes from king cabbage to hispi cabbage to fennel through the year. Isn't that just brilliant? They are saving the world one fat, juicy, spicy kebab at a time.

Lorne

London

What
Inventive, unfussy modern British food served with a local neighbourhood feel

Who
Katie Exton & Peter Hall, owners

When
Dinner Monday to Saturday, lunch Tuesday to Sunday

Address
76 Wilton Road, London, SW1V 1DE

+44 (0)20 3327 0210

lornerestaurant.co.uk

Bookings
Phone, website, or resdiary.com

Price guide

What they say
"Lorne focuses on the things that matter the most to us – good food, good wine, and good hospitality in an unfussy and relaxed atmosphere. We're also very passionate about the team who work at Lorne. Our staff work hard so we try to ensure we're giving back to them via learning and training to reflect how much they give every day at work. We are working on a system whereby our food waste will eventually turn into the compost that fertilizes our veg produce."

Signature dishes
Hogget sirloin with garlic, polenta, St George's mushroom, and monk's beard; Yorkshire rhubarb with ginger, custard, pumpkin seed oil; and spiced monkfish cheeks, celery, cucumber, sorrel, grape, peanut.

What we say
An oasis of peace, tranquility, and refinement amid the head-banging chain restaurants of modern Victoria. We visited on a parched city day and found the inside calm and cool, nicely lit, with a plain, almost puritanical menu of five starters, five mains and five puddings on a creamy sheet of A4. Plus recommended aperitifs of the day at the top, which is always a lovely touch. Sweetbreads stood out: two sweet lobes of pancreas with peas and fresh borlotti beans, caramelized shallots, and a lovely fresh jus. As did the monkfish, broccoli, squid, chilli, garlic, celtuce, and cashews: perfect fish and shellfish arced around a pretty plate with long leaves of the celery-lettuce hybrid, shards of nut, and specks of chilli – firm, sweet, and fresh.

Lupins

London

What
A neighbourhood restaurant serving modern seasonal British sharing plates

Who
Lucy Pedder & Natasha Cooke, chefs/owners

When
Lunch & dinner, Tuesday to Saturday, lunch Sunday

Address
66 Union Street, London, SE1 1TD

+44 (0)20 3908 5888

lupinslondon.com

Bookings
Phone or opentable.com

Price guide

What they say
"Using seasonal British ingredients is at the heart of our ethos, but we wanted to use unexpected flavour combinations and borrowed techniques to really bring them to life. Sustainability is a no-brainer for us – we use the best British fish and meat that we can get our hands on and try to stick to seasonal ingredients wherever possible. Matthew Stevens, HG Walter, and Natoora all help us to maintain integrity, quality, and sustainability in our food. We try hard to champion other small businesses in the community who we think have a similar ethos to us. London Beer Factory are excellent for the beer and Vino Beano and Smashing Wines help us give an exciting wine offering that we're truly proud of."

Signature dishes
Crispy spring onions with chipotle mayo; bream carpaccio with asparagus; and pigeon Wellington.

What we say
Lupins is a small, bright, two-storey space run almost exclusively by women. The downstairs is a very open kitchen with an eating bar for half a dozen people and a couple of tables, upstairs is a small, sunny dining room with lovely pale pinks and greeny greys in the paintwork. The single A4 sheet of menu offers ten or twelve small things priced between £7 and £12, of which we ordered six. They came sequentially at a perfect pace. The best kitchen-to-table service we have seen anywhere. And every single dish was perfect. What are you waiting for?

Lurra

London

What
Basque cuisine with a focus on produce, sourcing & simplicity

Who
Nemanja Borjanovic & Melody Adams, owners

When
Dinner Monday to Saturday, lunch Tuesday to Sunday

Address
9 Seymour Place, London, W1H 5BA

+44 (0)20 7724 4545

lurra.co.uk

Bookings
Phone or website

Price guide

What they say
"Lurra, meaning 'land' in Basque, is a supply-led restaurant. Our team's focus is to follow the seasons, bringing the best of the Basque region to the UK. We don't only ensure quality produce at a fair price, but can see first-hand the ethics and sustainability behind everything we source. To ensure this, for our fish produce we only use dayboat catch, wild fish from sources who have been certified by genuine sustainability bodies, and we only serve beef from old Galician Blond cows that have had a good and long life."

Signature dishes
Galician Blond prime rib; turbot; and octopus.

What we say
We love this beautiful modern eating space with its fridges of spectacular meat, outstanding cooking, and knowledgeable staff. It was here they first brought aged dairy cows from Galicia to the UK as beef. Previously thought of in this country as a farming byproduct and sent for burgers or pet food, it proved to be the meat sensation of the decade. Marbled like something Michelangelo might have worked in and with more flavour than anything we had known, it changed the way we thought about beef. Now Lurra has started, in Thirsk, a project to create a dual-purpose UK cow. When each cow's milking life is over she will be retired to lush Yorkshire grass for three more years, bouncing from a "spent" animal to a happy fat cow. A delicious, happy, fat cow.

Lyle's

London

What
Modern British restaurant

Who
James Lowe, head chef &
John Ogier, general manager

When
Breakfast, lunch & dinner,
Monday to Saturday

Address
Tea Building, 56 Shoreditch
High St, London, E1 6JJ

+44 (0)20 3011 5911

lyleslondon.com

Bookings
Phone, website, or email
info@lyleslondon.com

Price guide

What they say
"We love providing people with a snapshot of the best produce that's available in the UK at any given time. We provide food that is great value for money, served by people who care about what they do in a relaxed and inclusive atmosphere. The food at Lyle's is always seasonal. We work as often as possible with small-scale and local producers. The best example of this is during the summer, when we have daily (every evening) deliveries of salad leaves grown by Chrissy at Keat's Farm in Bexley Heath, South London. All of the fish we serve is from small dayboat co-ops, it is all line-caught and MSC-certified, and we buy whole animals and use the entire carcass."

Signature dishes
Asparagus with cured Mangalitsa belly, and pheasant eggs; chicken of the wood mushrooms with wild onions, and sweet cicely; and Speckled Face mutton with ramson, Jersey Royals, and yoghurt.

What we say
Chef James Lowe comes with a solid grounding in the best of modern British at St John Bread and Wine via one of the benchmark moments in the glorious hipster history of restaurant London, The Young Turks residency at The Ten Bells in Spitalfields. Lyle's is a perfect restaurant of its kind, marrying the experimentalism of The Ten Bells with the minimalism and sheer devotion to quality produce of St John. We've had some of our best meals in recent years here.

Mac and Wild

London

What
A restaurant obsessed with extreme provenance & everything Scottish – venison, whisky, beef, & beer

Who
Andy Waugh & Calum Mackinnon, co-founders

When
Lunch & dinner, Monday to Saturday, lunch Sunday

Address
65 Great Titchfield Street, London, W1W 7PS

+44 (0)20 7637 0510

macandwild.com

Bookings
Website

Price guide

What they say
"We are a restaurant obsessed with the term 'extreme provenance' and everything Scottish. We are in the fortunate position of having all of our venison and game sourced directly from Ardgay Game, my family business. This means we can tell you the name of the butcher, the breed of deer, the exact area that it was shot, and even the name of the person who shot it.

"This ethos extends to our other suppliers and we only order when there is extreme traceability. I want to create a connection between the food on the plate and the people who worked their socks off to get this incredible produce to us."

Signature dishes
Haggis pops: crispy balls of haggis with Red Jon (a sweet, zingy, earthy sauce); "VeniMoo": a banging burger of wild venison patty, aged beef patty, caramelized onion, pickles, and Béarnaise; and venison chateaubriand: wild venison fillet sold by the gram and served rare.

What we say
We came away from dinner at Mac and Wild saying, "This is the best restaurant in the world". But that was partly the whisky talking. So much whisky. Delicious whisky. But the whisky was not necessarily wrong. There is something about a mouthful of piping hot haggis, breaded and deep-fried, with a homemade dipping sauce of redcurrant jelly and mustard, washed down with a slosh of good single malt that makes you wonder why Scottish cuisine hasn't taken over the world.

Manna

London

What
Vegan fine dining

Who
Roger Swallow, owner/partner

When
Lunch & dinner, Tuesday to Saturday, lunch Sunday

Address
4 Erskine Road, Primrose Hill, London, NW3 3AJ

+44 (0)20 7722 8028

mannav.com

Bookings
Website

Price guide

What they say
"We celebrated our fiftieth anniversary in 2017 and are the oldest vegetarian restaurant in the UK (and possibly the longest-standing vegetarian fine dining house in Europe). Manna has been exclusively 100 per cent vegan for over a decade, serving plant-based and nutritious cuisine that nourishes a community and a string of excellent suppliers."

Signature dishes
Black quinoa maki rolls in the Japanese tradition; Caribbean platter: array of coconut-based broths and aromatic Jamaican delicacies; and bangers and mash: organic seed sausages with root vegetable and herb mash, and rich jus topped with sweet and tender gluten-free onion rings.

What others say
"The knockout dish ... was a delicious special of aubergine wraps with almond cheese."

Time Out

What we say
While Primrose Hill has changed beyond all recognition over the past twenty years, transforming into a super-fashionable film set of a place inhabited mostly by the staff of the Russian, French, and American ex-pats who don't actually live in the houses they've bought, with endless posh delicatessens and coffee shops, Manna has remained unchanged. There it is, still there after celebrating its fiftieth anniversary in 2017, tucked away off the Main Street in leafy and exclusive Primrose Hill. Vegetarian since the beginning, Manna has now been fully vegan for over a decade serving simple but elegant traditional, international recipes somewhat from a Californian prospective.

The Marksman Public House

London

What
A pub & restaurant in East London, focused on craftsmanship & seasonality

Who
Tom Harris & Jon Rotheram, owners

When
Dinner Monday to Thursday, lunch & dinner, Friday to Sunday

Address
254 Hackney Road, London, E2 7SJ

+44 (0)20 7739 7393

marksmanpublichouse.com

Bookings
Phone, website, or resdiary.com

Price guide

What they say
"Tom and Jon are passionate about craftsmanship, a theme reflected in the pub's original Victorian atmosphere and decor, while still appealing to the modern-day diner. The menu compliments and respects the pub's history, focusing on exceptional London food with a spotlight on traditional practices, such as authentic British baking and curing of native fish and meats."

Signature dishes
Beef and barley bun with horseradish cream; veal, wild garlic, and girolle pie (braised veal neck, seasonal wild garlic, and Scottish girolles encased in an all-butter puff pastry); and brown butter and honey tart (brown butter and honey custard in a shortcrust pastry).

What others say
"If there's a better lunch to be had in Britain right now than the beef and barley buns with horseradish, the kid goat curry with the fried potatoes

and the brown butter and honey tart served at the Marksman pub on the Hackney Road, I want to know about it."

–Jay Rayner, *The Guardian*

What we say
The wood-panelled dining room is one of the glories of East London, not a poncey modern bolt-on or faux-distressed pastiche of old-world glamour but a magnificent real pub dining room with leather banquettes and stools, big windows, mirrors, and a telly. Tom Harris comes from the St John stable of British chefs, Jon from Jamie Oliver's Fifteen and the lessons of those great places are there to see in the simplicity and ballsiness of the cooking.

Native

What
A wild food restaurant that uses locally sourced British produce with a zero waste initiative

Who
Ivan Tisdall-Downes & Imogen Davis, co-owners

When
Lunch & dinner, Tuesday to Saturday

Address
32 Southwark Street, London, SE1 1TU

+44 (0)20 3638 8214

eatnative.co.uk

Bookings
Phone, website, or email bookings@eatnative.co.uk

Price guide
●●●○○

What they say
"The main incentive of Native is to provide guests with an original dining experience using the country's best wild food that is native to the UK. Our aim is to be as sustainable and resourceful as possible while creating something amazing. This goes for our food as well as the way we run the restaurant from a business perspective. We're passionate about trying to use entirely British produce, using local producers and micro farms; our dishes intend to reflect indigenous Britain. We enjoy going foraging and incorporating our finds into the menu. In the past, we've pickled fruit from a tree that fell over in Ivan's mum's garden to use in the restaurant, too."

Signature dishes
Fallow deer with caramelized cauliflower and carrot top salsa verde; fish from the market with parsnip, wild garlic, and smoked lardo; and bone marrow fudge with ants.

What we say
Native is a true labour of love. For their new site they crowdfunded £50,000 on Kickstarter – so that is some seriously committed supporters. The whole team mucked in to clean up and redecorate the site to make it fit for opening. They made their own tables with cement and plywood, chairs were kindly donated, and everything in the kitchen was found on eBay. They were recently crowned champions at the Rude Health Porridge Championships (using only real ingredients – no additives, preservatives, colourants, or synthetics) with their parsnip, bone marrow, and sea buckthorn porridge.

Nutbourne

What
Barbecue grill restaurant

Who
Gladwin Brothers, owners

When
Breakfast & lunch, Tuesday to Sunday, dinner Tuesday to Saturday

Address
29 Ransomes Dock,
35–37 Parkgate Road, London,
SW11 4NP

+44 (0)20 7350 0555

nutbourne-restaurant.com

Bookings
Website

Price guide

What they say
"With Nutbourne we wanted to create a community restaurant for Battersea locals. We both live in and love Battersea, and we hope that we've created a space that caters to all the tastes of our local community. We serve wild British food in a farm-to-table style from our barbecue open grill. We source our fruit and vegetables from local farmers in the countryside, and this ensures trade into the local community. We also source meat from our brother and wine, fruit, and vegetables from our neighbours, as well as wine from our parents' vineyard, so we all know where it comes from and are personally invested in how it's grown."

Signature dishes
Barbecue-grilled Sussex beef rump with homegrown red pepper salsa; superfood salad; and honeycomb crunchy with mascarpone and tarragon sugar.

What we say
Nutbourne is bringing the joys of Sussex country life and country community values to the city. For example, they have a communal coffee table where locals can sit and enjoy the sunshine and they have organized a farmers' market out the front on a Saturday so locals can come and purchase their weekly fruit and vegetables, then stop in for a coffee or glass of Nutty (their nickname for wine from the Nutbourne vineyard).

OXO Tower

London

What
Restaurant, bar, & brasserie offering the very best in modern British cuisine

Who
Jeremy Bloor, executive chef

When
Lunch & dinner, daily

Address
Barge House Street,
London, SE1 9PH

+44 (0)20 7803 3888

oxotowerrestaurant.com

Bookings
Phone or website

Price guide
●●●●○

What they say
"We love to bring people together to celebrate the very best of British ingredients, rare wines and delicious cocktails and to enjoy the stunning London skyline. Being an SRA member is a source of pride for us, as well as the work we do with the local community and not-for-profit organisations. Many of our ingredients are organic (all of our milk), fair trade (such as our sugar and chocolate), direct trade (such as our illy coffee), and ethically sourced or produced (such as our Tregothnan tea). We have an extensive nurturing and mentoring programme for our team and have an exceptionally high rate of staff retention."

Signature dishes
Dorset crab with apple jelly and crab ketchup; lamb hotpot, belly, and cutlet with lemon quinoa and buttermilk gel; and English strawberry and basil mousse.

What we say
For a place known as a brilliant spot for evening drinks and food with staggering views over the city and a decent chance of a party in a steepling landmark building, it is wonderful to know that the feet of OXO Tower Restaurant, Bar and Brasserie are planted so firmly in the ground. They have worked to reduce CO2 emissions, have an extremely environmentally friendly kitchen (which won a CEDA award), and have supported the City Harvest charity that distributes surplus food, with donations and staff volunteering. Recently they have increased their vegetarian and vegan offerings to encourage guests to reduce their intake of animal products.

Noble Rot

What
Wine bar & restaurant

Who
Paul Weaver, chef

When
Lunch & dinner,
Monday to Saturday

Address
51 Lamb's Conduit Street,
London, WC1N 3NB

+44 (0)20 7242 8963

noblerot.co.uk

Bookings
Website or resdiary.com

Price guide

What they say
"At Noble Rot we are passionate about creating a welcoming environment, serving unfussy, delicious food and exciting fine wine at accessible prices with friendly, knowledgeable service. Treating and training our staff well is very important to us, too, and we care about creating a happy, fulfilling and rewarding workplace (our service charge goes to the staff). We filter water and offer it for free to customers and encourage this instead of stocking bottled water, and we work with a forager in Norfolk for sea vegetables and other grasses and herbs. A supplier in West London supplies us with herbs from his roof garden in Notting Hill and, when we need elderflower, Myles, our sous-chef, brings some in from Peckham."

Signature dishes
Lincolnshire smoked eel with Jersey Royals, and horseradish; slip sole and smoked butter; and roast Anjou pigeon and peas à la Française.

What others say
"Relentlessly, gaspingly good."

–Grace Dent, *London Evening Standard*

What we say
What a wonder Noble Rot was when it crept quietly onto Lamb's Conduit Street, surely the first restaurant to grow directly out of the pages of a wine magazine. Or possibly not. Who cares? It must be the best. Redolent of boozy 1970s London wine bars, with its naughty nooks and crannies and heavy booze focus, Noble Rot also happens to serve some of the most interesting small plates in London, brilliantly conceived each day to pair with the miraculous offerings of the wine list.

Padella

What
A high-quality, affordable, fresh, handmade pasta bar in Borough Market, London

Who
Tim Siadatan, owner

When
Lunch & dinner, daily

Address
6 Southwark Street, London,
SE1 1TQ

padella.co

Bookings
No bookings taken

Price guide

What they say
"At Padella, we aim to make the best pasta in the world and make it accessible for everyone. We use local wherever we can, for example we get our guanciale from Cobble Lane Cured, a charcuterie based in Highbury (so on our doorstep) and it tastes fantastic. Padella's menu is dictated by seasonality. This means we have built strong relationships with our suppliers, working closely with them far in advance in order to get the most delicious-tasting fresh produce as possible and ensuring a short supply chain. We work closely with small producers in Italy who have single-estate olive groves and press in-house. Despite it being further from us, we buy in one bulk order, limiting our carbon footprint as much as possible."

Signature dishes
Tagliarini with courgettes, brown shrimp, lemon, and chilli; *matalacci* with guanciale, peas, *grellots*, and pecorino Romagna; and our eight-year-old sourdough.

What others say
"Then an absolute barnstormer, barrelling straight to the top of my desert island dishes: those pici [*cacio e pepe*] ... utter, head-turning alchemy."

–Marina O'loughlin, *The Guardian*

What we say
Trullo was already one of London's most talked about and original new restaurants when it opened Padella, which has gone on to be probably the single-most sought-after restaurant destination in town. The queues are immense and the nay-sayers are as close to zero as we've ever seen. Padella is more than just a pasta joint. It is a revolution.

Palatino

London

What
A new Italian restaurant focused on the food of Rome from Stevie Parle

Who
Stevie Parle, founder

When
Lunch & dinner, Monday to Saturday

Address
71 Central Street, London, EC1V 8AB

+44 (0)20 3481 5300

palatino.london

Bookings
Phone or website

Price guide

What they say
"Palatino focuses on cooking the true cuisine of Rome – both Italian capital and melting pot of cuisines from across the wider region. Our menu changes with the seasons and we only work with the best quality, most sustainable suppliers, whether it's vegetables, seafood from British fishermen, or meat from our butcher in Yorkshire (Swaledale Foods). We work consistently on our environmental impact and we banned plastic straws from all our restaurants in 2017. We also work with a number of charities throughout the year and all staff are sent on research trips to meet our suppliers and better understand provenance of product."

Signature dishes
Tonarelli cacio e pepe with tellicherry pepper, and pecorino; *gnocchi alla Romana*; and chicken and pistachio meatballs with Aleppo chilli, and polenta.

What others say
"Better than in Rome."

–Jay Rayner, *The Guardian*

What we say
Pasta is having a real moment in this country, a welcome return to one of the great world foods after a few years in the carb-dodging doldrums, and nobody does it better than Stevie Parle. Our meal here was a true eye-opener, a dazzling transportation to Rome in the most unlikely of office-block settings. Purists whang on about the joys of *cacio e pepe*, but until we tried Parle's we had never really known what they meant – his had a silkiness, a depth, a poetry that we had never encountered in a bowl of spaghetti before. We kneel and pay homage.

The Palomar

London

What
Modern-day Jerusalem food, with influences from southern Spain, North Africa & the Levant

Who
Zoë & Layo Paskin, partners

When
Lunch & dinner, daily

Address
34 Rupert Street, London, W1D 6DN

+44 (0)20 7439 8777

thepalomar.co.uk

Bookings
Phone or opentable.com

Price guide

What they say
"Our suppliers are aware that using local and seasonal ingredients is very important to us, and so they keep us in the loop about when certain ingredients are at their best so that we can make informed decisions about what to include on our menu. We only buy British free-range eggs and organic milk. The majority of our seafood is sourced from British waters. The squid we use is sourced from either Scotland or Cornwall depending on availability. Our scallops and mackerel are sourced from Scotland. We choose to buy in our sea bream and octopus from Turkey and Spain respectively, as more local alternatives are not available, and both of these fish are farmed responsibly and sustainably."

Signature dishes
Kubaneh bread with tomato and tahini; polenta with mushrooms, asparagus, and truffle; and baba ganoush with coriander and pomegranate seeds.

What others say
"These are dishes that demand to be shared, talked about, Instagrammed and fought over."

–Tracey MacLeod, *The Independent*

What we say
In the evenings, people treat this wonderful place as a very distant extension of the Tel Aviv party scene, enjoying the music, shouting, and cocktails alongside the miraculous food. By day, it's more about hunkering down over the best Levantine cooking in town (it's been a huge influence and game-changer for the genre) to rave and gobble and, above all, Instagram the hell out of...

Paper and Cup

London

What
Provides work experience & employment training for people recovering from drug/alcohol addiction

Who
Spitalfields Crypt Trust

When
Breakfast & lunch, daily

Address
18 Calvert Avenue, London, E2 7JP

+44 (0)20 7739 5358

paperandcup.co.uk

Bookings
Email info@paperandcup.co.uk

Price guide

What they say
"We love the fact that we can provide tasty treats to our customers while, at the same time, help rebuild lives! The café offers a professional and safe environment where people can grow, learn, and move on. We help people to get back into the world of work after rehab by offering formal barista training and we skill them up on customer service and care. This helps them to get back into work, which will make their recovery sustainable. We've introduced new KeepCups to cut down on takeaway coffee cups and our leftovers are given to Spitalfields Crypt Trust's (SCT) drop-in and recovery accommodation."

What we say
Reducing the stigma around addiction is one of the central aims of Paper and Cup. They want to bring recovery out into the community and out of the mystery of rehabs and AA rooms. That is a hell of an aim for a small London café to set out with. And if Prince William is liking the tea then we are liking the whole thing all the way to heaven and back.

Parsons

London

What
A very classic take on seafood in the British Isles

Who
Will Palmer & Ian Campbell, owners

When
Lunch & dinner, Monday to Saturday

Address
39 Endell St, London, WC2H 9BA

+44 (0)20 3422 0221

parsonslondon.co.uk

Bookings
Website or opentable.com

Price guide

What they say
"We just love providing the best and freshest ingredients in a relaxed, affordable setting. Having always had a love of classic English fish restaurants, we wanted to create something new and exciting, where the wine and the simply prepared fish play equally important roles in the experience. An unassuming (and fun!) restaurant where you are just as welcome to drop in for a glass of wine and a few oysters at the bar as you are to sit down for a longer meal. Our fish is sourced as sustainably as possible using dayboats, mostly in Cornwall, and the menu is designed so that all the fresh fish items can be changed daily/hourly to reflect what is available at the time. We recreate classic British dishes into something recognizable but more thrilling."

Signature dishes
Potted shrimp croquettes; brown crab pissaladière; and daily fish selection, representing the restaurant's efforts to be sustainable – this is what they have and when it's gone, it's gone.

What we say
Parsons is right up there with the finest fish restaurants in London – Scott's, J Sheekey, Bentley's – but half the price. A small room with a lovely feel, brilliantly designed to maximize the space and with a spare, white-tiled elegance reminiscent of the great Sweetings in the City. Well-chosen wine and a commitment to helping keep as much of the best British fish as possible in Britain rather than letting it all go abroad.

Petersham Nurseries Richmond

London

What
A place of beauty, an emporium of goods, a celebration of the seasons

Who
Boglione family, owners & Damian Clisby, chef director

When
Lunch Tuesday to Sunday

Address
Church Lane, Richmond, London, TW10 7AB, plus other locations – see website

+44 (0)20 8940 5230

petershamnurseries.com

Bookings
Phone or website

Price guide

What they say
"Respecting the Slow Food philosophy of good, clean, and fair, focusing on the finest seasonal produce, quality ingredients, and Italian flavours. We aim to use certified organic produce or use produce grown using organic methods. We do sometimes source items from small artisan suppliers that do not have the means to be certified organic, but all of these suppliers have been chosen specifically for the quality of their produce and sustainability."

Signature dishes
Petersham Nurseries Café (mozzarella *di bufala* with varieties of courgettes, mint, and *taggiasca* olives); The Petersham (loin of Haye Farm lamb with sweetbreads, spinosa artichoke, chard, and basil; and La Goccia (wood-fired mussels and clams with Vermentino, courgettes, chilli, garlic, and parsley).

What we say
Since opening in Richmond in 2004, Petersham Nurseries has recently opened a second destination in Covent Garden, which includes two restaurants, The Petersham and La Goccia. Strong in so many areas, we particularly admire their attention to waste management and recycling – which are by no means the most glamorous or visible aspects of the business. They have been separating waste for over ten years, working alongside Quantum Waste – a socially conscientious company that uses lighter vehicles to collect in a local radius, lowering carbon emissions. They are also committed to reducing food waste from their kitchens, prep from entire carcasses, and are committed to composting. They use imitation greaseproof paper made from sustainable forest paper and have swapped from clingfilm to compostable bio-film.

Petersham Nurseries Richmond (p. 97)

Pizarro

London

What
Spanish restaurant

Who
José Pizarro, owner/chef

When
Lunch & dinner,
Monday to Saturday

Address
194 Bermondsey Street,
London, SE1 3TQ

+44 (0)20 7378 9455

josepizarro.com

Bookings
Phone or website

Price guide

What they say
"We love creating an eating space that makes people feel a part of our family, relaxed and comfortable as if they were at José's house. Being a Spanish restaurant in London, it is difficult to have 100 per cent local produce. But it is so important to us to work with our neighbours and local suppliers to showcase their produce and to be able to offer the best price and quality guarantee to our guests."

Signature dishes
Artichoke a la plancha with egg yolk and *jamón ibérico* 100 per cent, 5J, acorn fed; red mullet a la plancha with confit fennel, and citrus salad; and grilled veal loin with cabbage, wild garlic, sprouting broccoli, and anchovy vinaigrette.

What we say
José Pizarro, one of the London food heroes of the century, used to be head chef at Tapas Brindisa, the Spanish import company that did so much to bring great Iberian produce to the UK. In opening his Bermondsey Street restaurant he took that import principle further, bringing serious Spanish vibes to a tapas scene that was previously derivative and moribund. At this place you will eat delicious food, drink excellent sherry, and spill into a street that has become a food mecca mostly thanks to José.

The Pear Tree

London

What
The quintessential Victorian pub – privately owned, one of the last true free houses in West London

Who
Daz Seager, owner/chef

When
Lunch & dinner, daily

Address
14 Margravine Road, London, W6 8HJ

+44 (0)20 7381 1787

thepeartreefulham.com

Bookings
Phone or website

Price guide

What they say
"Hidden in the backstreets of Hammersmith, The Pear Tree is a nostalgic vision of a Victorian family-owned pub with a thriving and loyal local community. Our extensive bar selection includes constantly rotating beers from the best of English and European breweries with fine wines from the New and Old Worlds. We use the London markets as well as our local butcher and fishmonger (Steve and Jim), who are friends of ours and never let us down. We harvest our eponymous pears in late summer for chutneys, poaching, and the odd bottle of pear vodka from time to time!"

Signature dishes
Sea bass, filleted, seasoned, and pan-fried with a lemon caper dressing, Jersey Royals, and seasonal vegetables; Herefordshire sirloin medallions with Béarnaise and Maris Piper triple-cooked chips; and vegan tart with roasted beetroot, butternut, smoked

garlic, wild mushroom pesto, basil oil dressing, and kitchen salad.

What we say
A lovely old pub doing its bit to keep Fulham real. The Pear Tree celebrates fresh, quality ingredients by creating simple dishes that allow the flavour and freshness to shine. Their Herefordshire sirloin medallions are a testament to this, highlighting this prime meat in one exceptional dish. They also have delicious meat-free options, like a vegan tart, full of earthy goodness.

Pidgin

London

What
A small neighbourhood restaurant in Hackney, serving a weekly-changing four-course set menu

Who
James Ramsden & Sam Herlihy, owners

When
Dinner Tuesday to Thursday, lunch & dinner, Friday to Sunday

Address
52 Wilton Way, London, E8 1BG

+44 (0)20 7254 8311

pidginlondon.com

Bookings
Phone or website

Price guide

What they say
"Before we opened Pidgin we ran a supper club, so, for us, there's always been that element of the homely, intimate dinner party, of inviting people into your place and giving them an incredible time. That's the most important thing for us – having people leave our restaurant absolutely buzzing about what they've just experienced, not just because the food is great but because the whole package is special."

Signature dishes
A four-course menu that changes weekly.

What others say
"This fixed-menu idea is nothing new, but the Pidgin team have made it fresh and vibrant as a citron pressé. I'd happily go back for their home-churned Jersey cream butter alone."

–Marina O'loughlin, *The Guardian*

What we say
A brilliant little restaurant offering endless surprises and delights in an unlikely part of town (although Henry Dimbleby, founder of Leon, lives a few doors up the road) where, because they change the menu each week and have a very accurate idea of how many covers they are doing, food waste is almost non-existent. Presently, they have created around 560 dishes since opening, plus snacks and vegetarian dishes. Fixed-menu dining is one of the best ways to take restaurants – especially small restaurants – into a sustainable future and Pidgin is leading the way with style and class.

The Pig and Butcher

London

What
Gastropub serving a daily-changing menu that you would see on farmhouse tables around Europe

Who
Noble Inns Group

When
Dinner, daily, lunch Friday to Sunday

Address
80 Liverpool Road, London, N1 0QD

+44 (0)20 7226 8304

thepigandbutcher.co.uk

Bookings
Phone or website

Price guide

What they say
"We adore great food that has been raised well and looked after. We specialize in butchering our own meat and use rare and native breeds. All of the care and attention, from our farmers to our chefs, comes through in the quality on the plate in front of our customers. We only use ingredients in season and sourced locally. By changing our menu daily, we can ensure we utilize everything, this keeps waste to a minimum and we recycle all food waste."

Signature dishes
Thirty-five-day aged Ballindalloch Aberdeen Angus sirloin with crispy onion, portobello mushroom, horseradish creamed spinach, and double-dipped chips; Lyons Farm Iron Age pork brawn with Granny Smith, celeriac rémoulade, and sourdough toast; and Dorset snails and bone marrow gratin with crispy kale and cornichons.

What others say
"... the steak is almost unimprovably delicious."

–Amol Rajan, *The Independent*

What we say
We'd say this is a terrific country pub that just happens to be in Islington but that fact is that pubs as good as this, taking in whole carcasses of White Park beef, Iron Age pork, and Hebridean lamb and butchering on-site, drilling down into the supply chain to ensure sustainability and quality is something you're more likely to find in Islington than almost anywhere else. Filtered water is sold and the proceeds sent to Great Ormond Street Hospital, they do good work for Action Against Hunger, and... it's a bloody good pub.

Popolo

London

What
Sharing plates inspired by regional Italy with a touch of the Middle East, from an open kitchen

Who
Jon Lawson, chef/proprietor

When
Dinner Monday to Saturday

Address
26 Rivington St, London, EC2A 3DU

+44 (0)20 7729 4299

popoloshoreditch.com

Bookings
Phone, website, or email info@popoloshoreditch.com

Price guide

What they say
"Building a sustainable model to serve people with skill, love, and care, while creating experiences that will leave a lasting impression. A true labour of love, in which we have poured our craft and hearts at every detail; from the sourcing of local and sustainable produce, to the creativity of dishes inspired by the seasons with a lack of pretension. Service is attentive yet informal, while the food is beautifully partnered with a select list of raw and biodynamic wines coming from small independent producers. At Popolo we all care for and take pride in what we do and how it affects the people around us. Staff are treated and made to feel the way we want our customers to feel: cared for and respected."

Signature dishes
Freshly rolled *taglierini* with handpicked Dorset crab and wild fennel; Sardinian bottarga paired with a glass of Aleatico bianco "Alter Alea"

Lazio; and burnt honey panna cotta with pistachio *advieh*.

What others say
"I'd go back weekly if I could."

–Marina O'loughlin, *The Guardian*

What we say
Foodies rave and rave about the flawlessly realized Italian classics, reimagined with Moorish, Spanish, and Middle-Eastern touches. But there is a beautiful simplicity at the heart of everything Jon Lawson does, as there is at the heart of all great things.

Portland

London

What
A modern European restaurant, serving simple but imaginative & refined food in a calm setting

Who
Merlin Labron-Johnson & Zachary Elliott, head chefs

When
Lunch & dinner, Monday to Saturday

Address
113 Great Portland Street, London, W1W 6QQ

+44 (0)20 7436 3261

portlandrestaurant.co.uk

Bookings
Phone or website

Price guide

What they say
"Our ambition is to serve food that is light, yet full of robust flavours. Our menus are inspired by the produce delivered to us daily by the small growers and producers that we work with. Our wine list is given just as much attention as our menu and changes almost as frequently. Merlin is a key figure in London for championing the fight against food waste. He, Zach, and their team look at every kitchen process to work out how all leftover produce can be turned into something that is delicious, rather than throwing it away or composting it. Their aim is to be as inventive as possible with all offcuts."

Signature dishes
Wye Valley asparagus with ricotta *gnudi*, egg yolk, and nettles; St Bride's chicken with white asparagus, *calçots*, and mustard; and Kernow monkfish with root vegetables, nasturtium, and smoked beurre blanc.

What we say
At a time when the London restaurant scene was disappearing down a monochromatic path of sharing plates, barbecue, and big spicy flavours, Portland had the confidence to to bring refinement back to the kitchen, thrived beyond all expectation, and made a star of the brilliant but modest Merlin Labron-Johnson. That so much of his cooking philosophy comes from best environmental practice shows how a deep commitment to sustainability – they don't even serve garnishes in their drinks that they know will be thrown away – is the way to take hospitality to the next level.

Primeur

London

What
Small, intimate space serving small plates & low-intervention wines from a 1920s garage

Who
Jeremie C. Lingenheim & David Gingell, owners

When
Dinner Tuesday to Thursday, lunch & dinner, Friday to Sunday

Address
116 Petherton Road, London, N5 2RT

+44 (0)20 7226 5271

primeurn5.co.uk

Bookings
Phone, website, or opentable.com

Price guide

What they say
"When we found the old garage on a sunny day with its wide-open doors, we knew we could do something special here. We spent money from a shoestring budget where we should – i.e. the kitchen – and used the Shakers' utilitarian aesthetics for the rest, which suited simplicity and business constraints. We cook all the fresh produce in the morning and tend to sell everything on the night so we have virtually no wastage. Our wine producers work biodynamically with respect for the land, encouraging biodiversity and observing the law of return as well as feeding the soil, not the plant, which increases soil health and fertility."

Signature dishes
Jamón de Teruel; pig's head and nduja croquette; and chocolate pot and peanut caramel.

What we say
We have always loved the sense of "rus in urbe" about Primeur's location on a quiet, leafy street in what was once a motoring garage but has the feel of a village blacksmith. Then there is the enthusiasm of the staff for their fresh, organic produce, their biodynamic wines, and sublime cooking. The owners have small children and organize staff shifts to allow lives to be led outside work, and owner Jeremie has renounced houses, sold all his belongings, and moved into a horsebox to live autonomously and with a low impact. At least that's what they said in our survey. And you wouldn't take the mickey in a survey. Would you, boys?

The Quality Chop House

What
Offering modern, innovative cooking based around the finest ingredients in the British Isles

Who
Shaun Searley, head chef

When
Lunch & dinner, Monday to Saturday, lunch Sunday

Address
88–94 Farringdon Road, London, EC1R 3EA

+44 (0)20 7278 1452

thequalitychophouse.com

Bookings
Phone or website

Price guide

What they say
"As far as possible, we use local, sustainable ingredients. This ethos is at the heart of everything we do. We write our menus daily, which allows us the flexibility to use seasonal, sustainable produce. All of our meat comes from small UK farms. For example, we source rare-breed meat from rare-pedigree animals: longhorn beef, Middle White pork, and Ryeland lamb from Huntsham Court Farm in the Wye Valley, heritage pork from Hugh and Kathy at Penlan Farm in Herefordshire, as well as beef, milk-fed spring lamb, pork, and mutton from Farmer Tom Jones in the Welsh border. We work closely with the charity Action Against Hunger and their Love Food Give Food campaign."

Signature dishes
Cornish mackerel with smoked bone broth, Sichuan, kohlrabi, and seaweed; Cornish monkfish with marsh vegetables and langoustine hollandaise; and Madagascan chocolate with milk jam and caramelized white chocolate.

What others say
"Hear me now: do not make the mistake of dying before you have eaten here."

–Giles Coren, *The Times*

What we say
The very essence of the recycled restaurant. First opened in 1869 as a working man's eating house, repurposed as retro chic in the 1990s with its wonderful grade II listed Victorian interior, then most recently turned into one of the most wonderful restaurants in London by the guys who would go on to give us Clipstone and Portland. The wine list is dazzling, the cooking is off the clock, and the Victorian vibes are pure poetry.

Quo Vadis

What
An iconic British restaurant & members' club in Soho

Who
Sam, James & Eddie Hart, owners & Jeremy Lee, chef

When
Lunch & dinner, Monday to Saturday

Address
26 Dean Street, London, W1D 3LL

+44 (0)20 7437 9585

quovadissoho.co.uk

Bookings
Phone, website, or email info@quovadissoho.co.uk

Price guide

What they say
"Beautiful, simple, produce-led seasonal food and exceptional, attentive service in a characterful building where you are greeted with an astonishing array of beautiful flowers. We are blessed with the producers we get to work with, who farm and grow and produce in almost every county in the British Isles. One example is Fern Verrow, the biodynamic farm in Hereford. We are working with the SRA to help lower our carbon emissions and lessen our environmental impact."

Signature dishes
Smoked eel sandwich; baked salsify with Parmesan; and chocolate profiteroles.

What others say
"Lee is one of those rare phenomena in the London food world: a chap everyone agrees is a good thing."

–Jay Rayner, *The Guardian*

What we say
The takeover of this famous and beautiful old restaurant by the visionary Hart brothers, Sam and Eddie, and the installation in the kitchen of Chef Jeremy Lee, with all his extravagant genius, was the best thing to happen in Soho for a generation and arguably kick-started its gastronomic revolution over the last decade. The space is pale, breezy, and sexy, the cocktails are top hole, the brothers – when they are there – are charm personified, and Jeremy's cooking is in a class of its own when it comes to doing extraordinary things with the best of British produce. His eel sandwiches deserve a restaurant – indeed a whole chain of restaurants – all of their own.

Rabbit

London

What
Local & wild restaurant

Who
Gladwin Brothers,
founders/chefs

When
Dinner Monday, lunch &
dinner, Tuesday to Saturday,
Lunch Sunday

Address
172 King's Road, London,
SW3 4UP

+44 (0)20 3750 0172

rabbit-restaurant.com

Bookings
Phone or website

Price guide

What they say
"Our policy is 100 per cent green
energy usage throughout all our
restaurants. We deliver all our
produce directly from the farm into
our restaurants which reduces extra
supplier deliveries. Our vegetable
produce is all bought without the use
of pesticides and herbicides. We make
use of local and wild produce from our
own farm and vineyard in West Sussex
as well as the surrounding farms."

Signature dishes
Mushroom Marmite éclair; roasted
hake with lemon potato vinaigrette
and wild foraged sea spinach (coastal
foraging is the best); and Sunday on
the Farm, roast beef from the farm
with all the trimmings.

What we say
Having grown up in beautiful Sussex,
the Gladwins are making it their
mission to share the bounty of the
English countryside with all their
customers. Their own farm in West
Sussex produces the beef, pork, and
lamb served in the restaurants, the
brothers and their team forage their
garnishes from the Sussex countryside
and clean urban areas, and although
the wine list has round-the-world
representation, fifty per cent of
their wine sales are from their own
vineyard in West Sussex, driven up and
delivered to the restaurant only when
incorporating a trip back to the family
home. Bloody marvellous.

Restaurant Story

London

What
Tasting menu restaurant

Who
Tom Sellers, chef patron

When
Dinner Monday, lunch &
dinner, Tuesday to Saturday

Address
199 Tooley Street, London,
SE1 2JX

+44 (0)20 7183 2117

restaurantstory.co.uk

Bookings
Phone, website, or email
dine@restaurantstory.co.uk

Price guide

What they say
"We have a strong focus on our small
and dedicated team, who drive the
energy that we put into the food,
beverages, and the service we love to
give! From our greenhouse (in central
London) we creatively sculpt a menu
of seasonal and British produce. Our
suppliers are carefully chosen to align
with our philosophy and we aim to
highlight the best of all the seasons.
We thoroughly enjoy being part of
local charities, from Hospitality Action
to UNICEF and Cancer Research.
From pickling to programmes for
aspiring staff: it's all a part of our
'Restaurant Story'."

Signature dishes
Scallop with cucumber and ash; Story
salad (changes each season and
on every menu); and almond and
dill dessert.

What we say
Nordic chic in a glass cube at Tower
Bridge from an outrageously talented
chef who has done time at Noma. The
standout thing for most people is the
beef-dripping candle that melts as it
burns down (obviously) so that you
can dip chunks of delicious artisanal
bread in it. Talk about sustainable:
this is the rendered fat of an animal
you are eating anyway, turned into a
candle to light your romantic dinner,
which you can then eat as it burns! If
only all our lighting could come from
delicious spreads made out of animal
waste. What a green, green planet this
would be.

Roast

London

What
British restaurant passionate
about local suppliers

Who
Roast Restaurant Group

When
Breakfast, lunch, & dinner,
daily

Address
The Floral Hall, Stoney Street,
London, SE1 1TL

+44 (0)2 0300 66111

roast-restaurant.com

Bookings
Phone, website, or email
info@roast-restaurant.com

Price guide

What they say
"At Roast, we are extremely spirited
about working with and building
relationships with local suppliers
and farmers. It is so important to
us that we deliver to our customers
not only the best quality ingredients
but that these are sourced locally,
where possible, as we truly believe
that Britain has so much to offer.
We use seasonal produce and local
produce wherever we can – all of our
fish is sourced from Cornwall and
Dorset, beef from Colchester, lamb
from Wales, etc. With such great
quality so close to home, we believe
in making the most of what we have
on our doorstep."

Signature dishes
Pork belly roast (represents what
Roast is all about – each ingredient is
locally sourced and the flavours are
traditionally British); Roast (the dish
at the very heart of Roast's ethos – you
can't beat a comforting roast dinner);
and vegan roast.

What we say
You can't beat a comforting roast
dinner. This well-established and
beautifully designed restaurant has
long been a champion of the best of
British food values. With all of their
fruit and veg coming from the stalls of
Borough Market at their very doorstep
the carbon footprint of the delivery
schedule is light. They are also tackling
food waste by encouraging diners to
take their leftovers home with them
with handy recipe cards to make the
most of the ingredients – an innovation
of quiet genius. Don't miss the pork
belly roast – it's the most popular dish
on the menu for good reason.

Rok London

London

What
New Nordic-influenced dining focusing on preservation & cooking over an open flame

Who
Matt Young, Frida Lindmark & Charles Bakker, co-founders

When
Lunch & dinner,
Monday to Saturday

Address
26 Curtain Road, London,
EC2A 3NY

+44 (0)20 7377 2152

roklondon.com

Bookings
Website

Price guide

What they say
"Preservation and fermentation are our passions at the restaurant. We culture our own dairy for fresh cheeses, yoghurts, and crème frâiche. We ferment vegetables for pickles and fruits for wines and ciders. We also dry ferment our herring to make our own Scandi-style dashi. Even though we are a Nordic-influenced restaurant, we source all our meats from small British farms (our guinea fowl is actually reared by Matt's friend purposely for the restaurant)."

Signature dishes
Scallop cooked in the shell with nduja; pork chop with apples and sauerkraut; and soused mackerel with onions, crème frâiche, and flatbread.

What we say
In a small Victorian building in Shoreditch that is spookily dwarfed by the empty spaces of the vast towers soon to be erected all around it, you will find possibly the only Swedish barbecue in London. It is odourless, white-washed, and woody in a Scandi-meets-hipster way and both the cooking and outlook of these guys is quite delightful. The pickles, such as the fennel and wild garlic and the cucumber and gin, are quite simply outstanding. On our visit, little scotch quail's eggs of beef and pepperoni were rich and porky with pungent parsley mayo; perfect hot alder-smoked salmon was served on a sweetish salad of charred broccoli, quinoa, and seeds, a wedge of iceberg under anchovy mayo and crispy onions had a pleasing Burger King tang to it; and a salad of heirloom tomatoes was at perfect ripeness. Skål!

Rotorino

London

What
Chef Stevie Parle's Southern Italian restaurant & wine bar

Who
Stevie Parle, founder

When
Dinner Monday to Saturday, breakfast, lunch, & dinner, Sunday

Address
434 Kingsland Rd, London,
E8 4AA

+44 (0)20 7249 9081

rotorino.com

Bookings
Phone, website, opentable.com, or bookatable.co.uk

Price guide

What they say
"Providing top-notch Southern Italian food in a relaxed neighbourhood environment. Our menu changes a little bit every day and we put new specials on the blackboards every week. Our pasta dishes are available in small and large sizes and we encourage sharing of plates as much as possible."

Signature dishes
Pistachio *campanelle* with basil, garlic, and parmesan; watermelon salad with tomato, chilli, mint, and salted ricotta; and SASSO chicken with lemon, thyme, roast garlic, ricotta, and toast.

What others say
"A burrida of white fish and clams in a chickpea broth is another glorious thing, and a reminder of why we all took Parle to our overfed hearts in the first place."

–Jay Rayner, *The Guardian*

What we say
Another quite brilliant Italian restaurant from the incomparable Stevie Parle where hipster vibes and shameless good times go hand in hand – for once – with really top-notch, old-fashioned Italian cooking. Try the watermelon salad for a burst of freshness and flavour.

Sabor

London

What
A Spanish restaurant that takes you on a journey through Spain

Who
Nieves Barragán & José Etura, owners

When
Lunch & dinner, Tuesday to Saturday, lunch Sunday

Address
35–37 Heddon Street, London, W1B 4BR

+44 (0)20 3319 8130

saborrestaurants.co.uk

Bookings
Phone or email
info@saborrestaurants.co.uk

Price guide

What they say
"We are about quality – from the quality of the ingredients we use to the quality of experience had by our guests. We want to take our guests on a journey through Spain, from the tapas bars of Andalucía through to the asadors of Castile and the seafood restaurants of Galicia. We source the highest quality food and drink to bring an authentically Spanish experience – from the food to the warm and friendly service – to our corner of Heddon Street."

Signature dishes
Suckling pig (in El Asador); *arroz con salmonete* (at the counter); and *camarones fritos* with fried egg (in the bar).

What we say
Nieves Barragán helped Sam and Eddie Hart change the world in her time with them at Barrafina and now in her own place she goes from strength to strength. Nowhere outside Segovia itself have we witnessed piglet-cookery of this beauty, the perfect young animals treated to wood-roasting of a kind one sees now almost nowhere – the result soft, unctuous, sticky, and full of sweet barnyard flavours. The salads alongside are immaculate, the tapas sublime, the wine list a thing of wonder, and the service very good-natured and very, very Spanish. Viva!

Salon

London

What
A modern British restaurant in Brixton Market, serving food guided by the seasons

Who
Nicholas Balfe, founder/head chef

When
Lunch & dinner, Tuesday to Saturday, lunch Sunday

Address
18 Market Row, Coldharbour Lane, London, SW9 8LD

+44 (0)20 7501 9152

salonbrixton.co.uk

Bookings
Website, phone, or email
info@salonbrixton.co.uk

Price guide

What they say
"We believe sustainability is a prerequisite for any hospitality business. Our guiding principles where food is concerned are to source the best ingredients we can, ideally as locally as they are available, and cook these ingredients with care and great attention to detail, and serve them with a combination of grace and informality. The great thing about Brixton is that it has connected us to a huge community of like-minded people, both in and out of the industry. The biggest development has undoubtedly been meeting Roy, who looks after our allotment in West Norwood – about a mile from the restaurant."

Signature dishes
The Peashooter: pea pod elderflower liqueur with mint stalk cordial and a dash of organic Macabeo; raw brill with elderflower and chayote; and fresh house-made curd cheese, using "spent milk" from generating frothy milk for coffees.

What others say
"Salon by day is homely and at night is experimental, possibly challenging to some diners, but completely worth leaving one's postcode for ... there are wonderful things happening in SW9."

–Grace Dent, *London Evening Standard*

What we say
From the brilliance of the food on the plate and the slickness and professionalism of the operation in the restaurant, you would never know that the heart and soul of Salon lay deep in the stink of the compost heap, in the mud of the land, and in a redoubtable commitment to waste reduction and carbon neutrality. But it does. So everyone's a winner.

The Shed

What
Local & wild small sharing plate concept

Who
Gladwin Brothers, partners

When
Dinner Monday, lunch & dinner, Tuesday to Saturday

Address
122 Palace Gardens Terrace, London, W8 4RT

+44 (0)20 7229 4024

theshed-restaurant.com

Bookings
Website

Price guide

What they say
"Growing, foraging, great cooking, and great company have always been the order of the day and this ethos has been brought to life at The Shed. The menu is made up of small plates of British food, changing daily according to availability of produce, whether from the farm or locally foraged or freshly caught off the South Coast. All our produce is sourced from around our parents' family home in Sussex, where they produce English wine which we sell in The Shed. We source our meat from our brother's farm, fruit and vegetables from our neighbours in Sussex and our wine from our family vineyard."

Signature dishes
Grilled Lulworth scallop with Sussex red pepper salsa; yoghurt-marinated pork tenderloins; and salted caramel espresso martini.

What we say
The shed was one of the first places to bring rustic hipster chic to Notting Hill. When we visited we were impressed by the beef tartare, the brawn terrine, some curls of warm chorizo with crispbreads and tangy labneh, a delicious dish of cuttlefish with almonds, and some things they called "lamb chips", which were deep-fried pucks of pulled lamb. Also the wonderful, humongous roasties rescued from the ashes of a burnt-out log cabin and reeking weepily of Bonfire Night. These we had with thin, sweet slices of beef heart and brandy butter. All good. All very good indeed.

Scully St James's

London

What
Scully's first solo venture based on a range of culinary traditions from his family heritage

Who
Ramael Scully, director/ executive chef

When
Lunch & dinner, Monday to Saturday, lunch Sunday

Address
4 St James's Market, Carlton Street, London, SW1Y 4AH

+44 (0)20 3911 6840

scullyrestaurant.com

Bookings
Website

Price guide

What they say
"Having the ability to learn about new food items daily, train the team, match with a wine, and then, the best bit, pass on our wealth of information to our guests for them to make their decisions. Our guests seem to really enjoy us talking to them about the menu and heritage of Scully. They are always wowed by our knowledge of ingredients and methods. We use The Modern Salad Grower (based in Devon) delivered by Natoora from farm to table/preserve jar within forty-eight hours. For our meats, we use Cabrito and Lake District farmers – all based in the UK. Our rapeseed oil we use is from a company called Duchess based in Oxford and we use the byproduct to produce our rapeseed and bay leaf ice cream!"

Signature dishes
Arepa with eggplant sambal and bergamot labneh; monkfish with sambal belacan and *sothi*; and beef short rib pastrami with horseradish and pistachio.

What we say
Having learned his trade under Yotam Ottolenghi and run the magnificent Nopi for seven years, it was time for Ramael Scully to spread his wings. Here, imperious purple beef ribs jostle with monkfish as big as labradors in the huge display fridges. The look is hard and futuristic but the cooking is assured, elegant, and precise. There was a new season tomato, green strawberry, and coconut salad on offer when we visited that we will remember as long as we live.

Six Portland Road

London

What
Small European restaurant & wine bar in Holland Park

Who
Oli & Ra Barker, owners, & Pascal Wiedemann, chef

When
Lunch & dinner, Tuesday to Saturday, lunch Sunday

Address
6 Portland Road, London, W11 4LA

+44 (0)20 7229 3130

sixportlandroad.com

Bookings
Phone, website, or resdiary.com

Price guide

What they say
"Simple seasonal cooking. Pure wine. Great vibes, man... When sourcing delicious produce, we try to keep it local (but being in London, of course a lot comes from outside the city). For example, our beer, which mostly comes from East London, and gin, which comes from down the road. We focus on our environmental impact by serving filtered water as an option to bottled, and are constantly striving to recycle in all the areas we can."

Signature dishes
Marinda tomatoes with mozzarella, crème fraîche, and mint; turbot with monk's beard, grapefruit, brown butter, and capers; and veal chop with white sprouting broccoli, *boquerones*, and almonds.

What we say
A rare restaurant of beauty in the Royal Borough of Kensington and Chelsea, which, despite being one of the wealthiest postcodes in the world, is poorly served for eating out. Six Portland Road has the local look and feel of a louche old London bistro from the 1970s, except that it serves incredibly good modern food with a super-smart list of mostly natural wines. The chatter is loud. And the big, fat roasted leg of chicken, served in two pieces with crispy golden skin, on asparagus, peas, morels, and spaetzle is a dish for the ages.

Smoke & Salt

London

What
Cuisine celebrating modern dining & ancient techniques by bridging cultures & traditions

Who
Aaron Webster & Remi Williams, founders/chefs

When
Dinner Monday to Saturday

Address
Pop Brixton, 49 Brixton Station Road, London, SW9 8PQ

+44 (0)74 2132 7556

smokeandsalt.com

Bookings
Website

Price guide

What they say
"Most cultures have some form of ancient food techniques, such as smoking, curing, and preserving. We take influence from these and adapt them to the modern dining scene, presenting food beautifully and humbly, while taking care to keep guests feeling at ease while they dine with us. We operate a fully transparent organization. All staff are paid above the London living wage and are of mixed ethnic backgrounds."

Signature dishes
Grilled Wiltshire beef heart with chimichurri, Gorgonzola and new potatoes; cured Chalk Stream Farm trout, sriracha mayonnaise, puffed taco, red onion, and jalapeño salsa; and grilled flatbread, variegated leaves, pickled garlic, caramelized onion peanut butter.

What others say
"What issues from their minuscule kitchen is little short of bravura ... tin box or not, this is how to create a restaurant."

–Marina O'loughlin, *The Sunday Times*

What we say
What Remi and Aaron have done with this tight little shipping container space at Pop Brixton (formerly home of the estimable Kricket) is nothing short of miraculous. The look is lean and futuristic and so is the cooking, which takes to new heights the sharing-plate and foraging genius these guys showed in their pop-ups and at The Shed, where they first met and learned so much. Service is always bumptious, confident and smiling, and Smoke & Salt will always have a special place in *Truth, Love & Clean Cutlery*'s heart, because we once supplied them with Jerusalem artichokes; they made them into ice cream.

Smokehouse

London

What
Original smoked & grilled food with a focus on quality, seasonality, provenance & great hospitality

Who
Maria & Scott Hunter, founders

When
Dinner, daily, weekend lunch

Address
63–69 Cannonbury Road, London, N1 2DG

+44 (0)20 7345 1144

smokehouseislington.co.uk

Bookings
Phone or website

Price guide

What they say
"We aim to offer the best and most original smoked and grilled food in London, have the best beer list (twenty on tap, sixty in the bottle), and we source wine from small family-owned vineyards only. Provenance is a large focus. Fish is delivered daily from Cornish markets and caught on dayboats, meat changes weekly with carcasses arriving from the best farms in the UK, and fruit and vegetables are from Natoora greengrocer. We grill over charcoal and roast and smoke using sustainably sourced English oak. We don't sell bottled water, but filter tap water, and we give the profits to Great Ormond Street Hospital."

Signature dishes
Short rib bourguignon; lamb heart with charred broccoli, anchovy, and sumac sour cream; and pan-fried fish of the day with whitebait, curried cauliflower, and chickpeas.

What we say
One of the first restaurants in London to go barbecue-crazy when the great Neil Rankin showed us the big five flavours were now salt, fat, smoke, fire, and carbon. Like guzzling the aftermath of the pig-barn fire in Charles Lamb's *A Dissertation upon Roast Pig*. Rankin has moved on but all the fire and spirit is still there. A glance at the website shows you what they're butchering today, maybe a Hereford from Charles Ashbridge or an eleven-month-old lamb from Lavinton Farm in Lincolnshire. With twenty beers on tap, sixty in the bottle, and wine from small family-run vineyards, Smokehouse is still on top of its game in every way.

SMOKESTAK

London

What
Barbecue restaurant driven by quality produce

Who
David Carter, owner

When
Lunch & dinner, daily

Address
35 Sclater Street, London, E1 6LB

+44 (0)20 3873 1733

smokestak.co.uk

Bookings
Website or email
book@smokestak.co.uk

Price guide

What they say
"We're proud to be part of the British Isles and do what we can to buy from within. This is why we value our relationships – it's so much more conducive to productivity when you can ring the supplier and have a conversation about what you're after and how you can work together. Great friendships have evolved from this. We work with Kernow Sashimi and Wild Harbour for all our dayboat fish. They only sell what the fisherman catches that day creating their own economy, for the fishermen especially, which is great. Philip Warren and Swaledale are our meat bosses – they care as much about the farmer and animal as they do about the customer, which is perfect as we get the best product! Our food is super simple, super delicious, and we do very little to it. It's all about sourcing the right product."

Signature dishes
Thirty-day aged beef rib with pickled red chilli; sea bream crudo with blood orange, jalapeño, and ginger; and charred greens with tahini and pomegranate.

What we say
Oh, Dave Carter, with your beard of Thor, your Bajan accent, and your forearms of Vulcan himself, toiling at the smithy of your ineffable barbecue, cooking with fire like nobody did untill you came along, how we adore you. We loved you just doing your street food thing at Dinerama and Dalston Yard but at SMOKESTAK – the ribs, the brisket, the ox cheek – you changed our lives forever.

Spring

What
Celebrating food for its conviviality & the joy of sharing seasonal produce

Who
Skye Gyngell, restaurateur

When
Lunch & dinner,
Monday to Saturday

Address
Somerset House, New Wing,
Lancaster Place, London,
WC2R 1LA

+44 (0)20 3011 0115

springrestaurant.co.uk

Bookings
Phone

Price guide

What they say
"Our cooking is heartfelt, wholesome, produce driven, and cooked by a team of people who are passionate about what they do and who feel truly privileged to work with beautiful ingredients. We hope to create an experience which not only sings on the plate but lingers in the memory. All our produce is seasonal – our menu is based entirely on what produce we receive from the biodynamic Hertfordshire farm Fern Verrow, with whom we have a partnership, taking all of the produce they grow."

Signature dishes
Morel and broad beans arancini with grilled spinach stems and wild garlic aïoli; halibut with slow-cooked tomatoes, olives, spring greens, and Capezzana; and selection of house-made ice cream.

What we say
Spring is without question one of the most beautiful restaurants to open in London in years. Such opulence! The white walls, the vast mirrors, the columns, the luscious floral displays, the staff in their jaunty neo-nautical uniforms. On a spring or summer's day, there is nowhere in central London one would rather be. And it is here that Skye Gyngell has chosen to lavish upon her lucky, well-heeled clientele, the superlative, produce-driven creations that made her a superstar at Petersham Nurseries.

Sorella (p. 118)

Sorella

What
A neighbourhood Italian-inspired restaurant with a menu driven by farm produce

Who
Robin & Sarah Gill, Dean Parker, Dan Joines, owners

When
Dinner Tuesday, lunch & dinner, Wednesday to Saturday, lunch Sunday

Address
148 Clapham Manor Street, London, SW4 6BX

+44 (0)20 7720 4662

sorellarestaurant.co.uk

Bookings
Phone or website

Price guide

What they say
"We're a family: from the team in the restaurant to our small group of unique suppliers. From the vegetables we get from our farm in West Sussex who collect all our food waste to plant our crops in, to Dylan Bean from Kernow Sashimi who we source our fish from via a small fleet of dayboats (of which Dylan's father is still the skipper). We take pride in being very much a local neighbourhood restaurant and look after part of a community garden on a council estate where we grow herbs for the restaurant."

Signature dishes
Jersey milk ricotta with caramelized Parmesan, and black olive; linguine mussels with Devon mussels and bottarga; and saddleback pork nduja ragù with sweetheart cabbage.

What we say
Sorella is a staggering place to find up a small side street off the main Clapham drag: a big, airy, relaxed restaurant staffed by cool, well-informed, prettily tattooed young people baking bread, curing meat, pickling vegetables... and cooking dishes of an incredible quality, so focused, so well balanced, so adventurous and hearty. One of the most promising London openings of 2018.

Smoking Goat

London

What
Inspired by Bangkok's late-night canteen spots

Who
Ben Champan & Brian Hannon, owners & Ali Borer, head chef

When
Lunch & dinner, daily

Address
64 Shoreditch High Street, London, E1 6JJ

smokinggoatbar.com

Bookings
Website

Price guide

What they say
"Here at Smoking Goat, we focus on using quality ingredients and creating a great atmosphere. From an ingredient perspective, we work closely with farmers and fishermen and have our own in-house butchery as well as growing all our vegetables in Cornwall, which allows us to have seasonally evolving menus. We are also really passionate about providing guests with the best possible experience. Atmosphere is incredibly important to us and the layout of Smoking Goat reflects this, with an open kitchen allowing guests to see behind the pass. We work with a producer who grows our Thai herbs and vegetables in Cornwall and Dorset as well as sourcing underrated, native seafood from Cornish waters."

Signature dishes
Sour curry; freshly made rotis; and barbecue pork jowl.

What we say
Leaving aside the explosive brilliance of the cooking here, a fiery, dense-flavoured, mouth experience that blows us from here to Bangkok and back every time, the way these guys look for ecological harmony at the very point of conception is close to tear-jerking. They grow their Thai herbs and vegetables in Cornwall and Dorset rather than import and support their farmer in his endeavour to use an organic chicory mix as his cover crop, thereby making it edible to his Tamworth pigs, giving them greater movement as they feed, making them taste great and tying everything into a great big beautiful circle of life.

St John

London

What
A lively London restaurant & bar

Who
Trevor Gulliver & Fergus Henderson, owners

When
Lunch & dinner, Monday to Friday, dinner Saturday, lunch Sunday

Address
26 St John Street, London, EC1M 4AY

+44 (0)20 7251 0848

stjohnrestaurant.com

Bookings
Phone, or opentable.com

Price guide

What they say
"We believe that a restaurant should have a sense of permanence, and be something of value to customers and community alike. A restaurant should be something to look forward to! We apply common sense to our sourcing, working within Britain where we can (there are no olive groves here) and locally where we can. Our smokies come from Arbroath and our game from the field, fish is sourced by an overnight call to the coast. We bake our own breads using organic flours from local mills that follow good principles and best practice. We change our menu twice daily which delivers a happy rigour and immediacy to the dishes."

Signature dishes
Roast bone marrow and parsley salad; grilled ox heart with carrots and horseradish; hake with salsify and sea aster.

What we say
Is this the greatest British restaurant in the world? We think it might be. Occasionally rated in The World's 50 Best Restaurants despite still being a modest urban refectory, this is a restaurant whose Michelin-star recognition in 2009 did more for the reputation of the old French tyre company than it did for St John. And it all started with the produce. With Fergus Henderson's mission to take the very best of British meat, fish, and vegetables, strip away all the nonsense and serve them up as close to the way God (who is an Englishman, with English tastes) intended. *Truth, Love & Clean Cutlery* – it all started here.

Street Feast

London

What
A collection of five street food arenas & night markets

Who
Jonathan Downey, CEO

When
Dinner, daily, weekend lunch

Address
19 Great Eastern Street, London EC2A 3EJ, plus other locations – see website

+44 (0)20 3931 1270

streetfeast.com

Bookings
Website

Price guide

What they say
"Supporting and mentoring the new generation of street-food traders. Since launching in 2012, Street Feast has transformed derelict and disused spaces into unique eating and drinking environments. From car parks to old markets and rooftops to office blocks, Street Feast has taken over locations including Dalston, Lewisham, Canada Water, Battersea, and Bermondsey, with more coming soon. In each new borough we choose a local charity to support, usually where our expertise in food and drink can help. In Hackney, for example, we support the excellent Made in Hackney charity, a vegan community kitchen teaching cooking skills to older people."

Signature dishes
Pork dumplings from Yumplings; tempura cauliflower tacos from Pocho; and pala-shroom burger from What The Fattoush.

What others say
"For a snapshot of the exciting food-and-drink scene in London, there is probably nowhere more stimulating, nor better value, for a fun night out."

–Nicholas Lander, *Financial Times*

What we say
Street food by its nature is low on food waste. Street Feast's traders specialize in only one or two things and they always plan to sell out. When it's gone, it's gone. They rarely have more than one or two red meat traders at a venue and almost all offer vegetarian options. Sixty per cent of the materials used to build the venues is recycled or repurposed. When a venue closes (they operate on short leases), they take most of what they have and use it somewhere else.

Temper

London

What
Unique barbecue & open fire pit restaurant with a huge New World wine & mezcal list

Who
Neil Rankin & Sam Lee, owners

When
Dinner Monday, lunch & dinner, Tuesday to Sunday

Address
25 Broadwick Street, London, W1F 0DF

+44 (0)20 3879 3834

temperrestaurant.com

Bookings
Website

Price guide

What they say
"Temper is all about having a good time. We turn the music up, we put a huge open fire in the middle of the room, and we serve food and drink that doesn't pull any punches. We're also about sustainability, minimum waste, and excellent produce. We only buy whole animals in Temper Soho – for us, this is the cornerstone of our sustainability – which means we can purchase from small trusted farms where we know the animal and its history, supporting small farms in their mission to keep native rare breeds alive while paying them a better price than the market."

Signature dishes
Beef fat tacos: cubes of aged beef fat served on a fresh corn tortilla with coriander, lime, and chipotle sour cream; slow-smoked pulled *cabrito* taco served on a fresh flour tortilla; and deep-dish cookie: cookie dough filled with chocolate and condensed milk.

What others say
"Temper is one of the most exciting restaurants to open in London this year. I'm not quite self-regarding enough to think people open restaurants with me in mind. But if they did, the restaurant would be Temper."

–Jay Rayner, *The Guardian*

What we say
This is a staggering place. Wonderful eating. One of those rare restaurants where you stuff yourself to the nuts, turn nothing down, swallow everything that's offered, and then fall back into a taxi afterwards, not regretting a single mouthful. Temper, we salute you!

Terroirs

London

What
Natural wine bar serving
modern European cuisine

Who
Erik Narioo, owner

When
Lunch & dinner, daily

Address
5 William IV Street,
London WC2N 4DW

+44 (0)20 7036 0660

terroirswinebar.com

Bookings
Website, or opentable.com

Price guide

What they say
"Terroirs has been serving true food
and pouring natural wine since 2008.
A London institution and industry
favourite, after ten years we are
still a must-visit place for foodies
where you can rub shoulders with
international winemakers. We care
about nature and simplicity – that's
why is so important for us to choose
the best products on the market made
by people for people. All the wines
we serve are sourced from small
artisan growers who work sustainably,
organically, or biodynamically in the
vineyard and with minimal intervention
in the winery."

Signature dishes
Pork and pistachio terrine; duck
rillettes; and Lincolnshire smoked eel
with celeriac remoulade.

What we say
Whatever you think about natural
wines – and the foodie world seems
to be very much split on this – there
is no question that Terroirs did an
immense amount to bring knowledge
of this important area, and indeed
the very concept of terroir, to the
UK. Their cooking – and the cooking
in the restaurants that split off from
the mothership – has always been
excellent and the attention to the
sourcing of ingredients second to none.
And the homemade pâtés? Divine.

Tom's Feast

London

What
Sustainability consultancy,
cheffing, events, recipe writing
& cooking demonstrations

Who
Tom Hunt, founder/chef

When
As required

Address
14 Sanford Walk, London,
SE14 6NB

+44 (0)78 9102 3426

tomsfeast.com

Bookings
Email tom@tomsfeast.com

Price guide

What they say
"I prioritize people and the environment
within my work and believe in a world
with a fair global food system, where
our actions benefit other people and
nature. All my work is focused on
protecting biodiversity and promoting
equality through raising awareness
about the issues affecting our food
system, while empowering people and
businesses to act responsibly through
my consultancy, collaborations, food
writing, presenting, and events. We
source our ingredients following Slow
Food's mantra that 'food should be
good, clean, and fair for everyone'.
We believe organic and biodynamic
farming is the future and buy from
community farms wherever we can."

Signature dishes
Roast cauliflower steaks with crispy
leaves and hazelnut sauce; spelt flour
soda bread farls with foraged seaweed;
and single origin chocolate truffles.

What others say
"Tom Hunt is a cook with a difference.
He not only champions wild, local
and seasonal food and but also
embraces unwanted & unappreciated
ingredients"

The Flexitarian

What we say
The "root to fruit" sustainability
philosophy defines Tom's Feast's
holistic approach to food –
encompassing all aspects of a
sustainable food system including
people, the planet, and, importantly,
the pleasure created through their
cooking. They have a strong focus on
vegetables and look to serve meat and
fish that has had a positive impact
on the environment. The food is
nutritional, seasonal, vegetable-centric,
and made with whole foods and non-
processed ingredients. Go, Tom!

Vanilla Black

London

What
Contemporary vegetarian restaurant

Who
Andrew Dargue, chef/co-founder, & Donna Conroy, co-founder

When
Lunch & dinner,
Monday to Saturday

Address
17-18 Took's Court,
London, EC4A 1LB

+44 (0)20 7242 2622

vanillablack.co.uk

Bookings
Website

Price guide

What they say
"Vanilla Black was established in 2004 with the intention of changing the image of vegetarian and vegan cuisine. We use as many local and small suppliers as possible: a cheesemaker in London, a microbrewery in South London, and some small wine producers, including an English sparkling wine company. We strive to serve a twist on traditional English and French classical dishes, reinvented as vegetarian food. The dishes we cook here are forward-thinking. Our food is challenging. It's different. We're smashing stereotypes."

Signature dishes
Jerusalem artichoke sponge withbbrazil nut milk, cabbage, spiced artichoke, turmeric, and curry leaf; tomato shortbread with sheep's milk, broccoli, gem lettuce, and egg yolk; and cep mushroom fudge with roasted cocoa, brioche with mushroom crisp, and honey ice cream.

What we say
When we first ate at Vanilla Black, we didn't even notice it was vegetarian until halfway through the meal. And that is a clever trick: to curate a post-minimalist, sexy, modern space with exciting, progressive dishes that just happen not to involve any meat or fish. When it opened ten years ago, I thought Vanilla Black might change the face of vegetarian restaurants in London, but it seems still to be ploughing a lonely furrow in that regard. So hats off to them for some serious perseverance – and some seriously good food.

Wahaca

London

What
Mexican market eating

Who
Thomasina Miers &
Mark Selby, owners

When
Lunch & dinner, daily

Address
66 Chandos Place, London,
WC2N 4HG, plus other locations – see website

+44 (0)20 7240 1883

wahaca.co.uk

Bookings
Website

Price guide

What they say
"Wahaca was born from a love for the flavours of the markets of Mexico – it's the most incredible, fresh, and vibrant cuisine in the world. Wahaca is the first carbon neutral restaurant group in the UK. We've always worked hard to ensure we're minimizing our impact on the environment and reducing our carbon emission. To take that to the next level, we've committed to converting any carbon we're not able to eliminate into funds that are donated to communities in Mexico – to build more efficient cook stoves, which allow them to reduce the amount of fuel they burn and reduce the amount of harmful fumes they are exposed to."

Signature dishes
Chorizo and potato quesadilla with Trealy Farm *sobrassada*; fish tacos with sustainably sourced MSC-certified cod lightly battered and served with shredded slaw, chipotle mayo, and house pickled cucumber; Mexican bowls with salsas, slaw, herb-spiked rice, and slow-cooked Yucatecan pork or roasted vegetables.

What we say
When a restaurant group as big as Wahaca shows a commitment to something as radical as carbon neutrality, you know we are at a tipping point, when restaurants really can begin to change the way we think about the world in which we live. As for the food – creative, flavoursome and delicious. Need we say more?

Waterhouse Restaurant

London

What
A social enterprise, offering a live restaurant setting to upskill young people as chefs

Who
Shoreditch Trust

When
Breakfast & lunch, Monday to Friday

Address
10 Orsman Road, London, N1 5QJ

+44 (0)20 7033 0123

waterhouserestaurant.co.uk

Bookings
Phone or email eat@ waterhouserestaurant.co.uk

Price guide

What they say
"Waterhouse Restaurant is home to the Blue Marble Training programme, which works with sixteen- to twenty-five-year-olds who are experiencing challenging circumstances in their lives as they transition into independent living. The programme offers ongoing pastoral support alongside kitchen-based chef training to young people whose needs cannot be met by traditional models of education, training, and employment."

Signature dishes
The Waterhouse chicken curry; the Shoreditch breakfast; and jerk chicken.

What others say
"… if you're looking for a healthy sized portion of delicious and affordable food, whilst helping to support a great charity, then look no further."

Guilt Free London

What we say
Waterhouse Restaurant is an unexpected find amongst the offices and residential quarters of Haggerston. But it is modern and bright thanks to window walls overlooking the Regent's Canal, and the outdoor tables overlooking the water are a rare find in the capital. As well as all the wonderful work done here to train young people facing challenging situations for a life of independence and sustainable employment, great stuff is done around all areas of physical and mental health, equality, and diversity. And you can get a really decent feast for not very much money at all.

Wild Food Cafe

London

What
Raw-centric plant-based eatery created around the art of feeling great

Who
Joel & Aiste Gazdar, owners

When
Lunch daily, dinner Tuesday to Saturday

Address
First Floor, 14 Neal's Yard, London, WC2H 9DP

+44 (0)20 7419 2014

wildfoodcafe.com

Bookings
Walk-ins or phone bookings for 10+

Price guide

What they say
"We celebrate the idea that food alone (though inspiring and delicious) is not the answer to our health, wellbeing, and happiness. We are a heart-centred enterprise that focuses on all aspects of holistic nutrition and individual and collective thriving. Our mission is to transform humanity's relationship with food by providing innovative, delicious, organic, seasonal, wild, crafted dishes and heartfelt hospitality to all our guests. Our menu changes seasonally, so we strive to use seasonal and local ingredients that are available to us to make our dishes."

Signature dishes
Ayurvedic Salad (wild rocket, courgette, cucumber, marinated artichoke, avocado, red pepper, heirloom tomatoes, buckwheat, amaranth, wild nettle, sea purslane pesto, hijiki, pink olives, hulled hemp, mango and lime dressing, and seasonal berries); Samurai Burger (nutrient-rich combination of in-house seeded butternut squash bread, burger patty featuring pink olives, dulse, shiitake, chickpea tofu, teriyaki sauce, wasabi guacamole, grilled aubergine, with sweet potato cubes and sunflower seed mayo); and chocolate tart (popular dessert of avocado, cacao powder, *lúcuma*, vanilla, coconut oil, coconut sugar, and creamed coconut).

What we say
For years the raw vegan food movement looked from here like the crazy indulgence of a handful of nutjob celebrities in certain small districts of Los Angeles. But these guys are showing London how it is done, and we are loving it. Try the beautifully balanced and deeply nourishing Ayurvedic Salad and prepare to be amazed.

Westerns Laundry

London

What
Seafood produce from the British Isles & clean, natural wines

Who
Jeremie Cometto & David Gingell, founders

When
Dinner Tuesday to Saturday, lunch Friday to Sunday

Address
34 Drayton Park, London, N5 1PB

westernslaundry.com

Bookings
Website or opentable.com

Price guide

What they say
"We use only fresh fish that has come from dayboats the previous day and work with what is available. Although they gut the fish (so that it transports better), we portion everything in-house so that we can use the entirety of each fish. In that sense, we are zero waste.

"The menu changes each night and we usually change two or three of the dishes daily to incorporate the most seasonal produce. We use high-quality fruit and veg from Europe from a selection of specialist independent farms, for example, the Sicilian basil that we buy is picked from boards so there is no damage to the crop, and transported with the roots so that it stays fresher for longer."

Signature dishes
Jersey or Morecombe Bay oysters with shallot vinegar; cuttlefish croquette with saffron aïoli; and turbot with seaweed hollandaise.

What we say
From the guys who created Primeur comes a bigger, brasher, even more brilliant restaurant. The buzz, the blackboards, the big communal tables, the bustling staff, the energy and enthusiasm here are all so infectious you want to eat here every day. And we LOVE them for eschewing sous vide machines (so beloved of other fish restaurants to keep fish longer) because they believe it is a waste of plastic and the fish is better when it's fresh.

Westerns Laundry (p. 124)

The Zetter

What

A contemporary, converted Victorian warehouse in Clerkenwell with all-day dining

Who

Ben Boeynaems, head chef

When

Breakfast, lunch, & dinner, daily & weekend brunch

Address

86-88 Clerkenwell Road, London, EC1M 5RJ

+44 (0)20 7324 4455

thezetter.com

Bookings

Phone, website, or email eat@thezetter.com

Price guide

What they say

"Head Chef Ben Boeynaems brings a light and contemporary approach to the menus, showcasing only the freshest seasonal British produce. Ben's cooking style is simple and well balanced, allowing the produce to really shine. It is this seasonal spontaneity that is a big part of the draw of Ben's menu, where the food is entirely ingredient-led. In keeping with The Zetter's approach to sustainability and environmental awareness, Ben has forged burgeoning relationships with local suppliers and producers, ensuring consistent access to the highest quality ingredients."

Signature dishes

Pan-roasted halibut with buttered Sussex crab, saffron gnocchi, young fennel, and orange; Hampshire asparagus with pheasant egg, toasted hazelnut, and chamomile; and rhubarb with custard and vanilla shortbread.

What we say

One of the founders of The Zetter was Mark Sainsbury, who was also one of the founders of the Sustainable Restaurant Association. So, how much *Truth, Love & Clean Cutlery* would you expect to find here? The answer is: a lot. And you do. It is arguable that The Zetter invented boutique hotels in London, and its restaurant is a wonderful space: light, modern, airy, and bang in the heart of one of London's primary eating locations. The food speaks for itself – refined, interesting and fresh.

The Zetter (p. 128)

64 Degrees

Brighton

What
Innovative, eclectic, small-plate dining with an open kitchen

Who
Michael Bremner & Carla Grassy, co-owners

When
Lunch & dinner, daily

Address
53 Meeting House Lane, Brighton, BN1 1HB

+44 (0)12 7377 0115

64degrees.co.uk

Bookings
Email info@64degrees.co.uk

Price guide

What they say
"We aim to provide an eating experience for our customers and an enjoyable place for our staff to work, and to have great relationships with our local farmers and suppliers. We get our fish pretty much exclusively from Brighton and Newhaven Fish Sales (BNFS), who are big advocates for sustainable fishing. When a certain fish is in abundance, for example, we will buy this and put it on the menu."

Signature dishes
Monkfish ceviche with blood orange and chilli; charred hispi cabbage with almond crumb and shaved Spenwood cheese; and smoked braised ox tongue with marinated tomatoes and wild garlic pesto.

What we say
There is a wonderfully urgent atmosphere here, in a sexy little room at the heart of the Brighton Lanes. Devotees crowd the small corner bar watching local superstar Michael Bremner at work, piling impeccably chosen Sussex specialties onto cute, eclectic plates of grey, blue, black... whatever suits. Flavours are sharp and bold, the attitude is muscular and uncompromising, the cooking, on a good day, is out of this world. This is super-sustainable Brighton at its gastronomic best.

Green Kitchen Brighton

Brighton

What
100 per cent vegan café serving breakfasts, lunches, burgers, salads & specials

Who
Catherine & Katie Gregson-Bourke, owners

When
Breakfast & lunch, Wednesday to Sunday

Address
8 Preston Road, Brighton, BN1 4QF

+44 (0)12 7368 4158

greenkitchenbrighton.com

Bookings
Phone or email hello@ greenkitchenbrighton.com

Price guide

What they say
"We are most passionate about providing great vegan food and showing that being vegan definitely doesn't mean missing out. Our menu is 100 per cent vegan, all of our food waste, coffee grounds, teabags, etc. are composted, and we work to ensure as little as possible is thrown away. We recycle absolutely everything we can, use compostable packaging (wherever possible) and drinking straws, and offer a 20p discount to those using their own cup for takeaway coffees."

Signature dishes
Full English breakfast: a vegan version of the British classic with tofu to replace egg and handmade rashers to replace bacon; Sunday roast: homemade nut roast or Wellington with seasonal vegetables and vegan Yorkshire pudding; and burgers: homemade nut and bean burgers or meat alternatives with a range of fresh toppings.

What we say
There is no question that vegan food eliminates the use of intensively produced and environmentally damaging meat while arguably better preserving the farmland of the world to feed us in the future. But we can't all be vegans. We'd miss the pure joy of a proper British fry-up too much. Unless we lived around the corner from this place, where joy and fun and colour are everywhere to be seen. The menu is full of vigour and excitement, and the breakfasts are simply unbeatable in their class. No wonder Brighton has more vegans per capita than any other town in Europe. Probably.

Lucky Beach Cafe

Brighton

What
Delicious local & sustainable food & drink right in the middle of Brighton beach

Who
Mike Palmer, owner

When
Breakfast, lunch & dinner, daily

Address
183 Kings Road Arches, Brighton, BN1 1NB

+44 (0)12 7372 8280

luckybeach.co.uk

Bookings
No bookings taken

Price guide

What they say
"We really want to surprise people with the quality of the food and drink on offer, and we want to make sure we have taken into account our impact on both the environment and the people who work with us. Most of the food we serve is locally sourced – the fish is landed here in Brighton, the meat is organic and local, the milk, the organic eggs. We balance the needs of the team, our guests, the business, and our suppliers. When that happens we end up with great, happy people serving up delicious food that we are all proud of... and that makes our customers smile."

What we say
Despite being well-known (and three-star SRA-rated) for its organic hamburgers, Lucky Beach Cafe has reduced its reliance on meat over the last three years to the point that they now sell more vegetarian food than carnivorous.

They've just introduced burgers where the organic patty is mixed with fifty per cent mushroom, and this summer they launched an "impossible" burger, which has a plant-based patty – the first time this has been available outside of London. With so many vegetarian and vegan restaurants in Brighton, it is great to see the virtues of plant-based food being preached to the as-yet-unconverted.

Pascere

Brighton

What
An elegant yet homely independent restaurant with an award-winning wine list

Who
Amanda Menahem, owner

When
Lunch & dinner, Tuesday to Saturday, lunch Sunday

Address
8 Duke Street, Brighton, BN1 1AH

+44 (0)12 7391 7949

pascere.co.uk

Bookings
Phone or website

Price guide

What they say
"Here at Pascere, we love providing a home-from-home ambience and take pride in giving a personalized experience. We use local and seasonal produce wherever possible – our fish and seafood is caught off the Sussex coast a few miles from us. We have Sussex wine on our award-winning wine list. Our cheese is from Neal's Yard. We also collaborate with and support other local restaurants, chefs, and producers in the events we run."

Signature dishes
Slow-braised beef cheek with aged Parmesan and homemade tagliatelle; roast chicken croquettes with roast chicken skin mayonnaise and roast chicken skin powder; and Wye Valley asparagus with sourdough croutons, summer truffle, and confit egg yolk.

What others say
"... can stand shoulder to shoulder with the country's best."

–Tom Parker Bowles, *Mail on Sunday*

What we say
This is a lovely little spot just on the edge of the famous Lanes, cute and stylish downstairs, light and breezy upstairs, where half a dozen chefs work with quiet devotion in the open kitchen. The small plates are all astounding, simply a riot of taste and beauty. Memories of the tiny Portland crab tartlet and the ingenious cauliflower croquettes will linger long in the mind, as will the unbelievable saddle of rabbit with tortellini of rabbit leg, and leek, chestnut, and lobster foam. They bake beautiful bread and the treacle tart is a dessert of true wonder.

Terre à Terre

Brighton

What
Vegetarian food that is more about indulgence than abstinence

Who
Amanda Powley & Phil Taylor, owners

When
Lunch & dinner, daily

Address
71 East Street, Brighton, BN1 3TD

+44 (0)12 7372 9051

terreaterre.co.uk

Bookings
Phone, website, or email mail@terreaterre.co.uk

Price guide

What they say
"Ultimately Terre à Terre is about quality ingredients served with flair, creativity, and playful exuberance. As active members of our community, we take part in charitable events and food festivals yearly. Our local suppliers provide us with amazing quality ingredients such as Hove honey, wild garlic, samphire, and even Brighton gin."

Signature dishes
KFC (Korean Fried Cauliflower): Asian-inspired starter with a twist; "Better Batter": vegetarian fish and chips with halloumi; "Snap Crackle and Choc": vegan dessert with silken tofu chocolate mousse.

What we say
For so many people, Terre à Terre is still the best vegetarian restaurant in Britain even after so many years. It's been there in that legendary spot on The Lanes, it sometimes seems, since before mankind had even thought of eating meat. And if all restaurants had been like this one then maybe we never would have. Dishes are unusual and extremely creative, the presentation is first class, and the way they manage to incorporate such an array of flavours, textures, and aromas without killing a single sentient thing is nothing short of miraculous.

Silo Brighton

Brighton

What
The United Kingdom's first
zero waste restaurant

Who
Doug McMaster, owner

When
Dinner Wednesday, lunch &
dinner, Thursday to Saturday,
lunch Sunday

Address
39 Upper Gardner Street,
North Laine, Brighton,
BN1 4AN

+44 (0)12 7367 4259

silobrighton.com

Bookings
silo.dinesuperb.com

Price guide

What they say
"Our restaurant is a real, live
demonstration that zero waste is a
natural system and utterly achievable.
We work closely with all our local
suppliers from food to beer to our
potter, Mark. All our produce is organic
and our weekly foraging allows us to
harvest the natural bounty in Brighton."

Signature dishes
Tiny potatoes with whey, blackcurrants,
and fennel pollen (highlights flaws in
the industrial system, throwing away
tiny potato pearls and whey); broccoli
with seaweed (championing the
idea that to maximize resources is to
minimize waste); and carrots cooked
in lemon compost (highlights waste
as an opportunity).

What we say
The energy and commitment that
has gone into this place are reflected
perfectly by the muscular, postindustrial space it inhabits, the
strapping, tattoo'd chefs, and the
thumping nose-to-tail approach to
meat-cooking in a place that, given its
zero-tolerance environmental fervour,
you might have dumbly assumed was
going to be vegetarian. Far from it. On
our visit they were clearly getting to
the end of an ox, because we were
served not only the tail but part of the
heart, sliced and seared, clean-tasting,
muscular and super-delicious, with
excellent horseradish mash. Chairs are
made from pulped wood waste and
soapless hand washing is done under
"intelligent taps". Silo does it all.

André Garrett at Cliveden

Taplow

What
Modern European restaurant
with three AA Rosettes

Who
André Garrett, executive
head chef

When
Lunch & dinner, daily

Address
Cliveden House,
Bourne End Road,
Taplow, SL6 0JF

+44 (0)16 2866 8561

clivedenhouse.co.uk

Bookings
Phone or website

Price guide

What they say
"André creates innovative dishes, has
fastidious preparation methods and
adds immaculate finishes to all his
dishes, and these techniques shine
through in each exquisitely crafted
creation. We are keen to support
local suppliers and champion British
produce. Where possible, André
selects the finest ingredients from
across the British Isles, even stocking
poultry from the local Copas Farms.

"We are also committed to providing
equal opportunities, training and clear
policies to keep employees happy and
productive. We engage with the local
community, schools and charities to
support the local people who support
our restaurant."

Signature dishes
Local fallow deer with braised shoulder,
watercress, chestnut and pickled
blackberry; Cornish turbot with gem
lettuce, clams, leeks, lemon, and

olive oil; and stuffed courgette flower
with quinoa, goat's cheese, hazelnut,
and truffle pesto.

What we say
To think that this magnificent country
house, once the scene of the Profumo
scandal and thus considered the
naughtiest location in England, should
now be a proud member of the
Sustainable Restaurant Association.
Isn't that simply delicious? André
Garrett is a West Country boy whose
evolution as a chef came out of a
deep commitment to the land, its
bounty, and its protection. So go
to Cliveden, be very, very naughty,
and know that you are making up
for it by eating responsibly sourced
food that is prepared with an eye to
waste management and caring for
local communities.

Artichoke

Buckinghamshire

What
Contemporary neighbourhood restaurant set in a sixteenth-century building with modern European cooking

Who
Laurie, chef patron & Jacqueline Gear, director

When
Lunch & dinner, Tuesday to Saturday

Address
9 Market Square, Old Amersham, Buckinghamshire, HP7 0DF

+44 (0)14 9472 6611

artichokerestaurant.co.uk

Bookings
Phone or website

Price guide

What they say
"Over the past seven years, Laurie has sourced a wonderful array of passionate suppliers. It has always been our mission to seek out the best produce that the British Isles have to offer and Laurie has been delighted to discover a collection of artisan producers right on our doorstep, many within the Chilterns. With the support of these producers and others who are slightly further afield, Laurie and his team are able to create the inspired cuisine served at the Artichoke. We work with various charities and some of our lovely gardening guests often contribute their surplus harvest to the restaurant menu."

Signature dishes
Wye Valley asparagus with Lancashire bomb sauce, black truffle, black pepper, and cheese wafer; Lyme Bay crab with Isle of Wight tomatoes, avocado cream, and passionfruit dressing; and rump of Jurassic Coast rose veal with broad beans, violet artichoke, orzo, almonds, and Berkswell cheese.

What we say
A long-standing and much-beloved fine dining restaurant set in a gorgeous medieval Old Town. There is a relaxed atmosphere for a restaurant of this sort and a real vim to the cooking, thanks, one suspects, to the spell Laurie did working at Noma when he was forced to close the restaurant for eighteen months in 2008 as the result of a fire. To emerge from the ashes of disaster so triumphantly is a lesson to us all.

The Hand and Flowers

Buckinghamshire

What
Two-Michelin-star pub

Who
Tom Kerridge, owner

When
Lunch & dinner, Monday to Saturday, lunch Sunday

Address
126 West Street, Marlow, Buckinghamshire, SL7 2BP

+44 (0)16 2848 2277

thehandandflowers.co.uk

Bookings
Phone, website, or resdiary.com

Price guide

What they say
"We're passionate about making an experience to remember for all of our guests. We want to create an environment where our guests feel comfortable and welcome. Surrounded by a relaxing setting, members of staff go out of their way to make sure the guests' needs come first, our food is big, bold, and flavoursome, to lead innovation within our industry. We're very conscious of our environmental footprint therefore try to reuse as much of our kitchen waste as possible. For example, all of our potato waste is given to a local farm for the pigs to consume."

Signature dishes
Omelette (with four simple ingredients elevated by the use of traditional cooking methods); Essex lamb bun (appears and simple, but hides layers of flavour and skill); and crème brûlée (the caramelization of the sugar is taken to its furthest point to allow a

bitter flavour profile, which balances all of the layers).

What we say
Little is left to be said about Tom Kerridge's legendary and inspirational pub. It remains as good as ever, despite his elevation to superstar status, and keeps coming up with new ideas for a changing restaurant world. Most recently, they have opened The Butcher's Tap (a traditional butcher's shop and bar combined) where their chefs do apprenticeships to become butchers, learning all the techniques required to graduate by sectioning a whole animal.

The Gallivant

East Sussex

What
A restaurant with coastal-inspired bedrooms & a beach hut mini spa

Who
Harry Cragoe, owner

When
Breakfast & dinner, daily, lunch Tuesday to Sunday

Address
New Lydd Road, Camber, Rye, East Sussex, TN31 7RB

+44 (0)17 9722 5057

thegallivant.co.uk

Bookings
Website or bookatable.co.uk

Price guide

What they say
"We are obsessed with making people happy. We do this by treating our guests as if they are guests in our own home, providing beautiful, relaxing spaces and serving food that is delicious, beautiful and inspiring. Everything is homemade in the kitchen or supplied by local producers and artisans. We are huge supporters of the burgeoning English wine scene and believe we now have the largest English wine list in the country, as well as a large selection of British spirits – it grows by the month. We serve some of the freshest fish you are ever likely to eat, supplied directly by local fishermen, who might call us while out at sea when they find something notable in their nets."

Signature dishes
Hand-picked Dungeness crab with heritage tomato and fennel; Romney salt marsh lamb with confit potatoes and local broccoli; and line-caught Hastings cod with foraged sea vegetables, pickled tomatoes, and garlic croutons.

What we say
This boutique hotel manages to be genuinely relaxed, thanks to its beachside vibes and the incredibly thoughtful way they look after their staff. Sure, the cooking is fantastic, the local sourcing is fanatical, and the work to involve local wineries is joyful. But clearly by looking after your own staff so well, employing the majority locally, paying a £9 minimum hourly wage, closing Mondays for training, and offering free yoga, you inspire them to pass on a lot of love to your guests.

The Wheatsheaf

What
Grade II-listed pub selling organic, seasonal, local food & drink

Who
Ollie & Lauren Hunter, co-owners

When
Lunch & dinner, daily

Address
Chilton Foliat, Hungerford, Berkshire, RG17 0TE

+44 (0)14 8868 0936

thewheatsheafchiltonfoliat.co.uk

Bookings
Phone

Price guide

What they say
"We love our suppliers and in return they allow us to connect with the nature and terroir around us – our aim is to express the land. We have a very strong synergy with Ollie's parents' farm, Hungerford Park, who specialize in incredible produce – organically fed rare-breed pigs, lamb, chickens for eggs, honey, organic vegetables, fruits and nuts, cider, and produce from their butchery including charcuterie, bacon, and sausages. Our aim is to create a vision for the future of pubs – serving only organic, local, or seasonal food and drink, and being a hub of creativity and expression within a community."

Signature dishes
Tagliatelle carbonara (ingredients all sourced within a five-mile radius); salmon pizza; and pressed apple terrine.

What we say
The Wheatsheaf only buys in whole animals – including beef, which is rare in the industry – which is possible as they work with Ollie's dad, who stores the meat at his butchery on the farm. So they only get a new animal in once they have used everything from the previous animal, thus promoting slow growing. They have a nose-to-tail ethos on all produce including vegetables to maximize the energy spent growing each vegetable or fruit. Then it's all cleaning with vinegar, converting pizza-oven energy waste to heat the building in winter, on-site composting, blackboards instead of paper menus, old receipts turned into waiter pads... and a hatful of ethical awards and nominations.

The Old Custom House

East Sussex

What
A small seafood restaurant & oyster bar in Hastings' historic Old Town

Who
Nick Hales, owner

When
Lunch & dinner Tuesday to Saturday, weekend breakfast

Address
19 East Parade, Hastings, East Sussex, TN34 3AL

+44 (0)14 2444 7724

theoldcustomhousehastings.co.uk

Bookings
Phone

Price guide

What they say
"The Old Custom House focuses on simply cooked food influenced by the classics, which allow the ingredients to take centre stage. We offer a range of oysters. Our sources vary depending on the season to ensure a quality product. We love making use of the large range of coastal vegetation by using locally foraged sea beets, sea kelp, and seaweed.

"Our menu consists of classics that are influenced by the seasons – this ensures the best flavour. For example, in the summer you can find our fridges rich with British strawberries, asparagus, wild garlic, and cherries. Alternatively, in autumn and winter, you can find greengage, squash, and locally foraged mushrooms. We undertake everything from butchering locally sourced meat, poultry, and game in-house, to setting up the West Hill Smokery, curing and smoking local meat and fish for use in the restaurant."

What we say
You know about the wonderful St Clement's – or, if you don't, you should – but this is their newer, smaller, more relaxed (not that they are in any way uptight) venture, focused on fish and seafood and a good range of oysters. All the same magnificent principles, just a bit smaller and quieter.

St Clement's

East Sussex

What
Michelin-star-nominated local seafood restaurant

Who
Nick Hales, owner

When
Lunch & dinner, Tuesday to Saturday, lunch Sunday

Address
3 Mercatoria, St Leonards-on-Sea, East Sussex, TN38 0EB

+44 (0)14 2420 0355

stclementsrestaurant.co.uk

Bookings
Phone or website

Price guide

What they say
"Here at St Clement's, we are dedicated to our local bounty of seafood and we have an extensive wine list with which to pair any one of our dishes. We purchase fish from local fishermen and use seasonal and, of course, local produce when available. Foraging is encouraged and we aim to serve food that is sourced within a twenty-mile radius of the restaurant."

Signature dishes
Smoked haddock with mussel, kale, and potato chowder; Sardinian fish stew with fregola and aïoli croutons (gurnard, salted cod, king prawns, scallops, mussels, and clams); and wing of skate with wild garlic mash, spinach, pickled mussel, and parsley butter.

What others say
"Every town deserves a St Clement's, which is one of those saintly places that straddles the border between Michelin standards and neighbourhood cosiness."

–Matthew Norman, *The Telegraph*

What we say
These guys are proud of their market-dependent, ever-changing menu to the point of defiance: it "outstrips the speed at which we can reasonably update this website", they roar when you go looking for menus. And they go on to warn that, "if you have dined with us before and really enjoyed a specific dish, it may not be available on your next visit". So that's telling you! And we admire the chutzpah. If you're going to overturn years of lazy assumptions based on lazy cooking and lazy hospitality and do things your own way (and the right way), you might as well be angry about it!

The Wellington Arms

Hampshire

What
Gastropub with rooms

Who
Jason King & Simon Page,
owner/chef/manager

When
Breakfast, lunch, & dinner,
daily

Address
Baughurst Road, Baughurst,
Hampshire, RG26 5LP

+44 (0)11 8982 0110

thewellingtonarms.com

Bookings
Phone

Price guide

What they say
"The Wellington Arms is a traditional
country pub offering carefully crafted,
unpretentious dishes using our
homegrown produce and the best from
the local area. Our food changes with
the seasons using the local produce
available, and the vegetables and fruit
we harvest from our gardens. All the
eggs used in the kitchen are laid by
our organic flock of free-range hens
and honey comes from our five hives.
Our wine list consists of many organic
and biodynamic bottles produced at
wineries around the world."

Signature dishes
Crispy-fried homegrown courgette
flowers stuffed with Beau Farm ricotta,
lemon zest, and pine nuts, with
leaves from the garden; slow-roast
leg of home-reared Jacob lamb with
tabbouleh, labneh, coriander, and
sumac; and jelly of house-made
elderflower cordial with homegrown
strawberries, and homegrown rhubarb
ripple ice cream.

What others say
"This is one of those labour-of-
love joints that have you cooing
with pleasure."

–Matthew Norman, *The Guardian*

What we say
A small place that has been doing
absolutely everything right since we
first visited eleven years ago and were
fair blown away by Jason and Simon's
commitment to sustainable, ethical
dining: eggs from their own organic
hens, milk from local organic herds,
food waste minimized through on-site
composting and the use of Green
Cones, local schools and hospitals
regularly supported through donations,
fêtes, and bazaars, LED lights, kitchen
water recycled, young staff nurtured...
but, most of all, incredible cooking
and a wonderful welcome. One of
our biggest little heroes.

Chewton Glen

Hampshire

What
A five-red-star hotel with two restaurants: The Dining Room & The Kitchen

Who
Luke Matthews, executive head chef

When
Lunch & dinner, daily

Address
Christchurch Road, New Forest, New Milton, Hampshire, BH25 6QS

+44 (0)14 2528 2212

chewtonglen.com

Bookings
Phone or website

Price guide

What they say
"We have a large kitchen garden within the estate where we grow herbs and crops for the chefs. Our local suppliers – sourced within a radius – are outstanding quality (e.g. Laverstoke Park Farm's delicious cheese). We also have seventy thriving beehives on site, which provide honey for the hotel and employment for a dedicated beekeeper. We are very passionate about using sustainable fish (we even won a five-star rating with the Sustainable Fish Pledge), and are members of the Sustainable Restaurant Association. It's wonderful to be able to share our ethos by promoting garden tours, local school tours, and supporting local food festivals."

Signature dishes
Chewton Glen cheese soufflé; Thai lobster curry with jasmine rice; and honeycomb parfait.

What we say
Chewton Glen is the most magnificent forest hotel in England. Bought by a family business, it is not just about ivy-clad walls and croquet lawns – here you'll find wonderful dining in a stunning conservatory, with impeccable old-fashioned service, afternoon teas, and shimmering Sunday roasts. It's about modern touches like the wood-fired pizza, the gourmet burgers, extensive catering for vegetarians and vegans, and a deep commitment to locavorism.

The Mill at Gordleton

Hampshire

What
The perfect place to relax with family & friends, enjoying delicious homemade food

Who
Upham Pub Company

When
Breakfast, lunch & dinner, daily

Address
Silver Street, Hordle, Hampshire, SO41 6DJ

+44 (0)15 9068 2219

themillatgordleton.co.uk

Bookings
Phone, website, or opentable.com

Price guide

What they say
"We are dedicated to fine food and wine here at The Mill, and work closely with local suppliers to ensure we get the best produce. We are also members of Hampshire Fare, allowing us an inside look at what's new on the market. The chefs pick fresh herbs from the garden to enhance the menu and we use free-range eggs and meat caught in the local area. Fish is sourced locally and is fresh to the plate. Our heat exchange unit, which is fitted to the base of the river, provides us with almost eighty per cent of our hot water and central heating for The Mill."

Signature dishes
The Mill twice-baked cheese and New Forest mushroom soufflé; Moroccan spiced lamb rump with chargrilled Mediterranean vegetables, sweet potato fondant, and olive dressing; and pan-fried fillet of cod with saffron and shellfish butter sauce, new potatoes, and sea asparagus.

What we say
A glorious old-fashioned bolthole (not one for the hipster crowd) barely seconds from the beach and the glories of the ancient New Forest, where wonderful efforts are made to marry a warm welcome with a devotion to rendering all the magic of the forest onto your plate.

The Goods Shed

Kent

What
A farmers' market, food hall & restaurant in a restored Victorian railway shed

Who
Susanna Sait, owner

When
Breakfast, lunch & dinner, Tuesday to Saturday

Address
Station Road West, Canterbury, Kent, CT2 8AN

+44 (0)12 2745 9153

thegoodsshed.co.uk

Bookings
Phone

Price guide

What they say
"With a strong farming background, we appreciate the industry needs to be sustainable. For example, when we sold raw milk we bought all the surplus to make yoghurt, and when we made butter we made a cocktail with buttermilk. We buy whole animals from a small local abattoir. By nature, we have to find a role for all of the animals on our menu and market. We have fishmongers, butchers, greengrocers, bakeries, cheesemongers, masters of wine, charcuteries, and general stores on-site. We all work together to create a shopping and restaurant experience from a time of pre-industrialized food production."

Signature dishes
Courgette flowers with garden weeds and honey; duck breast with ground elder and salsa; and rabbit with black pudding and wild garlic dumplings.

What others say
"I genuinely love the market in a draughty old railway goods shed in Canterbury ... the restaurant here has never let me down."

–Marina O'loughlin, *The Guardian*

What we say
This old railway was transformed in the early 2000s into a farmers' market where real people do their daily shop. But people love the handmade macaroons, too, and the slow-proved bread, local beer, cheese, and charcuterie, and the hairy, grubby, misshapen vegetables that we all know are far better for you than the ones that are round and shiny and look like the picture in the book. Each day, between 5.30 p.m. and 7 p.m., these are sold off at knockdown prices.

The Veg Box Cafe

Kent

What
Vegetarian café celebrating the best seasonal & organic local vegetables

Who
Liz & Adam Child, owners

When
Breakfast & lunch, daily

Address
17A Burgate, Canterbury, Kent, CT1 2HG

+44 (0)12 2745 6654

thevegboxcafe.co.uk

Bookings
No bookings taken

Price guide

What they say
"Think big colourful salads, soups, hotpots, and bakes. We are also obsessed with fermentation and have started a little sideline venture called Fermental. We make our own Kentish kimchi, sauerkrauts, and brine ferments, which we use liberally in all our dishes. We use a local biodynamic farm, Brockmans, for our fresh produce and top up from a local farmers' market, The Goods Shed. Our coffee is roasted locally by The Micro Roastery. Our sourdough is from an excellent baker in Faversham, Wild Bread, and our apple juice from Moors Organics. We get our wholefoods from Michaels Wholesale in Broadstairs."

Signature dishes
The Full Fermental: organic sourdough with fermented lemon hummus and a selection of seasonal fermented vegetables; buddha bowls: salad of leaves with grains, seeds, vegetables, hummus, olives, dressings, and sauces; and *farinata*: chickpea-flour frittata.

What we say
Twice runners-up in the Observer Food Awards' "Best Ethical" category, these guys sell only plant-based food (providing organic dairy for drinks). All takeaway packaging is 100 per cent compostable and food waste and other biodegradable items are collected by Biffa to be anaerobically digested commercially. They are wonderful advocates for that key proposition of the Hippocratic oath: *primum non nocere*, "first, do no harm".

Dalleth

What
A ticketed event business offering intimate tasting experiences that utilize wild British produce

Who
Jonathan Dowling, owner

When
Daily events – see website

Address
115 Glencoe Road,
Kent, ME4 5QF

+44 (0)77 0834 0545

dalleth.co.uk

Bookings
Website or email
jonathan@dalleth.co.uk

Price guide

What they say
"Dalleth menus encompass a large amount of foraged vegetation, wild meats, and fish, just like our ancestral hunter-gatherers would have eaten. We utilize ingredients that were once a staple in our diets but sadly have been forgotten with time. Reaching back into our ancestral memories, Dalleth's approach is one of reincarnation; projecting our interpretation of culinary possibilities had these traditions and values survived to the present day. We uphold pagan earthly values in regards to our menu design and how we gather our resources. We try our hardest to give more than we take."

Signature dishes
Squirrel and English mustard; St. George's mushroom and coastal succulents; and wood ants and mead.

What we say
Dalleth is an astonishing project, rooted deep in English pre-history and imagining forward to a better way of eating now, as if all the years of intensive farming, soil corruption, animal cruelty, and chemical toxins had never happened. What they do with grey squirrels (an imported pest) is the stuff of poetry – guests can dine on a crunchy oat-covered nugget of braised squirrel meat. A heroic way to end the scourge of the grey squirrel and make room for the return of the red (which we will NOT be eating!).

Belmond Le Manoir aux Quat'saisons

Oxfordshire

What
Raymond Blanc's Oxfordshire hotel & restaurant

Who
Raymond Blanc, owner & Gary Jones, chef

When
Breakfast, lunch & dinner, daily

Address
Church Road, Great Milton, Oxford, Oxfordshire, OX44 7PD

+44 (0)18 4427 8881

belmond.com/lemanoir

Bookings
Phone or website

Price guide

What they say
"Exemplary cuisine, comfort, and service using the very best seasonal ingredients. Raymond (president of the Sustainable Restaurant Association) passionately believes that it is up to each of us, be it a consumer, chef, or hotelier, to make a responsible choice. We also engage locally, nationally, and internationally with people and aim to create a more responsible society."

Signature dishes
Assiette Anne-Marie: a vibrant plate of vegetables representing the full cycle of spring (young carrots, white and green asparagus, pods of garden peas, broad beans, flower stamens and stigmas, and pea shoots); lobster plancha with red pepper jus and cardamom (the sweet, seared flesh of the native Cornish lobster with the sweet-acidic essence of the red pepper); and Le Café Crème, which

took owner Raymond Blanc six months to perfect.

What we say
It was a meal at Belmond Le Manoir aux Quat'saisons that first awakened us to the glory of great cooking, and it was a walk round the kitchen garden here that first impressed upon us the fact that sustainability, organics, and a reverence for every leaf, bud, and grain of soil is not just for hippies. Au contraire, it is where all the finest things in life begin. It was Ray White (as we affectionately think of M. Blanc) who first taught us this. And for that, we worship him.

The Crooked Billet

Oxfordshire

What
An unspoilt rustic country pub serving local & British produce

Who
Paul Clerehugh, owner

When
Lunch & dinner, daily

Address
Newlands Lane, Stoke Row, Henley-on-Thames, Oxfordshire, RG9 5PU

+44 (0)14 9168 1048

thecrookedbillet.co.uk

Bookings
Phone

Price guide

What they say
"Paul Clerehugh has run The Crooked Billet since 1989 and lives on his smallholding nearby, rearing beef and sheep and growing produce for the menu. We're serious about flavour and locality – and even encourage our community to bring in their homegrown produce to swap for lunch! We cook for our local village school every day, supplying them with fresh and nutritional food inspired by our love for the seasons and the great people in our local area. A renowned menu serving big and rustic flavours using our local produce (from Paul's farm) and sourcing from within Britain where we need to, is part of the reason why we're the favourite local spot."

Signature dishes
Wild rabbit with heritage carrots, purée potato and green sauce; venison pave with haggis and baked figs; and halibut with seashore greens, saffron, and cockles.

What we say
With a fair claim to having been the first gastropub (*The Daily Mail* coined the phase in 1989 describing The Crooked Billet), The Crooked Billet can call on some fairly impressive history both ancient (Dick Turpin visited – but didn't he always?) and modern (Kate Winslet got married here). It's a breathtaking, convoluted old English pub that is a job to find (not much in the way of passing trade), but a joy to discover. If you haven't brought a rabbit or a melon to trade for your lunch you can pay with money. You won't regret it.

The Hare

Oxfordshire

What
Charming Cotswolds village local – great food, great staff

Who
Sue & Rachel Hawkins, owners

When
Lunch & dinner, daily

Address
3 High Street,
Milton-under-Wychwood,
Oxfordshire, OX7 6LA

+44 (0)19 9383 5763

themiltonhare.co.uk

Bookings
Phone

Price guide

What they say
"We are lucky in the Cotswolds – there are literally hundreds of artisan producers, everything from cheese to gin. So we support local business and we buy a lot of our ingredients locally but by no means all. We do buy with integrity, though, so if we can't find local produce then we buy from a larger, less local supplier but one that we have met, liked, and enjoyed the ethics and service of. We have a daily changing blackboard (Marine Cuisine) where Head Chef Matt Dare – great name, great guy – indulges his personal passion of sourcing delicious fish from dayboats in Dartmouth and Cornwall, creating a sustainable daily dish."

Signature dishes
Scotch egg (beautiful, local free-range organic egg, encased in pulled ham hock and parsley with crunchy breadcrumbs – cut into it and it oozes its golden treasure all over your salt and vinegar crisps!); Marine Cuisine; and Sunday roast.

What we say
The menu looks at first glance like ordinary good gastropub stuff, but from the moment the food starts arriving you know that everything is going to be a cut above. And it is. Possibly two cuts. Every dish we ate was a marvel of precision and flavour. Staff are incredibly engaged and engaging, the evening mood is romantic and relaxed, and the prices are extremely good given the incredible fashionableness now of eating out in the Cotswolds.

The Kingham Plough

Oxfordshire

What
Dining pub in the Cotswolds with six bedrooms

Who
Emily Watkins, owner

When
Lunch & dinner, daily

Address
The Green, Kingham,
Chipping Norton,
Oxfordshire, OX7 6YD

+44 (0)16 0865 8327

thekinghamplough.co.uk

Bookings
Phone, website, or opentable.com

Price guide

What they say
"Our aim is for you to have a delicious dinner in a lovely atmosphere and, if possible, stay upstairs. Locality is hugely important – we take great pride in our ingredients and know all of our suppliers from meat to salad leaves, game to fish. Being a village pub, community is very important to us and as well as employing many people from the village, we also support the village school and nursery. Many of our artisans are very small and will only work with fellow small local farmers – our egg supplier takes such good care of his chickens he actually lives in a mobile home amongst them."

Signature dishes
Roast chicken and St George's terrine; duck breast with confit duck pie, chargrilled duck heart pie, hispi cabbage, and rosemary; and rhubarb and stem ginger panna cotta.

What we say
The late, great A. A. Gill once wrote that The Kingham Plough set the gold standard for all pubs. And he didn't even like the Cotswolds! It is hard to see why when visiting a village as pretty and well-served by great food and drink as Kingham. Emily Watkins is a masterful chef with a brilliant touch for both fine dining and folksier styles and her restaurant has become a foodie Mecca over the years, holding its position near the top despite the recent explosion of fantastic food pubs in the area.

The Magdalen Arms

Oxfordshire

What
A bistro pub & dining room serving modern British food with a strong Italian influence

Who
Tony Abarno, head chef & Florence Fowler, front of house

When
Dinner Monday, lunch & dinner, Tuesday to Sunday

Address
243 Iffley Road, Oxford, Oxfordshire, OX4 1SJ

+44 (0)18 6524 3159

magdalenarms.co.uk

Bookings
Phone

Price guide

What they say
"We use allotment produce that is local, homegrown, and priced fairly. All our fish is from Cornwall, always fairly fished. Most of our beef is from farmer Tom in Hereford – we've been lucky enough to work with him for over ten years! All food waste is either offered for takeout in compostable boxes or goes to food-waste bins and our head chef's allotment. Everything is made from scratch, so you know everything about your dish. We would always accept imperfections – all our produce from our allotments is imperfect, but it tastes the best!"

Signature dishes
Polpette in a wild dandelion broth; stuffed and baked globe artichoke with goat's cheese and black olive crumbs; and slow-cooked lamb shoulder for five.

What we say
A huge, magnificent, sprawling pub dining room of the kind that Oxford badly needed and still needs more of. Born out of the success of The Anchor and Hope, the Magdalen offers the same roiling pots of monstrous(ly beautiful) things: whole ducks for three-to-four, lamb shoulders for four-to-five, rabbit and mustard for two, roast rib of beef for three... but also delicate soufflés and sprightly green plates of new-season vegetables. The beer's good, the wine is better, the service is brilliant, the whole place throbs with the love and laughter of happy families and bloated students on a once-a-term blowout. We love it.

Nut Tree Inn

Oxfordshire

What
Fifteenth-century local village pub, serving award-winning food

Who
Michael & Imogen North, owners

When
Lunch & dinner, Monday to Saturday, lunch Sunday

Address
Main Street, Murcott, Oxfordshire, OX5 2RE

+44 (0)18 6533 1253

nuttreeinn.co.uk

Bookings
Phone, website, or bookatable.co.uk

Price guide

What they say
"Making sure people feel at home in our home. This is our home and has been now for twelve years and we are very fortunate to have a fantastic supportive team around us who share our passion. We strongly believe that the welcome should be the same whether you're joining us for a celebratory meal or a quick pint on the way home. We source the best quality ingredients available to us and treat them with respect and simplicity. We are by no means self-sufficient, but all the produce we grow, we use."

Signature dishes
Pavê of Nut Tree smoked Loch Duart salmon with horseradish cream, pickled cucumber and Avruga caviar; torte of braised lamb shoulder and potato with English asparagus, wild garlic and jus rôti; and vanilla custard soufflé with green apple sorbet.

What we say
A fifteenth-century pub with a thatched roof that offers guests a wonderful slice of English country life. Ducks waddle up out of the pond, across the lovely garden into the bar and out again. They have just under an acre of land under cultivation, producing salad leaves, herbs, and vegetables. In the summer months they raise their own pigs, and they have even had their own herd of Dexter cattle grazing in the paddock. As for the cooking itself? Well, that's had a Michelin star these last eight years, so you'll be fine.

Orwells

Oxfordshire

What
A restaurant serving nothing but top-quality ingredients with a major focus on sustainability

Who
Ryan and Liam Simpson-Trotman, owners

When
Lunch & dinner, Wednesday to Saturday, dinner Sunday

Address
Shiplake Row,
Henley-on-Thames,
Oxfordshire, RG9 4DP

+44 (0)11 8940 3673

orwellsrestaurant.com

Bookings
Phone

Price guide
●●●○○

What they say
"Orwells is a labour of love; we cook, work, and live together in our eighteenth-century former pub, which we launched in 2010 having won a Michelin star while working together at the Goose. We have our own small holding where up to seventy-five per cent of our fruit and vegetables are grown and we are expanding it every year. We do as much as we can to minimize our carbon output through small things that we feel all join together to make a significant impact. We only use LED lighting, provide staff training on energy output, and all the refrigeration that possibly can be is on a timer system."

Signature dishes
Mill Lane honey sponge; muntjac with girolles, elderberry, pickled cobnuts, and sea kale; and Norfolk asparagus and Cornish scallop with charcoal.

What we say
Two dishes tell you everything you need to know about the glory of Orwells: 1) The muntjac with girolles, elderberry, pickled cobnuts, and sea kale, because, you see, the muntjac forages for girolles, cobnuts and fallen elderberries so they serve it with its own forage. That, friends, is poetry on a plate. 2) The bowl of crispy whole Jerusalem artichokes with melted Stilton and almonds we ate on our visit there. They were steaming hot, crispy-crunchy, and caramel-sticky with length and depth in the surrendered fibre of the vegetable and then operatic high notes in the bubbling blue cheese. We still dream about them.

Field and Fork

West Sussex

What
A chef-led independent restaurant celebrating its tenth anniversary this year in Chichester

Who
Sam Mahoney, chef/owner, & Janet Mahoney, owner

When
Lunch & dinner,
Tuesday to Saturday

Address
4 Guildhall Street, Chichester, West Sussex, PO19 1NJ

+44 (0)12 4378 9915

fieldandfork.co.uk

Bookings
Phone or email
reservations@fieldandfork.
co.uk

Price guide
●●●○○

What they say
"Our bistro has the ethos of chef-prepared food, celebrating local suppliers and some truly great staff. Our spirit is to deliver quality food from happy staff, both front and back of house, while educating staff in service and cuisine. By using suppliers local to us, we are doing what we can to reduce our carbon footprint – as much as possible is local and our menus change as and when to reflect this."

Signature dishes
Maple-glazed peppered slow-roasted pork belly with smoked eel, carrot coleslaw, crackling, and ginger jus; local crab-stuffed homegrown courgette flowers with crab bisque and herbs; and asparagus parfait with crispy pekin bantam egg (from Field and Fork hens) and Cheddar crisp.

What we say
Most of the staff at Field and Fork have been there for the duration of its ten-year history to date, which is so, so unusual, even in a big-hearted restaurant in a relatively small town like this. To have retained so many staff in this industry and in this climate, the company must be treating them incredibly well. And it shows in the quality of the service, the knowledge, the kindness, and the warmth of the welcome. We also love their newest menu, the £12, three-course set lunch, created to take advantage of any bargains available from their suppliers and to utilize waste and surplus ingredients. Sustainable thinking that has the well-being and happiness of customers at its heart. Wonderful.

Turl Street Kitchen

Oxfordshire

What
An independent restaurant serving great local, seasonal food

Who
Adam O'Boyle, owner

When
Breakfast & lunch, daily, dinner Tuesday to Saturday

Address
16–17 Turl Street, Oxford, Oxfordshire, OX1 3DH, plus other locations – see website

+44 (0)18 6526 4171

turlstreetkitchen.co.uk

Bookings
Website or email
book@turlstreetkitchen.co.uk

Price guide

What they say
"Sourcing locally, working with local suppliers, being creative, and providing a laid-back, enjoyable experience for our customers is our passion. Our menus change weekly but we often source meat from Sandy Lane Farm, such as pork belly, and have that on the menu. Our vegetable tagine makes a regular appearance and we have a vegan full English on the menu permanently, an acknowledgment of the high number of vegetarians and vegans here in Oxford! We reduce food waste as much as possible within the kitchen itself, using what we can in the dishes, and any food waste produced is collected via the council food waste collection, not going into landfill. A third of our lunch and dinner menus are vegetarian and vegan and we also have permanent vegetarian and vegan dishes on our breakfast menu. We bottle our water in-house and use green energy throughout the building."

What we say
The Turl Street Kitchen is a lovely, relaxed, youthful canteen with impeccable local and sustainable-sourcing credentials, comfy pricing, and a pretty, historic location. The mazy old building (for many years a curry house) has been stripped back and lightened up and filled with nice young quasi-hipsters pushing a very small, very smart menu that changes twice daily. The Sandy Lane faggots and sausages were exceptional and the steamed ginger pudding with lemon custard a dessert for the ages.

157

England
South West

Dela

What
A restaurant & café with a seasonal, locally sourced menu with Scandinavian influences

Who
Lara Lindsay & Mike Orme, co-owners

When
Breakfast & lunch, Tuesday to Sunday, dinner Tuesday to Saturday

Address
Mivart Street, Bristol, BS5 6JF

+44 (01)1 7951 1499

delabristol.com

Bookings
Phone

Price guide

What they say
"We try to embody the Scandinavian approach to food and dining, creating a relaxed atmosphere, serving simple, delicious, seasonal food. We focus on pickling, fermenting, and preserving, with these methods bringing a focus to our menu. We make everything we can in-house, from the seasonal tinctures for our cocktails to ketchups and sauerkrauts. With fish as a focus of Scandinavian food, we make sure we are vigilant on where this comes from, only using locally caught and sustainable breeds. We have a blanket ban on cod and salmon when it comes to fish and instead focus on things like mussels, cockles, and mackerel."

Signature dishes
Pickled south coast mackerel with smoked salt butter and sourdough; Hasselback new potatoes with baby courgette, goats curd, cavalo nero, garlic, and parsley butter; and buttermilk pudding with *pepparkakor* and roast rhubarb.

What we say
Pure Bristol: surrounded by ethical growers, they can select all their produce from within a mile. Salad leaves are organically grown then picked and delivered by bike the same day by Edible Futures. Micro herbs are hydroponically grown in a carbon neutral environment and delivered by bike from Grow Bristol, and even the cheese comes by bike, too, from The Bristol Cheesemonger. The drinks menu is local where possible, with beers from within two miles and the cider and brandy from Somerset. Probably best not cycle after tucking into that lot though, even in Bristol.

Boston Tea Party (p. 162)

Boston Tea Party

Bristol

What
Ethically sourced, affordable, feel-good food

Who
Sam Roberts, managing director/co-owner

When
Breakfast, lunch & dinner, daily

Address
75 Park St, Bristol, BS1 5PF, plus other locations – see website

+44 (0)11 7929 8601

bostonteaparty.co.uk

Bookings
No bookings taken

Price guide

What they say
"Our food is healthy, of excellent quality and made on-site every day. Our speciality coffee comes from Extract Coffee Roasters, and all our baristas are Speciality Coffee Association trained, to make sure you get the very best. Our produce comes from the most caring of sources, free-range meat from the Dean family in the West Country, Severn Project social enterprise, and 100 per cent organic milk from Yeo Valley."

Signature dishes
The West Country breakfast: a traditional full English made with bacon and sausages from pigs reared especially for the restaurant, scrambled eggs, and Hobbs House bread; sourdough eggy bread with smoked bacon and avocado; and Cheddar and jalapeño cornbread.

What we say
It is fantastic to see such a quirky little place that is doing so much right in environmental areas – this summer they banned single-use coffee cups for good – growing first into a small chain and then branching out all across the West Country. They are at the cutting edge of water, waste, and power management while bashing out accessible, fun, healthy platefuls at decent prices that make them the go-to spot for harassed mums, hungry students, and, well, pretty much anyone passing by. With twenty-one locations other than Park Street, we can't wait for Boston Tea Party to spread even further afield in the years to come.

Bell's Diner & Bar Rooms

Bristol

What
A local restaurant & bar

Who
Connemara Coombes, owner

When
Dinner Monday to Saturday, lunch Friday to Sunday

Address
1–3 York Road, Bristol, BS6 5QB

+44 (0)11 7924 0357

bellsdiner.com

Bookings
Phone or email
questions@bellsdiner.com

Price guide

What they say
"We are really serious about a life of good food and great wine. Our staff are very enthusiastic about everything on Bell's menu, from the locally sourced produce to our wines, which are carefully chosen from small producers with help from our local buyers. We only source fish that are approved by the Sustainable Restaurant Association, ensuring that they are caught within season and with the knowledge that the fishermen involved in the catch are playing their part in sustainable fishing methods."

Signature dishes
Tempura Wye Valley asparagus with romesco sauce; radicchio with blood orange, pickled red onion, and basil; Cornish sardines with *muhammara* and *pangritata*.

What we say
With its history of good food and service stretching back to the 1970s, its vinyl-only music policy (played on a Bush Dansette), its resident artist and forager, and its newish management with a background at Rocinantes and the sainted Quartier Vert, this place just couldn't be more Bristol. Add to that the robust Mediterranean cooking with inspiration from Spain, North Africa, Italy, and France and the local sustainable sourcing that this city has nurtured longer than any other in Britain, and you've got, well, a hell of a diner and bar.

The Ethicurean

Bristol

What
A modern British restaurant situated within a Victorian walled kitchen garden

Who
Matthew & Iain Pennington, chef patrons

When
Lunch & dinner, Tuesday to Saturday, lunch Sunday

Address
Barley Wood Walled Garden, Long Lane, Wrington, Bristol BS40 5SA

+44 (0)19 3486 3713

theethicurean.com

Bookings
Phone, website, or resdiary.com

Price guide

What they say
"We source as close to the restaurant as possible, with approximately ninety per cent of the veg we use in summer coming from within the walled garden itself. Working so closely with the seasons has meant it's been a necessity to learn how to preserve the abundant produce for scarcer times. Pickling, fermenting, smoking, and curing are all techniques that feature widely on the menu. Culture here is celebrated from the soil all the way through to the food, then to the community that join us for annual events such as Wassail, Summer Solstice, and Apple Day."

Signature dishes
Cucumber and ewe's curd salad with garden flowers; duck breast with kimchi, carrot, and unripe fig; and sea buckthorn with honey and thyme cake.

What others say
"... it's impossible not [to] be infected by the energy in this ramshackle former orangery. From the poshest waitresses I've ever encountered ... to the handsome, industrious kitchen brigade, it's all outrageously jolly."

–Marina O'loughlin, *The Guardian*

What we say
Since winning best ethical restaurant at the Observer Awards in 2012, they have been runner-up every single year, only because the *Observer* can't keep giving first prize to the same place. From the beauty of the location to the quality of the garden produce to the effortless rightness of every plateful, The Ethicurean is just doing everything right, all the time.

The Olive Shed
Bristol

What
Mediterranean restaurant on Bristol's harbourside, serving freshly prepared food & organic wines

Who
Anastasia O'shea, owner

When
Lunch & dinner, daily

Address
Princes Wharf, Bristol, BS1 4RN

+44 (0)11 7929 1960 .

theoliveshed.com

Bookings
Email info@theoliveshed.com

Price guide

What they say
"A stone's throw from the waterside, we offer freshly prepared food with excellent service. Our coffee is fair trade, organic, and freshly roasted weekly to give that wonderful flavour. We source Cornish fish and local meats and vegetables. Most of our wine and soft drinks are organic or biodynamic, other wines are again from small artisan suppliers. Our milk (and whatever we can source) is organic and our artisan bread is delivered daily. Although we offer a range of dishes, we are also well known and loved for our extensive and delicious vegetarian options."

Signature dishes
Whole baked sea bream; thirty-six day aged ribeye (in a Himalayan salt chamber); and bouillabaisse with Atlantic wild prawns.

What we say
Nestled on Bristol's once-industrial harbourside, The Olive Shed's greatest strength is the sweeping, panoramic views it offers, from the masts of the SS Great Britain and the multicoloured houses of Cliftonwood across the shimmering water to Colston Tower. In the age of Instagram, that's all you really need to put bums on seats. But they have great cooking, too. Simple Mediterranean dishes made – because this is Bristol – with produce that is organic and fair trade wherever possible.

Poco
Bristol

What
A seasonal restaurant with a mission to operate as efficiently & sustainably as possible

Who
Ben Pryor, Tom Hunt, & Jen Best, owners

When
Breakfast, lunch, & dinner, daily

Address
45 Jamaica Street, Bristol, BS2 8JP

+44 (0)11 7923 2233

pocotapasbar.com

Bookings
Phone or email
info@pocotapasbar.com

Price guide

What they say
"We opened Poco because we believed that we could contribute to a considerable shift towards a more sustainable food system by creating our own best-practice benchmarks and spreading awareness through leading by example. We are also passionate about bringing people together through food and being part of a conscious community that provokes debate and initiates transformative action. We visit our suppliers every couple of months to develop a deep connection with the people that are growing our food and rearing our meat. Our suppliers often speak at our staff meetings as well. Nurturing this connection means we are serving the food consciously and that we are aware of the limitations of our own resources rather than overconsuming produce that our local soils cannot provide."

Signature dishes
Cornish mussels with capers, parsley, butter, and kelp; Wye Valley asparagus with labneh, lemon, and maftoul; and pressed pig's head terrine with crispy pig's ear, apple, walnut and celery salad, and sourdough.

What we say
Describing their signature mussels dish to us, Poco said: "Mussels are one of the most sustainable sources of protein available for consumption. They offer great food security in aquaculture as they do not require any feed and act as a localized filtration system, helping to prevent eutrophication and improving their habitat for other fish around them. This dish is also a perfect example of our efforts to promote healthy eating on the menu; it is packed full of nutrients." To our ears, that is pure poetry.

The Pony & Trap

Bristol

What
A gastropub serving tasty food in relaxed surroundings

Who
Josh & Holly Eggleton, owners

When
Lunch & dinner, Wednesday to Saturday, lunch Sunday

Address
Moorledge Road, Newtown, Chew Magna, Bristol, BS40 8TQ

+44 (0)12 7533 2627

theponyandtrap.co.uk

Bookings
Phone, website, or resdiary.com

Price guide

What they say
"First and foremost, our food has to be delicious, well balanced, and not too heavy. Second, we of course want it to be made from ingredients that are sourced from passionate suppliers – be that buttermilk from a local dairy, oysters from Porthilly, or radishes grown in the garden. In addition, our menus always reflect the seasons – whether produce from our own garden or from our suppliers. Another big thing is that we like to encourage the experience to be unstuffy, and there are dishes we would encourage to be eaten as finger food, for example the asparagus spears dipped in egg yolk and hollandaise, and front of house (or the chef) will always encourage you to do so."

Signature dishes
Mini Yorkshire pudding and steak tartare; Wye Valley asparagus with hazelnut dukkah, brown butter hollandaise, and hen's egg; and brown butter poached turbot with hay-baked oyster, buttermilk, peas, and radish.

What we say
Josh and Holly took over this 200-year-old pub with its gorgeous views over the Chew Valley in 2006, and it's now one of the country's great gastropubs, employing all the best principles but wearing the ethical commitment lightly so that guests focus mostly on the wonderful cooking. We especially like how they encourage children to enjoy smaller portions of à la carte dishes – such as poached white fish with vegetables, a small ploughman's lunch, a bowl of mussels – instead of just chucking chicken nuggets at them.

Root

Bristol

What
Relaxed & interesting dining experience, small plates highlighting local, quality ingredients

Who
Rob Howell, chef & Josh Eggleton, owner

When
Dinner Monday & Tuesday, lunch & dinner, Wednesday to Saturday

Address
Unit 9, Gaol Ferry Steps, Bristol, BS1 6Wp

+44 (0)11 7930 0260

Bookings
Phone

Price guide

What they say
"What we are aiming to do at Root is create a dining experience that is relaxed, interesting, and enjoyable for the customers. Honest, simple food that has come from using quality ingredients, treated with respect. Our menu represents our philosophy: most of our dishes are vegetable-based, however we always offer outstanding fish and meat plates, sourcing them from the surrounding areas and coastlines."

Signature dishes
Beetroot with blackberry, hazelnut, and seaweed oil; potato skin gnocchi with seasonal, organic vegetables; and doughnut dessert with soft cream cheese, carrot jam, and candied walnuts.

What others say
"Rob Howell is offering some of the best veg cooking in Bristol ... clever and delicious."

–Hugh Fearnley-Whittingstall, *Financial Times*

What we say
What a zappy, good-looking addition to Bristol's restaurant quarter this is. Huge floor-to-ceiling windows provide light and air for lush plants, walls are lined with shimmering green tiles and baskets of fresh produce loll sexily below blackboards of specials. The open kitchen throws open the debate between cooks and the cooked-for about a single-sheet menu that is predominantly vegetarian but peppered with occasional creations in meat and fish – which is exactly how the world is going to win, going forward: not by dividing into vegetarians and carnivores, but by eating less and less meat in a diet just loaded with plants.

The Thali Restaurant

Bristol

What
Showcases the hero dishes of India, from the backstreets of Bombay to the beach shacks of Goa

Who
Jim Pizer, co-founder/director

When
Breakfast, lunch & dinner, daily

Address
64-66 St. Marks Road, Bristol, BS5 6JH, plus other locations – see website

+44 (0)11 7951 4979

thethalirestaurant.co.uk

Bookings
Phone or website

Price guide

What they say
"Thali Restaurant is inspired by the heart and soul of India. We follow the Indian mantra *jugaad* (do more with less) and have been battling waste since serving our first curry at Glastonbury Festival in 1999.

"In line with our ethos of everyday India, we looked to the streets of Mumbai, where during Monday to Friday lunchtime, more than 200,000 tiffins are delivered by tiffin-wallahs to office workers. We now have 10,000 proud tiffin owners using the reusable box over and over again, instead of disposable packaging. The Thali Tiffin takeaway scheme aims to reduce packaging waste and currently saves the restaurant from half a ton of waste for takeaway orders. The team work on efficient delivery systems with Thali's suppliers, and oil that is collected from branches is then converted to biodiesel to power the company's delivery van."

Signature dishes
Keralan nandan chicken: free-range chicken thighs simmered in a creamy coconut, cumin, and green cardamom sauce; pumpkin *olan*: a vegan showstopper; and masala dosa.

What we say
When Indian food this bright, moreish, and satisfying gets a three-star rating from the SRA on the back of a seventy-six per cent overall score, there is nothing you can do but applaud. We may be going to hell in a handcart, but it might just be possible to row all the way back to heaven in a tiffin.

Alba

Cornwall

What
An award-winning seafood restaurant with a contemporary bar on the ground floor

Who
Grant Nethercott, chef patron

When
Dinner, daily

Address
The Old Lifeboat House, Wharf Road, St Ives, Cornwall, TR26 1LF

+44 (0)17 3679 7222

alba-stives.co.uk

Bookings
opentable.com

Price guide
●●●○○

What they say
"The whole dining experience, from the ingredients, to the decor, to the art we have displayed, is carefully thought out here at Alba. We want it to be a complete end-to-end experience. One of our chefs grows all our salad ingredients and herbs, as well as small batches of seasonal ingredients, and we work closely with our fish supplier in sourcing local and sustainably caught produce. Our pork is sourced from Primrose Herd, breeders and finishers of rare and traditional breeds of pigs, who produce an award-winning range of pork and bacon. Their farm is a small holding located in the Cornish countryside."

Signature dishes
Crab linguine (locally sourced Cornish crab); lobster niçoise (Cornish blue lobster caught just off the coast); and trio of mackerel (hand-lined mackerel from local fishing boats in the harbour).

What we say
Grant Nethercott is a classically trained chef with Michelin provenance and a strong French technique, but in the years he has been here the focus has moved firmly to modern British with, naturally, a seafood bias. The glass-fronted, two-storey building (bar downstairs, Alba upstairs) affords terrific views of St Ives Bay and the busy seafront. It's bright and modern and, as per their recent involvement in a Surfers Against Sewage charity dinner, you know they look after the sea, because they have to swim in it.

Ben's Cornish Kitchen

Cornwall

What
Small family-run bistro where the food & wine changes daily & flavour matters

Who
Ben Prior, owner/chef

When
Lunch & dinner, Tuesday to Saturday

Address
West End, Marazion, Cornwall, TR17 0EL

+44 (0)17 3671 9200

benscornishkitchen.com

Bookings
Phone or website

Price guide

What they say
"Quite simply, we love food with big flavour, a glass of quality wine, and a relaxed atmosphere to enjoy it in. We use local seasonal produce (grow a bit ourselves) and have close relationships with local dayboats and a fine independent butcher. Our food miles are tiny, waste is composted or recycled, and we're always looking for ways to reduce single-use plastic."

Signature dishes
Charred asparagus with Parmesan custard and pheasant egg; roast monkfish tail on the bone with spiced red pepper and chorizo ragout and smoked aubergine; and lemon tart with fennel meringue and yoghurt sorbet.

What we say
The most astonishing thing about this progressive little restaurant devoted to all the best things about Cornwall and its food is that Chef Ben works alongside his brother Toby (who's mostly on desserts) under the watchful eye of their mum, Jayne. And nobody (at the time of going to press) has killed anyone yet! Nothing has more truth and beauty in it than mothers and sons getting along like this. Ben's Cornish Kitchen, we love you.

Coombeshead Farm

Cornwall

What
Farm, guesthouse & bakery based in Cornwall

Who
Tom Adams & April Bloomfield, chefs

When
Dinner Thursday to Sunday, lunch Sunday

Address
Lewannick, Launceston, Cornwall, PL15 7QQ

+44 (0)15 6678 2009

coombesheadfarm.co.uk

Bookings
Phone or website

Price guide

What they say
"We hope Coombeshead is somewhere exciting, where people can come not just to eat delicious food, but perhaps to take away some learning back into their day-to-day lives and, importantly, relax and unwind. We are very aware of our impact on the environment and are taking steps towards our vision of self-sufficiency. We produce as much as we can onsite – from the soap in the bedrooms to the butter at breakfast – and have a brilliant network of farmers and growers who we work very closely with. We learn a huge amount from them and it's a great pleasure to work alongside people who will go to great lengths to create outstanding produce."

Signature dishes
Charcuterie; pickles; and butter.

What we say
To sustain a menu based on using whole animals throughout the year, you have to use everything and find ways of prolonging its presence on the menu. Coombeshead Farm only uses one pig a month, and this has to sustain the menu. Therefore, preservation is key. By curing, salting, and smoking, they are able to balance the menu through those times when fresh produce is sparse – as in the good old days. So they use charcuterie to balance a menu when there is less fresh produce in the garden or coming in from growers. The same is true of their pickles and ferments, which help to keep the shelves full through the darker months.

The Gurnard's Head

Cornwall

What
A dining pub with seven comfortable bedrooms on Cornwall's Atlantic coast

Who
The Inkins, owners & Chris Curnow, manager

When
Breakfast, lunch & dinner, daily

Address
Zennor, St Ives,
Cornwall, TR26 3DE

+44 (0)17 3679 6928

gurnardshead.co.uk

Bookings
Phone, website, or resdiary.com

Price guide

What they say
"We are located in the middle of an extraordinary landscape, a hub for the post-war group of West Cornwall artists, with the architectural handsomeness of an old-fashioned coaching inn. So we have to do our bit to make it work. Making sure people leave happy, tell their friends about us, and want to come back themselves. It underpins everything we do, upstairs, downstairs, behind the bar, in front of the bar, in the kitchen, in the office, and in the garden. Informality, but real attention to detail and the quality of the products we use, from the ingredients in the kitchen, to every element of our wine list, to the breweries we use, and where we buy our handwash from."

Signature dishes
Brawn scrumpet with smoked tomato ketchup and crispy pig's ears; rump of beef sith charred ox heart, asparagus, wild garlic hollandaise, and salsa verde;

and honey bavarois with sweet cicely, honeycomb, candied fennel seeds, and strawberry sorbet.

What we say
What a thoughtful place this is. Named (coincidentally) after a very sustainable fish of which people should eat more, it makes a great effort on behalf of vegetarians, vegans, and children (who are as welcome as their parents), they make a huge effort to provide hospitality (and work) all year round in a remote location, they support local businesses such as the Southwestern Distillery and the Wild Smoked smokehouse, and they organize foraging walks and art exhibitions.

Harbour Lights

Cornwall

What
Traditional fish & chips restaurant & takeaway

Who
Pete Fraser, owner

When
Lunch & dinner, daily

Address
Arwenack Street, Falmouth,
Cornwall, TR11 3LH

+44 (0)13 2631 6934

harbourlights.co.uk

Bookings
Phone or email
hello@harbourlights.co.uk

Price guide

What they say
"Our aim at Harbour Lights is to ensure that our guests leave with big smiles and happy tummies. We love serving our guests the nation's favourite comfort food, traditional fish and chips. We want our guests to feel that we have knocked it out of the park on freshness and quality while ensuring we minimize our impact on our oceans and environment. The crispiest batter, flakiest fish, and the most moreish of chips every time."

Signature dishes
The Famous Five (MSC codfish, chips, mushy peas, bread and butter, and a cup of tea); The Triple Treat (three local Cornish fish battered or grilled, served with half chips and half salad); and the children's meals, served in a beach bucket.

What we say
Any restaurant that has been awarded three stars by the Sustainable Restaurant Association is a friend (and hero) of ours. They do everything you would expect of such a highly rated establishment in terms of correct fishing practice, cleaning, recycling, and community involvement... AND in 2017 they inaugurated International Mushy Pea Day involving songs, dancing, recipes, and celebrities. Fish and chip shops as far afield as Canada, New Zealand, Singapore, and the Falkland Islands, joined in the silliness at mushypeaday.com. This year, they intend to make it even bigger and better. Talk about bringing the world together with great food: if you can do it with mushy peas, you can do it with anything!

The Hidden Hut

Cornwall

What
Outdoor beach café & wood-fired feast venue

Who
Simon Stallard & Jemma Glass, co-founders

When
Lunch, daily

Address
Porthcurnick Beach, Portscatho, Truro, Cornwall, TR2 5EW

hiddenhut.co.uk

Bookings
No bookings taken

Price guide

What they say
"The Hidden Hut is our outdoor restaurant, almost completely off-grid with no road access, where local ingredients are cooked outdoors, often over a wood fire, and you have to walk along the coast path to find it. The seafood is caught from the bay (in a handmade boat under sail and oar for minimum impact) that the hut overlooks, the beef is reared in the fields surrounding, and the vegetables grown locally and delivered direct from the farmer on his quad. It's unrefined, but that's what we love about it."

Signature dishes
Autumn vegetable dal; spider crab landing; and "black and blue" beef.

What others say
"The spirit of this place is infectious... I honestly can't think of anywhere I'd rather be on a warm summer's night."

–Jack Stein, *The Guardian*

What we say
Celebrity endorsements for this extraordinary restaurant just never seem to end. Not only does Rick Stein rave, but Oliver Peyton says it is the best beach café in the country, Xanthe Clay says it is possibly the hottest destination of any kind in the country, and Ben Fogle says the food is as stunning as the scenery. Fogle is the key here – he doesn't go anywhere that is easy to get to. And that is surely the glory of this place: the way its wild and beautiful location sings out everything you need to know about the beauty of its food and its philosophy. Quite simply the restaurant of your dreams.

The Old Coastguard

Cornwall

What
A fourteen-bedroom small hotel with a restaurant in an idyllic position above the Mousehole rocks

Who
The Inkins, owners & Louis Vanhinsbergh, general manager

When
Breakfast, lunch & dinner, daily

Address
The Parade, Mousehole, Penzance, Cornwall, TR19 6PR

+44 (0)17 3673 1222

oldcoastguardhotel.co.uk

Bookings
Phone, website, or resdiary.com

Price guide

What they say
"The Old Coastguard's restaurant is lucky enough to occupy a sensational position looking out over the usually shimmering waters of Mount's Bay. We have to match this position with sharp service and beautifully executed food that takes advantage of the ingredients of this part of West Cornwall. Fish and shellfish from Newlyn, meat from the farms around us, and fresh produce from market gardens and a community farm. We are also passionate about wine and have just been shortlisted by the IWC Awards in the Restaurant Wine List category. We try to be rooted in our community. This applies to how we source our produce, with ingredients from all over the west of Cornwall. It is reflected in how we employ locally, and how we support local events and charities."

Signature dishes
Tempura seaweed mackerel with alexanders and horseradish; Primrose Herd pork loin with nettle farro, black pudding, and mousseron sauce; and Cornish strawberries with cow's curd and lemon verbena shortbread.

What we say
Sister to The Felin Fach Griffin and The Gurnard's Head and with all the mellow beauty of those other two, The Old Coastguard has possibly the best view of all, over the inland waters and away to St. Michael's Mount and the Lizard. It is not hard for a restaurant to be local, seasonal, traditional, healthy, clean, beautiful, and delicious in this wonderful part of the world. But well done anyway.

Halsetown Inn

Cornwall

What
Country pub serving good food with locally sourced ingredients

Who
Stuart Knight, chef, & Julia Knight, manager

When
Lunch & dinner, Monday to Saturday, lunch Sunday

Address
Halsetown, St Ives, Cornwall, TR26 3NA

+44 (0)17 3679 5583

halsetowninn.co.uk

Bookings
Phone

Price guide

What they say
"We're lucky with our locality in the food we source here at Halsetown Inn. We source cider vinegar from a supplier a few hundred yards away, use Trink Dairy, who are just about a quarter of a mile away, and our asparagus is sourced from Splattenridden Farm half a mile away. Our menu focuses heavily on food that celebrates the seasons and the best of our local produce. We recycle everything we can. We return crates, etc. to suppliers, we recycle water from table jugs to water the garden, we recycle metals with a local reclamation company, and we send waste oil to be turned into biodiesel."

Signature dishes
Mussel with hake, smoked bacon, sweetcorn chowder, and toasted St Ives Bakery sourdough; crispy cinnamon potato tacos with sweetcorn and radish salsa, cashew nut and lime "sour cream", and rocket; and confit Cornish duck leg with squash, parsnip and caramelized onion mash, orange and star anise sauce, and watercress.

What we say
The Inn was built by a Victorian philanthropist called James Halse in 1831 and has a cosiness that feels very much of that time, with open fires, an old Cornish range, and walls of deep, deep red. Nestled here with good food and a bottle, one can't help but reflect on how old Mr. Halse, a great progressive of his age, would have approved of the wonderful environmental example being set here today.

Paul Ainsworth at No.6

Cornwall

What
Michelin-star restaurant located in Padstow serving modern British food using Cornish produce

Who
Paul & Emma Ainsworth, owners

When
Lunch & dinner, Tuesday to Saturday

Address
6 Middle Street, Padstow, Cornwall, PL28 8AP

+44 (0)18 4153 2093

paul-ainsworth.co.uk/number6

Bookings
Phone or email
info@paul-ainsworth.co.uk

Price guide

What they say
"I love running restaurants and love being in business for the very fact that I can watch the team grow. It is so rewarding to see a junior member of the team grow into restaurant supervisor or a brilliant chef – it really is the people that I am passionate about. For me, sustainability includes supporting your local area where you can, from suppliers to potters and florists, etc. Johnny Godden is our fish and shellfish supplier and a real hero – he's so passionate about what he does; we set up shop at the same time and he's now a really good mate of mine."

Signature dishes
The smoked haddock "quiche Lorraine"; aged soy-glazed duck with ginger and hoisin consommé; and "Trip to the Fairground".

What we say
A beautiful, tasteful, calm restaurant, muted colours, twinkling glass, an oasis in the summer madness of modern Padstow, and an opportunity to fall under the spell of a brilliant chef who is not Rick Stein. Cooking is adventurous, sprightly, very English, with exotic grace notes, and a perfect theatre for the sparkling performances of some of the best fish in the world.

Prawn on the Lawn

Cornwall

What
A fully licensed fishmonger & restaurant serving seafood small plates & sharing platters

Who
Katie Toogood, owner, & Rick Toogood, chef/owner

When
Lunch & dinner, Tuesday to Saturday

Address
11 Duke Street, Padstow, Cornwall, PL28 8AB, plus other locations – see website

+44 (0)18 4153 2223

prawnonthelawn.com

Bookings
Phone or website

Price guide

What they say
"We work so closely with our suppliers that we change our menu every day to ensure we make the most of their amazing produce. We work with small dayboats, rather than trawlers, to ensure our fish is as sustainable as possible. We also work with a local kitchen garden to ensure we get the freshest herbs and vegetables, as well as a local microbrewery and vineyard."

Signature dishes
Local Cornish (Mylor) prawns with Szechuan salt and lemon; whole lobster or crab (caught just outside Padstow) served either hot with lime and coriander butter or chilled on ice with garlic créme frâiche; and sole (from St Ives) a la plancha with garlic and parsley oil and lemon.

What we say
Cornwall is a wonderful place to be a fish, and Prawn on the Lawn is a wonderful place to be person who likes eating fish. What a perfect, clean, well-lit place this is. Tiled and cool, sharp-lined, crisp, and gleaming, with glossy seafood winking at you from the ice as you walk in. Blackboards, burners, a plancha grill. Simple food, at its peak, cooked with confidence and flair. Rick and Katie Toogood are both under thirty-five, own three restaurants already, have no investors, taught themselves everything they know, and recently published their first cookbook. If you live in London, visit the Islington branch. All the seafood there is sourced from the same suppliers in Cornwall and driven up each day.

The Scarlet

Cornwall

What
Restaurant in the heart of the Scarlet Hotel

Who
Michael Francis, head chef

When
Breakfast, lunch & dinner, daily

Address
Tredragon Road, Mawgan Porth, Newquay, Cornwall, TR8 4DQ

+44 (0)16 3786 1800

scarlethotel.co.uk

Bookings
Phone or website

Price guide

What they say
"We pride ourselves on working with the most amazing suppliers the county has to offer and we're proud of how blessed Cornwall is with innovative, organic, and sustainable growers, fishermen, and farmers. We have a number of Cornish spirits and beers in our bar, our coffee is roasted in Falmouth and some of our tea is grown on the Tregothnan estate in Cornwall. The fish we buy comes in fresh each morning, and the majority of our vegetable and dairy products come from no more that twenty-five miles away. We use small-scale producers, which means that our products change throughout the seasons to showcase this. Mostly these producers are really small and so only work with a few specific restaurants in Cornwall."

Signature dishes
Cornish crab salad on rye toast with pickled peppers and chilli; heritage beetroot salad with pumpkin seeds, honey, and goat's curd; and braised native beef with heritage carrots, horseradish potato, crispy oyster, and rainbow chard.

What we say
The building was designed with sustainability as a priority. There is grey water harvesting, underfloor heating, and no air-conditioning. There is no gas in the kitchen and all the heat from the fridges is cycled on to be used around the hotel. All paper for the menus is recycled, and crockery, cutlery, and glassware is all from within the UK. The natural pool uses no chemicals but you can swim in it thanks to filtration by the reeds around the edges.

Restaurant Nathan Outlaw

Cornwall

What
The finest sustainable seafood, caught off the Cornish coast by small dayboats

Who
Nathan Outlaw, owner

When
Dinner Wednesday, lunch & dinner, Thursday to Saturday

Address
6 New Road, Port Isaac, Cornwall, PL29 3SB

+44 (0)12 0888 0896

nathan-outlaw.com

Bookings
Website

Price guide
●●●●●

What they say
"Seafood, seafood, seafood is our passion. And having a great time while we're at it! Over ninety-five per cent of our seafood comes from boats fishing out of, and landing in, Cornwall. Our menu reflects our reliance on local growers for seasonal vegetables. We have worked closely with local farmer Richard Hoare for over six years now, who supplies the vast majority of our vegetables. We work with boats that are certified by the responsible fishing scheme, using low-impact fishing methods to help preserve our marine environment. We support Fishermen's Mission and work with Cornwall College and Academy Nathan Outlaw to create a space for students to access training."

Signature dishes
Cured gilt-head bream with cucumber, apple, and chilli; John Dory with hazelnuts and red wine dressing; and turbot with St Enodoc asparagus and smoked hollandaise.

What we say
Nathan Outlaw is an inspirational chef who has done so, so much for the way we buy, eat, and understand fish in this country. Dinner at Restaurant Nathan Outlaw is one of the most memorable eating experiences to be had in Britain, the young chefs he has trained over the years have gone on to spread the message to an ever-widening audience and he deserves all the accolades he gets.

The Seafood Restaurant

Cornwall

What
Famous for establishing an international reputation for the freshest fish & shellfish

Who
Rick Stein & Jill Stein, owners

When
Lunch & dinner, daily

Address
Riverside, Padstow, Cornwall, PL28 8BY

+44 (0)18 4153 2700

rickstein.com

Bookings
Phone or website

Price guide
●●●●○

What they say
"Opened by Rick Stein and Jill Stein in 1975, The Seafood Restaurant in Padstow is famous for establishing an international reputation for the freshest fish and shellfish, often landed on our doorstep. Head Chef Stephane Delourme and his team create simple seafood dishes with classic flavours using Rick's recipes. We use seasonal and local produce wherever possible and work with Clean Cornwall, the SRA and The Final Straw."

Signature dishes
Singapore chilli crab; the fruits de mer; and roast tronçon of wild turbot with hollandaise sauce.

What we say
What can be said that has not already been said about this temple to cooking from the sea and the pioneering fishmeister whose name it bears? We sat at the bar and scoffed a braised fillet of brill with a dun-coloured sauce of mushroom and black summer truffle on slivers of potato that was as deft and well conceived, as sprightly and full of meat and drink, as any fish dish you could imagine. The big, circular, central bar is very cool, affording a view of chaps cutting sushi and sashimi to order, which they do very well, with fine, fine fish. The wine list is magnificent and as we left we saw Stein himself – actual Rick Stein, rare as a bluefin tuna - sauntering along the street.

Snail's Pace Cafe

Cornwall

What
Solar-powered café & bike hire

Who
Linzi Hanscomb &
Nick Marcroft, owners

When
Hours change seasonally

Address
St Breward, Bodmin,
Cornwall, PL30 3PN

+44 (0)12 0885 1178

snailspacecafe.co.uk

Bookings
Phone

Price guide

What they say
"Beginning with a love of ecology, permaculture, community development, and good food, we have created a unique space within and about a recycled shipping container. The menu changes regularly according to availability and season, but there is always a healthy and hearty selection to choose from. Where possible and appropriate we do prefer to use fair trade products. Most of our teas are fair trade, and some are organic. Our coffee is roasted locally and sourced from a plantation that has family ties to the Cornish company that sells the final product. All our baking (which is done on-site) uses organic flour and local butter."

Signature dishes
Ploughman's with homemade pickled onions, local cheddar, local butter, local bread, and local ham; salad plate with sprouted legumes, grains, roasted nuts, dried fruit, micro greens, beetroot, and red cabbage coleslaw; and homemade roasted garlic and goat's cheese tart.

What we say
They are off-grid, solar powered, and have a composting toilet. They offer a wide range of both vegetarian and vegan food and keep food miles as low as possible. They have opted out of plastic straws and promote Clean Cornwall beach cleans on social media as well as Turn on the Tap, which provides free tap water refills to discourage the use of plastic bottles. That's what we call a soft footprint.

Star & Garter

Cornwall

What
A gastropub set on the water's edge of Falmouth Harbour

Who
Elliot Thompson, owner/
head chef

When
Lunch & dinner, daily

Address
52 High Street, Falmouth,
Cornwall, TR11 2AF

+44 (0)13 2631 6663

starandgarterfalmouth.co.uk

Bookings
Phone or website

Price guide

What they say
"With fish direct from the boat and meat is sourced from local farms and butchered and smoked by us. Our nose-to-tail philosophy underpins our ethos, with a wood-fired oven at the heart of the kitchen. This extends to our vegetables and our meat. All parts are used, for example, cauliflower ribs transformed into pickles and meat bones for rich broths. Even ash at the bottom of our big green egg is used in our ash-roast beets. This keeps our food waste down to an absolute minimum."

Signature dishes
Hake with chickpea chermoula, chard, and clams; octopus and fish ragù with crostini; and fourteen-ounce moorland ribeye with burnt onions and pistachio butter.

What we say
This historic maritime pub in the heart of Falmouth has been given a new lease on life by owners Becca and Elliot Thompson and their passionate troop of chefs, all from the local area. There is a noticeable Italian flavour to the energetic nose-to-tail cooking on offer here. Unfashionable cuts of meat, fresh local fish, and lots of on-site smoking and curing keep those flavours robust and rugged, and serious attention has also been given to the excellent drinks menu. The place looks an absolute treat, too, with its traditional wood-panelling a soothing shade of marine blue, an eclectically furnished back bar, and an elegant dining room with views over Falmouth Harbour.

beachhouse devon

Devon

What
Beachside seafood café, restaurant & takeaway in the South Hams of Devon

Who
Tamara Costin, owner

When
Breakfast & lunch, daily, dinner seasonally

Address
South Milton Sands, Kingsbridge, Devon, TQ7 3JY

+44 (0)15 4856 1144

beachhousedevon.com

Bookings
Email beach@ beachhousedevon.com

Price guide

What they say
"Uniquely situated at South Milton Sands, on the coast between Thurlestone and Hope Cove, we are a laid-back foodie destination on a stunning stretch of Devon coast. With panoramic views, beachhouse devon is a great venue for relaxing with friends or quietly soaking up the atmosphere whilst people and boat watching.

"We have the best local seafood and the best service. We work hard to source the very best of the organic produce of South Hams and surrounds – if it's not to our high standards, it's not on the menu! Our menu is fluid; if we are offered great turbot, for example, then we are quick to present the perfect dish… and once it's gone, it's gone!"

Signature dishes
Whole rough-dressed local cracked crab with aïoli and crusty bread; sizzling garlic and chilli prawns; and local mussels with miso, coriander, and lime.

What we say
There is nothing better than yaffing down piping hot platefuls of Devon's best seafood while staring out at the sea it swam in or the beach it crawled up. Sizzling hot prawns in garlic butter, cracked crabs as big as the car you drove here in with pungent garlic aïoli, and great haunches of white fish, charred to perfection. All washed down with rivers of rosé and the company, if you're lucky, of local girl Tamara Costin, who owns this place and is its heartbeat.

Ben's Farm Shop

Devon

What
Four farm shops, two cafés & a wine bar in South Devon selling good food from good farming

Who
Ben Watson, founder

When
Breakfast & lunch, daily

Address
Hole Farm, Buckfastleigh, Devon, TQ11 0LA

+44 (0)18 0376 2850

bensfarmshop.co.uk

Bookings
Phone

Price guide

What they say
"Our mission is to produce, sell, and serve simple, good quality, ethically produced food that tastes wonderful. Through our traditional butchers' counters and our fresh veg and grocery aisles, we aim to bring back the taste and quality of fresh food, traditional and otherwise, prepared from the best fresh ingredients. In our cafés and wine bar we use the same ingredients we sell in our shops. Much of what we sell and serve is certified organic, though we also offer spanking fresh, unsprayed, non-organic vegetables from growers just down the road. But what we like most is to produce foods ourselves from start to finish – from farm to table, our way. Food should tell a story and, because we know what it is, we can tell you."

Signature dishes
Mezze plates; soups; and our daily burger.

What we say
For thirty-odd years these were called Riverford Farm Shops, but the name changed recently (Ben Watson is the Watson who always ran the shops – the others are Guy, Rachel, Louise, and, Oliver) to avoid confusion with the Riverford Organic Farmers brand name, as they also wanted to support local, ethical, and interesting suppliers who aren't organic. They are what we might now, call "post-organic" (my, haven't we come a long way?), and they rock more than ever!

Cafe ODE

Devon

What
Family-friendly food & drink that does not cost the earth

Who
Tim & Clare Bouget, owners

When
Breakfast & lunch, daily

Address
Ness Cove, Shaldon, Devon, TQ14 0HP

+44 (0)16 2687 3427

odetruefood.com

Bookings
No bookings taken

Price guide

What they say
"Celebrating our region's finest food and drink, prepared and served with minimal impact to our environment. We are lucky to have incredible produce on our doorstep: herbs from our boundary wall, South Devon-bred beef, organic eggs, and dairy. We use plant-based packaging that is composted, have a sedum grass roof and solar thermal that heats our water, and we are actively educating the community in food sustainability."

Signature dishes
Teign sand eels, breadcrumbed and fried, served with a dipping sauce; wild Haldon fallow deer, humanely culled; and lentil *dal*.

What we say
Since beating Hugh Fearnley-Whittingstall's River Cottage to become the Sustainable Restaurant Association's Restaurant of the Year in 2012, this brilliantly conceived and entirely green stable-block conversion above Ness Cove in Shaldon has gone on to become a true legend in the field. Owner Tim Bouget has described Ness Cove as "a quaint drinking village with a fishing problem". Well, it's an eating village now, too, and possibly the highest rated sustainable restaurant in the country. Luckily for the drinkers, Ness Cove is also home to the Two Beach microbrewery, whose elderflower-tinged ODE Ale is a true beer hero.

Kingfisher Fish & Chips

Devon

What
An award-winning fish & chip shop with a passion for sustainability

Who
Craig Maw & Nikki Mutton, owners

When
Lunch Monday to Saturday, dinner, daily

Address
Chaddlewood Shopping Centre, 6 Glen Road, Plymouth, Devon, PL7 2XS

+44 (0)17 5233 5567

kingfisherfishandchips.co.uk

Bookings
No bookings taken

Price guide

What they say
"When we opened Kingfisher in 2012, we set about becoming MSC certified as we knew this was the gold standard for sustainable, responsibly caught and fully traceable fish. We currently serve twelve MSC-certified species, leading the MSC to declare ours as the "most sustainable seafood menu in the world". Sustainability is the top priority for sourcing our fish. This may mean it's not the most local catch but for us, knowing that it has been caught responsibly, in a way that will not damage delicate ecosystems or stocks and is fully traceable, is of the utmost importance."

Signature dishes
MSC-certified lobster; MSC-certified cod tongues; and MSC-certified Cornish hake.

What we say
We love how these guys actively promote fish and chips as a nutritious, delicious treat that is part of a balanced diet which can be eaten with a clear conscience. It is a source of protein, vitamins, minerals, and fibre and a portion of homemade mushy peas counts as one of your five-a-day. Using 100 per cent natural ingredients, they are doing everything in their power to maintain fish and chips' status as the nation's favourite dish. In October 2017 they were invited to Japan for three weeks to promote and champion sustainable fish and chips. While there, they cooked a record 9,000 portions of fish and chips in ten days and were asked to come again. What ambassadors!

The Old Dairy Kitchen at Trill Farm

Devon

What
An educational kitchen & community dining space based on Trill Farm in East Devon

Who
Chris Onions, owner

When
Lunch Wednesday & Saturday

Address
Trill Farm, Musbury, Axminster, Devon, EX13 8TU

+44 (0)79 9992 3089

olddairykitchen.co.uk

Bookings
Phone or website

Price guide

What they say
"Showcasing the organic ingredients from Trill Farm, supporting local producers, and promoting local food are the pillars of our ethos. We strive to improve our local food culture through our menus and various forms of education. Thanks to using the incredible produce straight from the farm, the bulk of our ingredients have zero food miles. What we do source from elsewhere either comes from local producers or is as local as possible. We are known for our creative approach to vegetarian dishes, using meat only as a supplement to the seasonal ingredients grown on the farm. We create as little waste as possible and use the whole animal when we do."

Signature dishes
Lyme Bay scallops with shaved Dalwood asparagus and lightly fermented dandelion buds; nettle choux bun with homemade feta and lovage; and Trill lamb leg cooked over coals, glazed with wild garlic and Trill Farm honey.

What we say
From the beginning, the idea wasn't to create a commercial kitchen. It was to create a community kitchen. They are one business in a community of small-scale enterprises based on a 300-acre mixed organic farm. This network delivers a wide range of educational courses and sustainable products, from organic herbs, vegetables, meat, and honey to willow weaving, woodworking, soap making, and cookery courses. They are also open for seasonal evening feasts – not to be missed. They are a product of their environment; there is nothing they serve that does not speak exactly to where they come from.

Percy's

Devon

What
Country hotel on fifty acres of undulating pasture & woodland

Who
Tina Bricknell-Webb, chef

When
Dinner, daily

Address
Coombeshead Estate, Virginstow, Devon, EX21 5EA

+44 (0)75 5334 4371

percys.co.uk

Bookings
Phone or email
info@percys.co.uk

Price guide

What they say
"Provenance, animal welfare, home-produced, and locally sourced ingredients are part of our ethos here at Percy's. We work with low food miles, organic, and biodynamic wines and offer restricted diets a dining experience to remember. Fantastic vegetables, freshly picked, lightly cooked with fresh homegrown herbs. Amazing dawn chorus, wild beavers (the only unfenced colony of wild beavers in the UK), and teeming wildlife are all part of Percy's magical charm."

Signature dishes
Home-reared organic lamb; seared diver-caught Cornish scallops with home-cured bacon; and Cornish dayboat line-caught sea bass with saffron glaze.

What we say
Since first visiting fifteen years ago, we have long regarded Percy's as one of the most inspirational restaurants in Britain. Indeed, it is one of the places that first formed our vision of what a sustainable restaurant is and what all restaurants should aspire to as far as they possibly can. Everything here springs from the local environment and so much is put back. In 2000, they planted 60,000 trees – sixty thousand! – in line with a "food from the forest" theme. They rear organic sheep and pedigree pigs, they send animals only to local slaughter and then tan the hides for sale. And for all this dreamy focus on the best meat, the soundness of their veg game means this is one of the best places in Europe to be vegan or vegetarian. Percy's, we salute you!

The Pig at Combe

Devon

What
A glorious restaurant with rooms in the heart of the Devon countryside

Who
Robin Hutson, owner

When
Breakfast, lunch & dinner, daily

Address
Gittisham, Honiton, Devon, EX14 3AD, plus other locations – see website

+44 (0)34 5225 9494

thepighotel.com

Bookings
Phone or website

Price guide

What they say
"There's a saying in Devon that 'if you stick your finger in the ground it will grow', and the kitchen garden is the beating heart of our new addition. The difference here is there are three walled gardens – the vegetable garden, the herb garden, and the infusion garden. Being eight miles from the coast, the menu consists of fresh fish as well as the very best Devonshire cheese and locally reared meat from butchers around the area. With all the Pigs, what cannot be grown in the kitchen garden will be sourced within a twenty-five-mile radius."

Signature dishes
Buckhouse lamb loin with walking onions, asparagus, and roasted beetroot; Lyme Bay hake fillet with Teign mussels, shore veg, radishes, and white wine sauce; and Gibbins Farm tomahawk pork chop with creamy spinach, pancetta, and mustard sauce.

What we say
We love the Pigs! They are all housed in fantastic buildings in beautiful parts of the English countryside that seem endlessly full of fun, silly people, larking about, eating fantastic food that is locally sourced, vibrant with life and tasty as hell, drinking, shouting, wassailing away and making you wonder how on earth we survived before. For so long, English country hotels were the stuff of chintzy nightmares, hushed dining rooms, and cold, wobbling, gelatinous food. The Pigs have blown all that away with their succession of superb sties and made our rural hospitality something to shout about to the world again!

Rockfish

Devon

What
Fresh local fish & seafood, an ethos grounded in sustainability

Who
Mitch Tonks, founder

When
Lunch & dinner, daily

Address
Brixham Fish Market, Brixham, Devon, TQ5 8AJ, plus other locations – see website

+44 (0)18 0385 0872

therockfish.co.uk

Bookings
Website

Price guide

What they say
"Here at Rockfish, we aim to change the way people eat seafood in the UK. Fish and shellfish caught and landed daily right outside our doors is served in our restaurants by the sea, and we work with local fisherman, brewers, and producers to buy in the best produce to create our menus. Our menus include classic fresh fried sustainable fish and unlimited chips, plus tacos, fritto misto, fresh local crab salads, and more. Thirsty passers-by can fill up their water bottles with our outdoor taps, too."

Signature dishes
Local Brixham scallops in the half shell with garlic and breadcrumbs; grilled MSC hake served with unlimited fresh cut chips, asparagus, peas, and mint; and crispy fish taco: crisp-fried MSC cod with guacamole, red onion, fresh lime, chilli, yoghurt, and mint coriander, in a grilled flour tortilla.

What we say
You could walk into any branch of Rockfish and think it was just a normal seafood restaurant or takeaway – albeit a clean, well-designed, well-staffed one with an incredibly diverse menu. All the work that the visionary Mitch Tonks has put in – here and throughout his life – to marine sustainability is worn incredibly lightly. Order seafood cooked to your preference and read up about what is being done here to champion the well-being and bounty of the seas. This is probably the best seafood group in the world.

The Riverford Field Kitchen

Devon

What
Dedicated to making seasonal organic veg the star of every plate

Who
Guy Singh-Watson, founder

When
Lunch & dinner, daily

Address
Wash Barn, Buckfastleigh, Devon, TQ11 0JU

+44 (0)18 0376 2074

theriverfordfieldkitchen.co.uk

Bookings
Website or resdiary.com

Price guide

What they say
"Vegetables are at the heart of what we do, and we are happy to be called veg nerds. We hope to bridge the gap between aspiration and reality; to make a turnip or courgette exciting and to prevent a cardoon or artichoke from being intimidating. We're not vegetarian, but meat and fish are used as a seasoning and organic seasonal veg is the star of every dish."

Signature dishes
Leek and ramsom *gribiche*; purple sprouting broccoli with tahini and dukkah; and beetroot *thoran* with cashew nut butter.

What we say
We all know that eating less meat is the key to the future of humanity, whether we are talking about the health of each individual or the health of the planet. We also know that ubiquitous compulsory vegetarianism is not the answer. The answer is less meat. Not none. Less. Like at lunch in this very Eden, where five or six eye-popping, unforgettable veg dishes are served up at communal tables along with a gleaming meat dish of which you really need take only a little. Maybe a fifth of your full meal intake. This is made possible by the quality of the veg they grow, through which you are invited to take a tour before you eat. Do – it will change your life. As will a spoonful of any of their utterly historic desserts.

The School House

Devon

What
Seafood café, takeaway & tearoom on the Flete Estate in the stunning South Hams

Who
Tamara Costin, owner

When
Hours change seasonally

Address
Mothecombe, Plymouth, Devon, PL8 1LB

+44 (0)17 5283 0552

schoolhouse-devon.com

Bookings
Phone or email
dinnerlady@schoolhouse-devon.com

Price guide

What they say
"Using local, seasonal produce is immersive in our restaurants. We grow our own leaves here at Mothecombe, and only use local fish from our beautiful Devon coastlines. Sourcing sustainable fish and seafood is an absolute must for us. We love our strong team and are constantly nurturing, educating, and mentoring staff where we can. We live in a lovely tight-knit community and so participate wherever we can with local community projects from the local primary school, running clubs, etc. We work hard to source the very best organic products from the South Hams and surrounds. If it's not to our high standards, it's not on the menu!"

Signature dishes
Bang bang crispy prawns with harissa mayo and shredded iceberg lettuce; crab rarebit with Mothecombe leaves; and local flatfish goujons with tartare, leaves, and thin chips.

What we say
We spent many wonderful summer afternoons and evenings here last year, eating beautiful local seafood prepared with real oomph and served by engaging young locals. The views across the fields are lovely and then a walk down to the beach is a must. Once private and accessible to the public only three days a week, it is now fully open. This means busy crowds at times, but wondrous solitude if you're lucky. And then a brisk march back up the hill for another basket of deep-fried calamari and perhaps a bottle of rosé...

The Seahorse

Devon

What
Award-winning seafood restaurant, private dining room & bar, overlooking the River Dart

Who
Mitch Tonks, chef

When
Lunch & dinner, Tuesday to Saturday, lunch Sunday

Address
5 South Embankment, Dartmouth, Devon, TQ6 9BH

+44 (0)18 0383 5147

seahorserestaurant.co.uk

Bookings
Website

Price guide

What they say
"At The Seahorse we cook our super fresh, just-caught seafood over the coals, taking special care with the provenance of our ingredients and keeping simplicity and attention to detail in our cooking. Sustainability is part of our DNA and not an add-on. It's just what we do. We've created a relaxing cosy space here in our little Devon sanctuary – so that it feels like walking into a good friend's house, warm and relaxing, where you know the food, drink, and company are going to be memorable."

Signature dishes
Local cuttlefish in ink with soft polenta; Dover sole cooked whole with lemon and olive oil over fire; and scallops roasted in the shell with white port and garlic.

What others say
"It's manna from Devon ... this corking quayside restaurant might be the best in Britain."

–Tom Parker Bowles, *The Independent*

What we say
The turbot cooked here on the Josper grill not long after it opened remains one of the most memorable things we've ever put in our mouths. The atmosphere on a dark evening when the wind whips in off the harbour and good wine is being drunk with great cooking is second to none.

Daylesford Organic Farmshop & Café

Gloucestershire

What
Offering seasonal, delicious food made with organic produce from the café's farm

Who
Carole Bamford, founder

When
Breakfast & lunch, daily, dinner Monday to Saturday

Address
Daylesford near Kingham, Gloucestershire, GL56 0YG, plus other locations – see website

+44 (0)16 0873 1700

daylesford.com

Bookings
Phone

Price guide

What they say
"Since the 1970s Carole Bamford has been passionate about organic farming and Daylesford has become one of the most pioneering and sustainable farms in the UK. We want to lead by example: farming, growing, and producing according to sustainable organic principles because we care for the land we work. We are committed to the preservation of rare and heritage breeds of animals as well as English heritage market garden produce. Eating well is sharing seasonal, local, organic food that nourishes our bodies. We believe that producing food organically, following the year's natural rhythms, is not only best for the future of our planet, it is better for our well-being, too."

Signature dishes
Cotswold chopped salad (Gloucester ham from the Daylesford smokehouse, our award-winning Cheddar, avocado, boiled egg, chicken, tomato, and beetroot with avocado oil and apple cider vinegar); beef burger with crisp truffle potatoes (grass-pastured patty, Cheddar or Bledington blue cheese, house-made bacon jam, pickled beets); and Welsh rarebit, with Daylesford Cheddar, chutney, and dressed Market Garden leaves.

What we say
Carole Bamford's journey and commitment to organic and sustainable farming began over thirty-five years ago. This passion and dedication is evident on entering one of Daylesford Organic's four other farm shops and cafes in London. It's about vibrant, quality, organic, sustainable, and seasonal produce. Try a guilt-free item from the menu to soak up some of Daylesford Organic's goodness.

Daylesford Organic Farmshop & Café (p. 182)

Arbor

Dorset

What
Serious food in a relaxed setting, without the pretence or the price tag, offering guilt-free dining

Who
Andy Hilton, chef

When
Lunch & dinner, daily

Address
4 Grove Road,
Bournemouth,
Dorset, BH1 3AX

+44 (0)12 0249 8900

arbor-restaurant.co.uk

Bookings
Website

Price guide

What they say
"We're lucky. Nearby, we have England's garden counties: Dorset ('daarrset', as we say), Hampshire, and Wiltshire, from where we get daily deliveries of the best meat, vegetables, and dairy products. On the south coast, we also get the pick of the country's fish and shellfish. We love our artisanal suppliers and we get a buzz out of finding new specialist providers to work with. The best thing is that you can enjoy all this with a clear conscience. The greenhouse was developed on sustainable principles – from the building materials and the energy systems to the beehives on the roof!"

Signature dishes
Pan-fried pork tenderloin with braised carrot and pulled pork shoulder lasagne; crab and scallop tortellini with crab bisque and pickled fennel; and tandoori lamb shank with lamb biryani and apricot chutney.

What we say
A tall white building surrounded by whispering oak and birch trees. Beautiful gardens that are an endless reminder of the beauty and bounty of nature. A five-minute potter down to the beach for a smell of the sea. Time to reflect on the pure green philosophy of this immaculate hotel and restaurant ahead of an elegant, season-driven supper that is unquestionably the best in Bournemouth.

The Green

Dorset

What
Small family-owned business where the words terroir & fresh have great influence on the menu

Who
Sasha Matkevich, chef/owner

When
Lunch & dinner, Tuesday to Saturday, lunch Sunday

Address
3 The Green, Sherborne,
Dorset, DT9 3HY

+44 (0)19 3581 3821

greenrestaurant.co.uk

Bookings
Phone or email
info@greenrestaurant.co.uk

Price guide

What they say
"We are lucky enough to be in the heart of the West Country on the Dorset/Somerset border, where we are spoilt for choice when it comes to local produce. We use ethically sourced, high-quality ingredients. We know our suppliers personally and are able to visit their businesses and farms: Harry's Cider, Montgomery's Cheddar, Dorset Blue Vinney, Professor S. J. Eykyn eggs, and many more are all on our doorstep. We work on people's strengths while accepting their imperfections.

"Sasha grew up in the Caucasus mountains, an area of Southern Russia particularly abundant in local produce. He has always been passionate about growing and foraging for food and spends as much time as he can with his family on the hunt for ingredients."

Signature dishes
Cornish mackerel escabeche on *borodinsky* toast; puy lentil ragout with roasted sunchoke; and wild garlic and meadowsweet mousse with walnut praline and Dorset sea buckthorn berries.

What others say
"[The] food is thoughtful and inventive, most of it based on locally sourced meat, game, fish, vegetables and fungi. An accomplished forager, [Sasha] knows where to find cepes and truffles. His ham hock was at least as good as any I have eaten, even when it was called jambon persillé in Burgundy."

–Bruce Anderson, *The Spectator*

What we say
All the foraging and devotion to local produce comes from the heart and soul here, not from a blind following of fashion. The ingredients are unimpeachable and the sly Russian twists are a delight.

Bangkok Canteen

Gloucestershire

What
A gluten-free Thai restaurant

Who
Wicha Kidhen & Kittima Manmaunjun, owners/chefs

When
Dinner Tuesday to Saturday

Address
72 Westgate St, Gloucester, Gloucestershire, GL1 2NZ

+44 (0)14 5230 6288

bangkokcanteen.co.uk

Bookings
Email
eat@bangkokcanteen.co.uk

Price guide

What they say
"Our fresh, vibrant flavours, along with locally sourced ingredients and the variety of vegan choices, are what make Bangkok Canteen so special. We grow our own produce for the restaurant and buy from local growers whenever possible. Our menu features our local farmer heroes, so you know what you're eating. From choosing fair trade coffee to local organic milk, and working in the restaurant on our eco-friendly policies, we care about the world we live in and we want to make it better with great food and a great ethos!"

Signature dishes
Longhorn massaman; old spot panang; and pad thai.

What we say
Gloucester is so lucky to have this adorable little Thai café with such committed staff working so hard to create authentic dishes that not only use entirely local produce, but are gluten-free as well – the first of its kind in the city – and cater admirably for vegans and vegetarians, too. That such a small restaurant, in a town not known for its wealth or foodiness, should be doing so much that is so good, is an example to us all.

Le Champignon Sauvage

Gloucestershire

What
A two-Michelin-star restaurant in Cheltenham which launched over thirty years ago

Who
David, owner/chef & Helen Everitt-Matthias, front of house

When
Lunch & dinner, Tuesday to Saturday

Address
24–28 Suffolk Row, Cheltenham, Gloucestershire, GL50 2AQ

+44 (0)12 4257 3449

lechampignonsauvage.co.uk

Bookings
Phone

Price guide

What they say
"My unwavering commitment to Le Champignon Sauvage is driven by my absolute love of cooking. It's not about expensive ingredients, it's about top-quality produce and being able to turn simple ingredients like everyday vegetables or a pig's trotter into a show-stopping dish. Ultimately it all comes back to remaining loyal to the seasons and using the absolute best they have to offer."

Signature dishes
Scallops, salsify with milk crumbs, cured jowl, onion dashi, and leek purée; rabbit loin with rillettes and parfait, heritage carrots, and mead jelly; and Shurdington lamb with wild garlic pesto and sheep's curd.

What we say
Since opening the restaurant thirty years ago, Chef David Everitt-Matthias and his wife Helen have never missed a service. Never. Missed. A. Service. We don't think there is another chef-prop couple in the country that can say that. Or possibly in the world. "It may be considered old fashioned", they say, "but we believe that guests expect to find the head chef cooking in the kitchen". The result is unwavering consistency and some of the best cooking anywhere.

Acorn

Somerset

What
A vegan restaurant without any vegan clichés. Modern gastronomic food made entirely from plants

Who
Richard Buckley, owner/chef & Jamie Taylor, chef

When
Lunch & dinner, daily

Address
2 North Parade Passage, Bath, Somerset, BA1 1NX

+44 (0)12 2544 6059

acornrestaurant.co.uk

Bookings
Website

Price guide

What they say
"We want to reverse vegan clichés by creating clever modern food that only happens to be made from plants. Our owner, Richard, is fanatical about good farming and quality ingredients, so we work closely with local farmers and artisanal producers to get the best raw ingredients that money can buy. All our staff are paid the same for the same work, and we work hard to ensure that catering is a sustainable career choice for those that work with us, staffing at levels that allows them to work only forty-five hours and to see their families occasionally (if they want to!)."

Signature dishes
Wye Valley asparagus, compressed with lemon oil and charred, with spring greens braised in porcini stock and whipped smoked almond curds; whole cauliflower with roasted florets, truffled purée, molasses-pickled core, braised leaves, and fenugreek croqueta; and Yorkshire forced rhubarb with fennel carpaccio and almond sorbet.

What we say
Acorn has been wowing vegetarians and non-vegetarians alike with its brightly coloured, complex cooking since opening four years ago in one of the oldest houses in Bath (which is saying something). This one is of gorgeous honeyed stone, naturally, with all the clean lines and invigorating natural light you'd expect of a Georgian masterpiece. A wonderful, muted palette in the decor, some quirky knick-knacks and really cheery service provide a relaxing and elegant backdrop to some of the best vegetarian cooking in England.

Simpsons Fish and Chips

Gloucestershire

What
A family-run, award-winning fish & chip shop based in the heart of the Cotswolds

Who
Bonny & James Ritchie, owners

When
Dinner Monday & Sunday, lunch & dinner, Tuesday to Saturday

Address
73-75 Priors Road,
Cheltenham,
Gloucestershire, GL52 5AL

+44 (0)12 4252 1964

simpsonsfishandchips.com

Bookings
Phone

Price guide

What they say
"Good quality, sustainably sourced, honest food. We're constantly striving to put fish and chips at the forefront of people's minds as an option for fast food. We want to educate people about the nutritional qualities of Britain's favourite dish and we're passionate about our ingredients, their provenance, and their preparation. We're also dedicated to supporting our local suppliers and businesses wherever possible. We won't compromise on quality, though, so if we have to travel further afield to get the right product, we will. All our seafood is MSC-certified and our specials always reflect the seasons. We have vegan and gluten-free options, too."

Signature dishes
Cod and chips; halloumi fries; and deep-fried asparagus.

What we say
This big, American-diner-style fish and chip shop is just the last thing you'd expect to find on the edge of the Cotswolds, about as far in Britain as you can get from the sea. But it is wonderful. The Cheltenham branch was the first MSC-certified chip shop in Gloucestershire, which led to a flurry of other outlets following suit – we love people who lead the way and the new shop in Stroud not only became the one hundredth MSC-certified fish and chip shop in the UK but has been endorsed by PETA for its vegan-friendly menu. Simpsons also does wonderful things for the local community – such as a "senior meal deal" – which gives this very forward-thinking restaurant a wonderfully old-fashioned feel.

Roth Bar & Grill

What
Classic British restaurant serving food from its 1,000-acre estate, often cooked over fire

Who
Steve Horrell, chef & Jules Horrell, manager

When
Breakfast & lunch, Tuesday to Sunday, dinner Thursday to Saturday

Address
Durslade Farm, Dropping Lane, Bruton, Somerset, BA10 0NL

+44 (0)17 4981 4700

rothbarandgrill.co.uk

Bookings
Website

Price guide

What they say
"Sustainable, local, and affordable food. Sourcing is important to us, with all beef, pork, and lamb coming from our estate. We love to cook over fire and host weekly feasts every Thursday evening. We love to work with like-minded people and often host guest chefs, speakers, and workshops. All our purchasing is sustainable, including fish, which is line-caught and scallops are hand-dived. Wild food is often a choice, game comes from the estate during the season alongside truffles, wild garlic, and other seasonal delights."

Signature dishes
Homemade merguez sausages with white beans and harissa mayonnaise; hand-cut Tomahawk steak (Hereford X Aberdeen Angus) with chips and Béarnaise, watercress; and whole roast Durslade Farm lamb cooked aside chimichurri, with kitchen salads.

What others say
"Roth Bar & Grill is exactly what a country restaurant should be: its combination of a laid-back dining room and a serious kitchen would not feel out of place in Shoreditch, while the twin rustic virtues of a friendly welcome and top-notch local ingredients make for a hugely rewarding meal."

–Bill Knott, *Financial Times*

What we say
Everything about Roth just blows us away. But get a load of their Feed the Team initiative, by which once a month they take their staff to visit a supplier, "to feed them with knowledge, which in turn, they pass onto our guests". They also take them fishing, stalking, shooting, and foraging to allow them to truly get to grips with where their food comes from. Outstanding!

Roth Bar & Grill (p. 191)

Talbot Inn

Somerset

What
Gastropub & bedrooms
in rural Somerset

Who
Dan Brod, Matt Greenlees
& Charlie Luxton, owners

When
Breakfast, lunch & dinner, daily

Address
Selwood Street, Mells,
Frome, Somerset, BA11 3PN

+44 (0)13 7381 2254

talbotinn.com

Bookings
Phone or website

Price guide

What they say
"Very simply, what's important to us
is making sure everyone who comes
through our doors has a great time.
This is, for us, at the heart of what
an English country pub is all about.
Of course food and drink needs to
be excellent, local, and delicious
but it is the overall experience of
being genuinely hospitable that is
most important, and having our staff
espouse this every day is what we
are most passionate about. We use
seasonal produce because it is obvious
to do so and source locally, not only
because of our great produce, but
also because it connects us with
our locality."

Signature dishes
Crispy lamb sweetbreads with pickled
Bromham beetroot, broad beans, and
garlic pesto; Somerset-cider-battered
fish and chips with mushy peas, and
tartare

sauce; and rhubarb (from the Inn's
walled garden) parfait with crème
patissière, gingerbread, and rhubarb
sorbet.

What we say
We had a wonderful night here quite
early in the new life recently granted
to this ancient inn. We ate and drank
and wobbled around, met great people,
talked of food and wine and the
countryside, and passed out quietly
in a corner, dreaming of the happier
world this magical hostelry transports
us back to. England is covered with
coaching inns like this, whose glory
days were once thought behind them.
But thanks to a new generation of
hosts – like Dan, Matt, and Charlie
– they are bringing huge pleasure to
thousands of us once again.

Thyme

Gloucestershire

What
Simple & honest food through
the love of the land

Who
Matt Wardman, head chef

When
Lunch & dinner, daily

Address
Lechlade, Southrop,
Gloucestershire, GL7 3NU

+44 (0)13 6785 0205

theswanatsouthrop.co.uk

Bookings
Phone or website

Price guide

What they say
"It's all about friendly service, a
relaxed environment, and a selection
of delicious seasonal dishes that
communicate generosity of spirit and
celebrate the bounty of the land. The
starting point for our menus is the
seasonal produce grown in the kitchen
garden and farm at Thyme: fruit,
vegetables, herbs, hen and duck eggs,
lamb, hogget, and mutton from our
sheep, and honey from our bees. We
have an ongoing dialogue with all our
suppliers to improve the sustainable
nature of our relationships. Thyme is
committed to the people who work
for us; their development is prioritized
within a nurturing environment with
leadership, inclusivity, transparency,
integrity, stewardship, and continuous
improvement at its heart."

Signature dishes
Rack of Cotswold lamb with spinach
and braised beans; whole mackerel
"the Flemish way" with a kitchen
garden salad; and chicken, bacon,
and wild garlic pie with potatoes
and greens.

What we say
It isn't just that so much comes from
Thyme's own farm garden, it is that
that garden is one of no-dig beds and
sustainable composting. They also
have a rigorous reuse and recycle
policy and all staff are working towards
"no waste kitchens". Their bottled
water is Belu, produced with the lowest
possible carbon footprint and all
profits used to combat water poverty.
And they are committed to green
technologies, with ground-source
heat pumps and biomass boilers as
well as sophisticated ventilation and
heat recovery systems. AND it's in the
Cotswolds – we love the Cotswolds!

Sharpham Park Pantry

Somerset

What
The restaurant of Kilver Court designer outlet village

Who
Roger Saul, owner

When
Breakfast & lunch, daily

Address
Kilver Court, Kilver Street,
Shepton Mallet,
Somerset, BA4 5NF

+44 (0)17 4934 0416

kilvercourt.com &
sharphampark.com

Bookings
Phone

Price guide

What they say
"We're ALL about our organic spelt, which is grown, harvested, and milled less than thirty minutes away at our sister company Sharpham Park. As well as having a strong spelt focus, the Pantry is focused on showcasing the best seasonal, local, and organic produce that Somerset and the South West has to offer. We work closely with local organic beef and dairy farmers, bakeries, and patisseries. We support Bowel Cancer UK and are involved in our local community group Sustainable Shepton, as well as offering the opportunity for local residents to volunteer in our gardens and organic veg patch. Sharpham Pantry is situated in a regenerated Victorian textile mill complex featuring RHS accredited gardens."

Signature dishes
Purple broccoli with spelt pasta, wild garlic, and hazelnut pesto; asparagus Caesar salad with spelt croutons and locally sourced cheese; and Moroccan spiced salad with slow-cooked lamb shoulder, spelt couscous, dates, and almonds.

What we say
We first met Roger Saul on a tour of Highgrove with the Soil Association fifteen years ago, when he was planting his first fields of spelt. He explained to us what spelt was, how it related to the wider wheat picture, and what it could do in terms of health and nutrition. A few years on, Roger is the undisputed King of Spelt, we (and millions of others) are converts, and the world has a chance of being just a little bit slimmer, healthier, and happier.

Yeo Valley Canteen

Somerset

What
Serving organic food to its staff & now the public

Who
Sarah Mead, director

When
Breakfast & lunch,
Tuesday to Friday

Address
Rhodyate, Blagdon,
Somerset, BS40 7YE

+44 (0)17 6146 1425

yeovalley.co.uk

Bookings
Phone or website

Price guide

What they say
"We are fanatical about supporting local and British farmers and sourcing local and organic produce. We use our own organic meat, which is all raised on the farm. Yeo Valley Dairy support the local community by purchasing vegetables, salad, cheese, and fruit from within six miles of our kitchen. We really are seasonal and have our suppliers to thank for that. We are running our own race and hope to take people along with us on that journey by talking about what we do and why we do it at every opportunity."

Signature dishes
Community farm leek and wild garlic tart with Strode Valley organic salad; Holt Farm's devilled lambs' kidneys on our house-made toasted sourdough; and Yeo Valley vanilla ice cream baked Alaska.

What others say
"The best staff canteen in the world."

–Gemma Mullin, *Mail Online*

What we say
It is an honour and a privilege to be welcomed into what was once the Yeo Valley staff canteen as a paying member of the public. For so many years Yeo Valley has a been a beacon of organic hope in a grisly world of exploitative farming. The sight of their logo in the dairy aisle of an otherwise hopeless supermarket, offering the chance of proper milk in your tea, butter on your toast, and yoghurt for your breakfast was always one to warm your heart. We knew they had to be eating something good. And it turns out they were.

Helen Browning's Royal Oak

Wiltshire

What
Pub, hotel, & restaurant on
an organic Wiltshire farm

Who
Tim Finney, general manager &
Helen Browning, owner

When
Breakfast, lunch, & dinner,
daily

Address
Cues Lane, Bishopstone,
Swindon, Wiltshire, SN6 8PP

+44 (0)17 9379 0481

helenbrowningsorganic.co.uk

Bookings
Phone or website

Price guide
●●●○○

What they say
"We're farmers first and foremost.
Providing hospitality is, at heart, really
a hobby, something we want to do.
We value our raw ingredients – and
who they're produced by – and we
treat them with a very light touch
in the cooking process to keep the
integrity of the flavour. Equality
is very important to us; we are a
woman-dominated business, and
most of the key skills and standards
are set by women. There's also no
obvious pay differential at any level
between genders. Our produce from
our organic farm is highlighted on the
very seasonal, ever-changing menu."

Signature dishes
Slow Eastbrook roast pork belly
carbonara with penne and Parmesan;
rare Eastbrook roast beef with
Bishopstone watercress and truffle oil
salad; and homemade gnocchi with
village wild garlic and burrata.

What we say
With its rambling and eclectically
furnished rooms, book-lined walls,
views over farms and countryside, and
wonderful, soulful food, this is one
of the great places to sit and while
away the Wiltshire hours. We've loved
this champion of organic farming
for many years and it's great to see
it still at the top of the pile. They
are currently planting fifty acres of
agroforestry – approximately 20,000
trees – so that livestock can graze
beneath and between. The trees' nuts
and fruit (walnuts, apricots, soft fruit,
perry pears, among others) will all
be available for consumption via the
pub and through local markets and
processors. The stuff of legend.

The Beckford Arms

Wiltshire

What
An English country pub with great food & stylish bedrooms, set in beautiful Wiltshire parkland

Who
Dan Brod & Charlie Luxton, co-owners

When
Lunch & dinner, daily

Address
Fonthill Gifford, Tisbury, Wiltshire, SP3 6PX

+44 (0)17 4787 0385

beckfordarms.com

Bookings
Phone, website, or email info@beckfordarms.com

Price guide

What they say
"Great English country hospitality with unpretentious country pub food and drink. It is only natural for us to work with the very best local producers, we have never done anything else. We take a common-sense approach to sustainability, preferring a long-term approach rather than short-term impact, and of course we recognize that a country pub fits within its community, which is equally valid for our suppliers as well as our customers."

Signature dishes
Local venison with kohlrabi and celeriac dauphinoise; suckling pig slow-roasted on the pub's open fireplace with garden-grown Bramley apple sauce; and local Chalk Stream trout smoked in-house with English heritage salad leaves.

What we say
The Beckford Arms was one of the first of the new wave of country hotels (partly inspired by Babington House and the Soho House vibe generally) that were youthful, fun, modern, hip, and up-to-date while at the same time very much more in tune with the timeless values of English countryside hospitality than the net-curtained, thickly-carpeted, fishy-smelling mid-late twentieth-century hostelries they replaced. This is a bar, restaurant, and small hotel that is just fun, fun, fun. When we visited, we got plastered on delicious cocktails and ended up arm-wrestling some sailor all night. So we barely remember the utterly historic dinner and terrific wine list. Only kidding, we do. (No, we don't.)

The Compasses Inn

Wiltshire

What
A beautiful fourteenth-century pub in rural Wiltshire with rooms

Who
Ben Maschler, owner & Paddy Davy, chef

When
Lunch Monday to Friday, weekend lunch & dinner

Address
Lower Chicksgrove, Tisbury, Wiltshire, SP3 6NB

+44 (0)17 2271 4318

thecompassesinn.com

Bookings
Phone, website, or opentable.com

Price guide

What they say
"Looking after people and allowing them to have a good time is important to us, as is serving really good, honest food in a beautiful environment. Ultimately, enabling people to enjoy their time here. We always buy locally where possible. It makes good sense to us on so many levels. Most importantly, it means that we can develop relationships with local producers who come to know about our standards and expectations. We have a fantastic veg supplier less than two miles from the pub and a lot of the beef that we serve is raised in the fields surrounding the pub."

Signature dishes
Scotch egg, made with locally sourced organic egg, pork mince, and black pudding; Chicksgrove home-salted beef with root vegetable hash, spinach, fried egg, and horseradish cream; and roasted hake fillet with risotto nero, mussels, and gremolata.

What we say
A beautiful pub in the heart of fantastic walking country that is dog-friendly and human-adoring. One of the coolest things they do is to offer customers a "Barter Board" accepting fish (trout) that people have caught locally, game that is shot during the season, and vegetables that the neighbours have grown in return for food and drink. An inn with such good food and such great vibes that is well on the way to abolishing money – that is surely the Arcadian dream in the heart of every true believer.

199

England
West Midlands

The Bookshop

What
A passion-project focused on crafting honest food using locally sourced seasonal ingredients

Who
Brothers Dorian, chef & Edwin Kirk, visionary

When
Dinner Thursday to Saturday, lunch Sunday

Address
33 Aubrey Street, Hereford, Herefordshire, HR4 OBU

+44 (0)14 3234 3443

aruleoftum.com

Bookings
Website

Price guide
●●●○○

What they say
"The Bookshop is big on responsibly produced, delicious food. Our ethos is to treat all the amazing produce that comes our way with the utmost respect. Our beetroot *borani* dish (roast beetroot, golden beetroot, beetroot crisps, candied walnuts, goat's curd, nigella seeds) is a great example of one way in which we choose to show our respect for the work and care put into sustainably grown produce. By drawing as much out of a product as is put into it, we are able to showcase a humble vegetable in all its glory. Our organic beets arrive in a crate, plucked straight from the ground, ready for us to transform them into an abundant vegetable dish that takes pride of place on the menu alongside the steak cuts."

What we say
From the same guys as Hereford's Rule of Tum and The Burger Shop, this place revels in its history as a former bookshop, still lining the walls with books and selling mostly... er, steak. Yes, it's not a bookshop anymore. Thursday to Friday, it's cuts of dry-aged Herefordshire beef and other seasonal local specialities. On Sundays it's a roast they say is "better than your mum's", which we will gladly believe. Our mum mostly opens tins.

The Burger Shop

Herefordshire

What
A passion-project focused on inspiring change in the food industry

Who
Brothers Dorian, chef & Edwin Kirk, visionary,

When
Lunch & dinner, daily

Address
32 Aubrey Street, Hereford, Herefordshire, HR4 0BU, plus other locations – see website

+44 (0)14 3235 1764

aruleoftum.com

Bookings
Phone

Price guide

What they say
"Our mission is to be a successful and profitable restaurant brand that delivers exceptional food experiences, with a vision of becoming one of the most highly regarded and sustainably led group of restaurants in the UK. We have built trusting relationships with those around us. By fostering partnerships with local farmers who grow produce specific to our needs, fostering connections with craftspeople who inject life and soul with their skills in ceramics, art, and horticulture, and fostering a drive for independent business culture, we ensure a reliable source of supply and demand within our community."

Signature dishes
Hereford Hop burger; Farmer Tom's beef burger; and Westcombe cheese curds.

What we say
It is only right and proper that a city with one of the great beef breeds named after it should have a humdinger of a burger joint in it. And this is certainly one. It is a rough-edged wooden space with bare bulbs and a heady whiff of rendering beef fat, as befits its status. This is not one of those annoying, poncey, burger-as-fine dining places. The food comes on plastic trays in cardboard wrappings, the beef is roughly ground for superlative heft and chew, there is a good char on the outside and the innards are medium-rare and pink as a summer evening sunset. It's a damned tasty burger.

Carters of Moseley

Birmingham

What
The philosophy of Carters is to be a true expression of British terroir within the moment

Who
Brad Carter & Holly Jackson, co-owners

When
Lunch & dinner,
Tuesday to Saturday

Address
2C Wake Green Road,
Birmingham, West Midlands,
B13 9EZ

+44 (0)12 1449 8885

cartersofmoseley.co.uk

Bookings
Phone, website, or
opentable.com

Price guide

What they say
"We aim to take the diner on a journey of discovery, helping people to learn about eating seasonally, sustainably, and responsibly – considering the provenance of ingredients and how human consumption affects the world we live in. Central to the cooking are British rare breeds, sustainable seafood, fresh herbs, fruits and vegetables, and wild food from the UK. There is particular attention to foraged ingredients indigenous to the UK. Carters aims to treat all ingredients with respect and admiration by limiting waste with a strong nose-to-tail dining ethos."

Signature dishes
Lichfield asparagus with Berkswell and three-cornered leek; Orkney scallop with grilled cream and Exmoor caviar; and Cornish ray with potato and sea truffle.

What we say
So great is their commitment to limiting foreign ingredients in their kitchen, that they do not serve lemon in the restaurant, instead using such substitutes as dock stems, sorrel, lemon verbena, and... ants! We all know that insects as wide-scale sustainable protein lie ahead, but to see formic acid as an alternative to citric, well, that's just visionary. They also use fig leaves to replace the flavour of coconut and plum stones for the taste of almond, although they have found a local UK grower of almonds. They work closely with producers capable of growing typically foreign ingredients in the UK, often pushing the experimental development themselves for things like Kaffir lime, wasabi, and yuzu. Inspirational.

Leon

Birmingham

What
On a mission to show the world what fast food would be like in heaven!

Who
John Vincent, CEO

When
Breakfast, lunch & dinner, daily

Address
25, Birmingham New Street Station, Birmingham, West Midlands, B2 4QA, plus other locations – see website

+44 (0)12 1643 5925

leon.co

Bookings
No bookings taken

Price guide

What they say
"LOVE: Love for good fast food. Love for natural food. Love for our guests, their taste buds, and their health. Love for our Leon family. And love for our planet. All Leon's produce is responsibly sourced from farmers, growers, and partners that we know and love. As much as possible is sourced in Britain and, if not, in Europe. We source British chicken and free-range British eggs, but our rice is Italian – because it's the best!"

Signature dishes
The Leon plant burger; Moroccan meatballs; and vegan falafel wrap.

What we say
Thirteen years ago, when it first opened, we hailed Leon as "the future of fast food" and we still believe that it is. The principles of good health, sustainability, fair trade, proper farming (organic where possible but not Messianically so), affordability, and great flavour were, back then, a revolutionary platform on which to build any restaurant, let alone a big nationwide chain with aspirations even further afield. Leon has gone from strength to strength, taking us all with it. They are even more plant-based than before, even more committed to our future well-being, and in so many places now, from train stations to shopping centres and high streets, the only option for people who care about what they eat.

Arthur's Farm Kitchen at Fordhall Farm

Shropshire

What
A community-owned organic farm offering a unique experience to all who visit

Who
The Fordhall Community Land Initiative, owner

When
Breakfast & lunch, Tuesday to Sunday

Address
Tern Hill Road, Market Drayton, Shropshire, TF9 3PS

+44 (0)16 3063 8696

fordhallfarm.com

Bookings
Phone or email
project@fordhallfarm.com

Price guide

What they say
"Arthur's food celebrates the diversity of seasonal ingredients with a menu that changes throughout the year. All the meat we use is reared on the farm. Dishes are made fresh and by hand with simple and traditional cooking methods. We want our customers to understand where their food comes from, appreciate the wonderful flavours of Mother Nature, and to try new things. We believe that our food culture needs reigniting, bringing back convivial sharing, conversation, and an appreciation of the meal and those who produced it."

Signature dishes
Spring nettle and potato soup with wild garlic pesto and foraged greens; slow-cooked Aberdeen Angus beef brisket with onion and bone broth gravy in a Yorkshire pudding wrap; and Fordhall farmhouse brunch with bacon, eggs, and bubble and squeak.

What we say
They do so many beautiful things so well here (free parent and toddler groups for local families; wonderful eco-build with hemp walls, lime plasters, natural clay paints, and sheep's wool insulation) that it is easy to forget the attention that goes into the cooking. But look at that brisket: Aberdeen Angus beef slow-cooked in a weekly-made seventy-two-hour bone broth, ensuring all the goodness is extracted from the organic grass-fed bones. Then the broth reduced to a gravy. With Yorkies that are made fresh in the morning. Is it in Shropshire or is it in heaven?

Russells Fish and Chips

Worcestershire

What
Best-quality fish & chips to eat in or take away

Who
Ross Cameron, chef & Andrew Riley, owner

When
Dinner, Monday to Saturday, lunch, daily

Address
20A High Street, Broadway, Worcestershire, WR12 7DT

+44 (0)13 8685 8435

russellsfishandchips.co.uk

Bookings
Email ross@
russellsfishandchips.co.uk

Price guide

What they say
"We serve only the finest fish alongside locally grown potatoes for chips all fried in Cotswold Gold rapeseed oil, in a relaxed and vibrant atmosphere in the beautiful Cotswold village of Broadway. The potatoes for chips are grown on the hill overlooking Broadway, the rapeseed oil is grown and refined less than two miles from the restaurant, and the pies we sell are made in the next village. As far as is possible we source locally produced drinks – local beers from Donnington Brewery, Purity Brewing, and a tiny brewer called Burke's Beers from Blockley, all within a few miles. Bottled local apple juice from Hayles Fruit Farm and our house gin, Cheltenham Gin, has its office based above the restaurant!"

Signature dishes
Cod and chips; The Supersize Snorker; and specials such as salmon, plaice, and sardines.

What we say
This is absolutely top-quality fish and chips, with the cod and haddock both immaculate, as is the plaice either breaded or grilled, whole tail scampi, fishcakes, or fish finger sandwich. We love the chalkboard that tells you each day what variety of potato they are chipping and there is a useful and well-priced children's menu. Service is knowledgeable, friendly, and quick, the village of Broadway itself is an utter delight and the ideal spot to consume what is without question the best possible way to eat cod that there is in this world.

The Vicarage

What
Locally sourced produce with a menu driven by responsible local gardeners, foragers & farmers

Who
Steven Tuke, executive chef

When
Breakfast, lunch & dinner, daily

Address
Knutsford Road,
Holmes Chapel, Cranage,
Cheshire, CW4 8EF

+44 (0)14 7753 3393

thevicaragecheshire.com

Bookings
Phone, website, or resdiary.com

Price guide

What they say
"Being positioned in rural Cheshire means it's not difficult for us to source exceptional produce from some of the country's best growers as well as various smallholdings just a stone's throw away. It's important to us to buy locally wherever possible to support responsible local businesses, to reduce our impact on the environment, and to ensure we serve the freshest food possible. We work very hard to keep our team happy and to treat them well. When our people find their work rewarding and satisfying it creates a happy and welcoming atmosphere for all our visitors."

Signature dishes
Beef fillet with English parsley, creamed potatoes, parsley crisps, shin of beef allumette, caramelised celeriac, creamed horse radish, and port jus; braised and rolled ham hock with homemade sultana, apple cider and pancetta black pudding, crushed broad beans and peas, heirloom pickled tomatoes, and brioche crisp; and Burt's blue cheese mousse with compressed pear, pear crisp, port jelly, and candied walnuts.

What we say
We have rarely encountered a place with such a wholehearted commitment to staff training and welfare. They do their best to employ and train as many local people in their hotel as possible. Age is not an issue. They believe certain people have hospitality in their DNA and that it is their job to find it and nurture it.

Cornichon

Cheshire

What
Independent bar & bistro
in Tarvin

Who
Ben & Lisa Green, owners

When
Lunch & dinner, Tuesday to
Saturday, lunch Sunday

Address
71 High Street, Tarvin,
Cheshire, CH3 8JA

+44 (0)18 2974 1391

cornichonrestaurant.co.uk

Bookings
Phone or resdiary.com

Price guide

What they say
"Ingredients and our customers having
a wonderful time are what drive
us. We get excited about certain
ingredients coming into season, and
we thrive off positive feedback and
the lovely buzz of a busy dining room
full of happy guests. Seasonal produce
guides our menu, and we source
locally where possible. Our milk is
from a local dairy, our asparagus is
grown a couple of miles down the
road, we make ricotta with raw milk
from another local dairy, our rapeseed
oil and honey is from a family in
Macclesfield, we buy flour from
Walk Mill down the road, where they
grow the wheat and mill it on an old
reconditioned mill."

Signature dishes
Burger: made in-house with chuck
burger patty, buttery brioche bun,
and Chester potato triple-fried fries;
Delamere asparagus with ricotta,
hazelnuts, and honey; and brunch:

home-cured bacon with Cumberland
sausage, house-made black pudding,
and sourdough.

What we say
The commitment to waste reduction
sees elements from the pastry section
used for cocktails, such as leftover
liquor from poaching rhubarb used
to make a delicious rhubarb gimlet.
They'll use offcuts of their homemade
brownies or two-day-old honeycomb
which has lost its crunch in ice cream.
All vegetable cuttings go to stock, and
leftover Sunday veg become soups.
Leftover prep will be used for staff
dinner where possible. They are happy
to hold stock and have fortnightly
deliveries rather than weekly.

The Pheasant Inn

Cheshire

What
Five-star gastro inn based
in the beautiful Cheshire
countryside

Who
Nelson Hotels

When
Breakfast, lunch & dinner, daily

Address
Pennsylvania Lane, Higher
Burwardsley, Chester,
Cheshire, CH3 9PF

+44 (0)18 2977 0434

thepheasantinn.co.uk

Bookings
Phone, website, or email
info@thepheasantinn.co.uk

Price guide

What they say
"Tucked in a peaceful corner of rural
Cheshire, yet sitting high atop the
Peckforton Hills, The Pheasant
enjoys some of the most magnificent
panoramic views in the area, stretching
across the Cheshire Plain to the Welsh
hills. Using fresh local and seasonal
produce simply with intelligent
pairings to create high-quality pub
fare and modern European dishes.
Providing friendly, first-class service
to all customers and creating a
welcoming and comfortable ambience,
so that customers leave having had a
memorable and enjoyable experience."

Signature dishes
Monkfish and king prawn curry; steak
and ale pie (homemade comfort food
and traditional British fare); and tiger
prawn *pil pil* (staple Nelson Hotels dish,
using Mediterranean concept).

What we say
Standard modern pub food done very
well and with a keen eye to the supply
chain makes these 300-year-old
Cheshire sandstone buildings, with
their open fires, panoramic views, and
flower-filled courtyard not far from
Chester, a popular base for anyone
planning to explore this part of
Cheshire or venture into North Wales.

The Brown Horse Inn

Cumbria

What
An 1850s coaching inn located in the heart of the Lake District

Who
Steve & Karen Edmondson, owners

When
Breakfast, lunch & dinner, daily

Address
The Brown Horse Inn, A5074, Windermere, Cumbria, LA23 3NR

+44 (0)15 3944 3443

thebrownhorseinn.co.uk

Bookings
Phone or email
info@thebrownhorseinn.co.uk

Price guide

What they say
"The Brown Horse Inn prides itself on using fresh homegrown produce. Anything we do not source from our estate is purchased from local farms within a five-mile radius. Owners Steve and Karen have developed the surrounding land and vegetable gardens to supply both The Brown Horse Inn and its sister property, the Lyth Valley Country Inn, with all their vegetables and herbs. We also farm our own game, such as pheasants and partridges. Our menu is adapted for each season to use fresh and seasonal produce. We have our own chickens so we are able to source our own fresh eggs."

Signature dishes
Hake with crushed Jersey Royals, English asparagus and parsley cream; fillet of salmon with sautéed Jersey Royals, baby beetroot, pak choi and dill yoghurt; and Winster Estate lamb cobbler with blue cheese scones and caramelized carrots.

What we say
This was one of those places we stumbled into for a pint after a long walk, ordered some ham and eggs, and didn't realize was going to be in any way special till we went out to the beer garden and found a chap brewing beer. This was 2011, when such things were simply not usual. Then came the food: thick gammon, slow cooked and "pulled" from pigs whose relatives we could see from the table under a quivering, super-fresh poached egg, breadcrumbed and quite beyond delicious with historic chips. Lovely dining room inside too. Oh, and the beer was superb.

The Cottage in the Wood

Cumbria

What
Foodie bolthole in the heart of Whinlatter Forest

Who
Kath & Liam Berney, owners & Ben Wilkinson, chef

When
Dinner Tuesday to Saturday, lunch Thursday to Saturday

Address
Magic Hill, Whinlatter Forest, Braithwaite, Keswick, Cumbria, CA12 5TW

+44 (0)17 6877 8409

thecottageinthewood.co.uk

Bookings
Phone or email
reception@cottageinthewood.co.uk

Price guide

What they say
"We aim to capture the flavour and terroir of Cumbria. From using ingredients such as Herdwick hogget and foraging for local delicacies, our land is our palette. We are supporters of Compassion in World Farming, RSPCA Freedom Foods, and the Marine Stewardship Council. We have also developed a culture of eliminating waste, recycling, and reducing excessive energy consumption. Local produce is kindly matched with the bounty of our northern neighbours, and further afield if necessary – we love Evesham asparagus and even Sicilian lemons."

Signature dishes
Cured Arctic char with cucumber and oyster; Herdwick hogget with onions, peas, and lamb "bacon"; and Douglas fir with lemon and fennel.

What others say
"A perfect tranche of turbot is partnered with a crisp disc of long-cooked pig's trotter and, to bring it all to life, a whizzy vinaigrette of cockles. Best of all is the big-flavoured Herdwick hogget served both roast and as a cylinder of something rich and braised, alongside a couple of pink fir potatoes and some baby leeks and glazed salsify. The plating may be delicate, but the cooking is big and bold."

–Jay Rayner, *The Guardian*

What we say
A rare wild adventure into the stormy heart of the last English wilderness, where views of unimaginable beauty provide a backdrop to cooking with a breathtaking sense of place. Rest assured that Head Chef Ben Wilkinson will present you with dishes full of flavour and creativity.

Lake Road Kitchen

Cumbria

What
Cold climate cooking – a representation of the North and its landscape

Who
James Cross, owner/chef/ partner & Sally Wilson, partner/general manager

When
Dinner Wednesday to Sunday

Address
Sussex House, Lake Road, Ambleside, Cumbria, LA22 0AD

+44 (0)15 3942 2012

lakeroadkitchen.co.uk

Bookings
Phone or email
info@lakeroadkitchen.co.uk

Price guide

What they say
"Our focus is entirely on the quality of the produce, the care and finesse with which we prepare and cook it, and the deliciousness of the finished dish. Our food is not about how good it looks on Instagram, it's about how it tastes. As we work within the unpredictable Northern climate, preservation is always present in our cooking. We also provide our regular guests with a unique culinary experience for each visit, all of which means that menus vary from night to night, and from table to table."

Signature dishes
Eleven-week dry-aged Saddleback pork chop cooked over fire with trompette purée, pickled white asparagus, ramson caper sauce; hand-dived Orkney scallop, LRK miso, and black truffle beurre monté; and lemon verbena custard tart with alpine strawberry ice cream.

What we say
We love how they use their location in Northern England to build a bond with the current power of the Nordic kitchen and get year-round beauty and flavour from a harsh landscape. They are also inspired by a practice from the South (originally Galicia in Spain) that has seen them turning local Holstein cattle that have finished their milking life into meat that is far more delicious than that which comes from younger animals. By doing this, their butchers not only lengthen the animal's life by seven to eight months, but double their value to the dairy farmers, helping to make dairy farming sustainable once again.

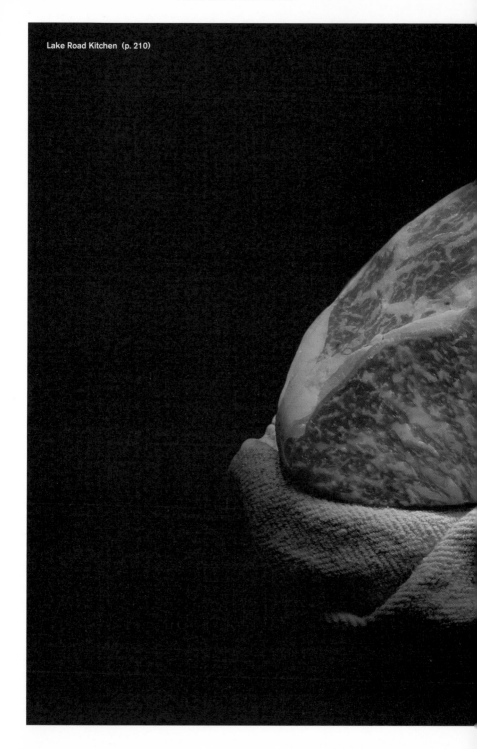

Lake Road Kitchen (p. 210)

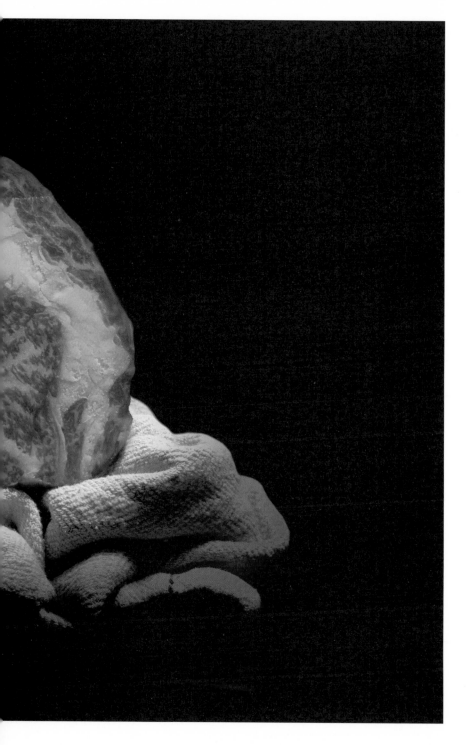

The Jumble Room

What
A small & funky, laid-back restaurant hidden in a quiet corner of Grasmere

Who
Andy, owner, Chrissy, chef & Emily Hill, manager

When
Lunch & dinner, Wednesday to Monday

Address
Langdale Road, Grasmere, Cumbria, LA22 9SU

+44 (0)15 3943 5188

thejumbleroom.co.uk

Bookings
Phone

Price guide

What they say
"The food is simple and superb, uncompromising in quality, nothing but the best, freshest, local, and, if possible, organic ingredients. Unfussy, skillfully married by Chrissy and the team.

"The experience, our restaurant, is about great food; soul food. Conversation, chatter, music, life, and enjoying time with friends, it's a collection of the senses. And yes, the food is great!"

Signature dishes
Pork and Morecambe shrimp *shumai*; Persian lamb rump; and Malaysian seafood curry.

What others say
"This is the heartiest, happiest restaurant in the Lakes, squashed into a corner cottage in Grasmere and serving hearty plates of stilton crostini, Lebanese lamb and pumpkin risotto.

The food is as eclectic as the decor, a mad melange of country kitchen, 1950s kitsch and tart's boudoir."

The Times

What we say
This small stone eighteenth-century cottage opened as a restaurant in 1996 in the hands of two people who just wanted to project their love of the locale into a room and onto a plate. Twenty years on, they have both a vigorously enthusiastic local clientele to keep them ticking over and pilgrims from all over the world booking months in advance for their little slice of heaven.

L'enclume

What
Showcasing the finest ingredients & harnessing the powerful connection between food & nature

Who
Simon Rogan, chef

When
Lunch & dinner, Tuesday to Sunday

Address
Cavendish Street, Cartmel, Grange-over-Sands, Cumbria, LA11 6PZ, plus other locations – see website

+44 (0)15 3953 6362

lenclume.co.uk

Bookings
Phone or website

Price guide

What they say
"From the precision we apply in sourcing the finest ingredients, to the creativity shown by the chefs in the kitchen, to the care and attention from the front-of-house team, we always strive to ensure that we give our guests a truly exceptional and unrivalled experience. Our farm was designed specifically to develop a harmonious relationship between cooking and growing. For my team, the produce is a driving force, so perfect that we barely have to do anything to it. Everything that we grow now has been carefully chosen to ensure it yields the best nutrients and retains maximum flavour. Our aim is to grow near-perfect produce in a natural and sustainable way. Growers and chefs work side-by-side to create the ingredients used in all of our restaurants – the farm is an extension of the kitchens."

What we say
Simon Rogan is in many ways the godfather of everything we treasure in restaurants. It was a visit here in 2004 that first opened our eyes to what a restaurant can be in terms of inhabiting its direct environment, encapsulating a specific moment in time and space, and presenting it on a plate. Rogan was foraging and serving edible flowers before anyone else, bringing his garden indoors and plating it before such things were really known. And his cooking is, of course, beyond compare.

The Punch Bowl Inn

Cumbria

What
Nine-bedroomed inn & award-winning restaurant in the Lake District

Who
Richard Rose, owner

When
Lunch & dinner, daily

Address
Crosthwaite, Lyth Valley, Kendal, Cumbria, LA8 8HR

+44 (0)15 3956 8237

the-punchbowl.co.uk

Bookings
Phone or resdiary.com

Price guide

What they say
"The Punch Bowl Inn is situated in the heart of the delightfully unspoilt Lyth Valley at Crosthwaite in Cumbria, alongside the parish church of St. Mary's. We offer a classic, contemporary-style formal restaurant and a traditional pub atmosphere in our bar with the same menu served throughout. Our produce from our gardens reduces our carbon footprint – from road fuels and use of fertilizers and pesticides. We love incorporating local freshwater fish and locally sourced shellfish in our menus, and we are constantly working on reducing food waste."

Signature dishes
Twice-baked Mrs. Kirkham's Lancashire cheese soufflé, onion chutney with thyme-infused cream; asparagus, hollandaise, and poached egg; and cod loin with warm tartare sauce, braised lettuce, and sautéed potatoes.

What we say
At The Punch Bowl Inn they forage for, grow, and preserve wild garlic, damsons, elderflower, pine shoots, rhubarb, beetroot, carrots, radishes, tomatoes, red currants, blackcurrants, gooseberries, raspberries, and watercress. The River Gilpin flows through Mirk Howe, where they cultivate the watercress. They source their paper for letterheads and slips from local mills at Beetham and Burneside. They use a locally sourced charcoal from Cartmel to barbecue appropriate dishes. The reception desk, which also doubles as the village post office, sells locally produced jams and preserves. This is the world of Beatrix Potter magically transformed into a restaurant! What absolute bliss.

Quince and Medlar

Cumbria

What
Fine-dining vegetarian restaurant on the edge of the Lake District

Who
Colin & Louisa Le Voi, owners/chefs

When
Dinner Tuesday to Saturday

Address
11-13 Castlegate, Cockermouth, Cumbria, CA13 9EU

+44 (0)19 0082 3579

quinceandmedlar.co.uk

Bookings
Phone

Price guide

What they say
"Great thought is put into each dish to ensure balanced nutrients (so often eating establishments provide, for example, vegetable dishes without protein). All dishes are prepared, cooked, and served by Colin and Louisa – when we are not here, the restaurant is closed. We have very little food waste, with peelings going to local horses and rabbits and leftover food eaten by us and our families."

Signature dishes
Baked courgette-wrapped Cumbrian cheese soufflé on rosemary garlic mushroom; beetroot with borlotti, and butternut patty, star anise-baked fennel, whipped salsify, truffle oil, and pine kernels; and gingered quinoa roast mooli root stack with hazelnut, pomegranate, wasabi-coated peas, peanut butter, and shallot sauce.

What we say
Sometimes the values and beliefs of *Truth, Love & Clean Cutlery* seem to us modern and forward-thinking to us, so millennial and downright hipsterish. And then we remember people like Colin and Louisa Le Voi – born just down the road in Workington and Whitehaven respectively – who have been creating terrific plant-based dishes at their listed Georgian townhouse restaurant since 1989. Nestling next to the castle in this beautiful riverside market town, Quince and Medlar is a friendly, welcoming place that has been easy on the eye, easy on the belly, and easy on the planet for thirty years now, with high hopes at this end for (at least) thirty more to come.

Three Hares

Cumbria

What
Field-to-fork, nose-to-tail café, bistro, & bakery focusing on quality seasonal produce

Who
James Ratcliffe, owner & Nina Matsunaga, chef

When
Breakfast & lunch, Tuesday to Sunday, dinner Thursday to Saturday

Address
57 Main Street, Sedbergh, Cumbria, LA10 5AB

+44 (0)15 3962 1058

threeharescafe.co.uk

Bookings
Phone or email
info@threeharescafe.co.uk

Price guide

What they say
"When our customers ask where their meat or game is from, I can often point out the window or they can visit close by. I strongly believe you can taste the landscape in a dish; the weather, the animal, the grass, the soil all contribute to the final product. We have our 'garden' of produce and it is our job to best represent it. We also focus on game (seasonally), which comes to us in abundance, and makes good use of a by-product of another local industry. Locally, we use a lot of fruit and veg grown by domestic gardeners, allotments, etc. We use fresh, and preserve what we can as it hits the peak of its season."

Signature dishes
Hare leg with Alexanders, celeriac, new season asparagus, and blood cake; wild sea trout with white asparagus, heritage potato, sea spinach, and verbena; and beetroot mousse with sweet cicely, gingerbread, and blood orange.

What we say
Few embarked on our survey with the application to detail of James Ratcliffe and Nina Matsunaga. On beef, they wrote: "Our favourite beef producer grows his own cereal, meaning no need for 'man-made cake' to finish the animal, so his farm runs a rotation system of grazing and growing, which is much better for the environment. Unfortunately purely 'grass-fed beef' does not quite work here – the quality of grass in parts of the North of England just isn't good enough." And so we learn a little something new.

Three Hares (p. 216)

Northcote

Lancashire

What
Luxury independent hotel located in the Ribble Valley, Lancashire, with a Michelin-star restaurant

Who
Craig Bancroft, managing director & Lisa Goodwin-Allen, chef

When
Breakfast, lunch & dinner, daily

Address
Northcote Road, Langho, Blackburn, Lancashire, BB6 8BE

+44 (0)12 5424 0555

northcote.com

Bookings
Phone, website, or email reception@northcote.com

Price guide

What they say
"Northcote is an oasis of gastronomic excellence that, alongside its restaurant, chef's table, and carefully curated wine cellar filled with unique wines, also boasts a truly interactive cookery school and a biodynamic kitchen garden. The Northcote kitchens have always held a deep loyalty to artisan producers and the great larder of Lancashire, with seasonality at its heart. The menus have a core of flavours that need to be true and dynamic, with a blend of modern influences. The ultimate aim is to delight our guests with flavours that are memorable, presentation that is sensational, and an overall experience that lingers forever."

Signature dishes
Chargrilled Wye Valley asparagus with Leagram's sheep's curd and sorrel; Northcote black bee honey with organic milk and lemon; and wild sea bass with young charred organic leeks and lettuce, and iron cross oxalis.

What others say
"Lisa Goodwin-Allen is a kitchen goddess. I've always thought so ever since she served up a sequence of brilliant dishes on the *Great British Menu*, and swept all before her."

–Matthew Fort, *northcote*

What we say
Nigel Haworth, who moved upstairs to become "chef ambassador" in 2017, was a barnstormer for everything Lancastrian and made this place the famous temple to local gastronomy that it has become. Lisa Goodwin-Allen, who took his place as executive chef, is a more modern, playful chef, but with roots equally grounded in the soil of Lancashire. Regulars and passing pilgrims alike are beyond lucky: nothing needed to change here, but now that it has, it's doubly wonderful.

Sticklebarn

Cumbria

What
Sticklebarn offers hearty food, a cracking pint & a warm welcome in the heart of the Lake District

Who
The National Trust

When
Lunch Monday to Saturday, dinner, daily

Address
Great Langdale, Ambleside, Cumbria, LA22 9JU

+44 (0)15 3943 7356

nationaltrust.org.uk

Bookings
Email
sticklebarn@nationaltrust.org.uk

Price guide

What they say
"As we're the only pub run by the National Trust, all of our thinking is around conservation and how we can help improve the surrounding area. This underpins everything from where we buy our meat through to what type of straws we use on the bar. This is guided by the National Trust's central food and beverage team in line with the Trust's strategy of looking after special places, forever, for everyone. Spirit of Place (SOP) is an all-encompassing set of standards that we set within our own specific property. SOP is what makes each property unique and is a guiding principle in every decision we make. For example, everything from the sympathetic heritage-style of food through to the rustic glass candleholders on the table is included."

Signature dishes
Herdwick lamb stew; superfood salad; and *ropa vieja* chilli.

What we say
The lamb here is some of the best meat you will ever eat. It comes from Herdwicks farmed by National Trust tenant Will Benson, who has fell rights in the area. The sheep are "hefted" to their patch of fell, which means they never leave it – a trait inherited by the breed over centuries. When ready, they are slaughtered locally, minimizing suffering and food miles. They are a slow-maturing animal so there is no "spring" lamb, they are all at least a year old at slaughter (making them "hoggets") and thus much fuller of flavour and denser of grain.

The Allotment

Manchester

What
A relaxed, unpretentious, fine dining, gluten-free & vegan restaurant

Who
Matthew Nutter, head chef/owner

When
Dinner Thursday to Saturday

Address
6 Vernon Street, Stockport, Manchester, SK1 1TY

+44 (0)16 1478 1331

allotmentvegan.co.uk

Bookings
Website

Price guide

What they say
"The most exciting thing about this restaurant is that we never know what we're doing. There are no recipes for vegan cooking. We are learning every day, and we are reinventing the wheel. It never stops being exciting. Our (mostly) organic produce comes from nearby producers, we use recyclable high-quality paper napkins, and we're aiming to go chemical-free within the year. Our little waste in the restaurant is shared amongst staff, who take home our nourishing food for their families to share."

Signature dishes
Shiitake mushroom parfait with truffle salt and pickled onion; confit aubergine steak with vegetable jus; and hibiscus meringue with jelly, fennel, and mint ice cream.

What we say
Matthew Nutter blew Manchester away last year taking chef of the year at the city's Food and Drink Awards from under the noses of some of the biggest names in the industry – Aiden Byrne of Manchester House, Adam Reid of The French, and Sam Buckley of Where The Light Gets In (terrific ventures all of them). This from a guy who doesn't touch meat, dairy, or any animal products, works solely with vegan produce, began his cheffing life working in a Harvester and had barely been open a year. Surely one of the great stars of the future!

Eighth Day Cafe

Manchester

What
A worker's vegetarian & vegan cooperative, considered a Manchester institution

Who
The Eighth Day Co-operative, owner

When
Breakfast, lunch & dinner, Monday to Saturday

Address
111 Oxford Road, Manchester, M1 7DU

+44 (0)16 1273 1850

8thday.coop

Bookings
Phone or walk-ins

Price guide

What they say
"We provide incredibly stunning veggie eats, with a myriad of vegan mouthfuls, while maintaining a caring and sustainable business. From our utility supplier, Ecotricity, to many of our food suppliers, our ethos is to keep our environmental impact as low as possible. We recycle all our cardboard, paper, tin cans, plastic bottles, and glass. Our mission statement is: Eighth Day Cafe exists to encourage the optimum health of its customers and staff by providing quality vegetarian food and advice, while maintaining a caring, sustainable, democratic, and ethical business environment for its workers."

Signature dishes
House *dal*; full house vegan breakfast; and red dragon pie (red-bean cottage pie with beetroot ketchup).

What we say
This worker's cooperative, located in the university area of Manchester, has become a legend since opening in the 1970s, since when it has provided arguably the largest selection of vegetarian, vegan, and organic food in the North West. The menu is inherently healthy, centred as it is around fresh veg, legumes, and wholegrains in every dish. They offer a predominantly dairy-free menu with a 100 per cent vegan salad and have four different dairy-free milk choices for their organic, fair trade, and locally roasted coffee. As well as stocking cold-pressed juices and serving made-to-order juices, they keep a keen eye on allergens in their food, ensuring their team is well educated about the dangers and is on top of any nutritional information you might need.

Greens

Manchester

What
Long-established vegetarian & vegan restaurant

Who
Simon Connolly, owner

When
Dinner Monday to Saturday, lunch Tuesday to Sunday

Address
43 Lapwing Lane, Manchester, M20 2NT

+44 (0)16 1434 4259

greensdidsbury.co.uk

Bookings
Phone or website

Price guide

What they say
"Greens Didsbury is a lively and popular dining experience that focuses on imaginative dishes packed with flavour. Set up by Simon Rimmer and Simon Connelly (Simon & Simon), we were somewhat pioneers in the vegetarian food scene and we are as passionate about it today as we were back then. We take care with our thoughtfully selected local produce, from local vegetable suppliers to gin, beer, and even water. We aim to create a relaxed, unpretentious atmosphere with great service."

Signature dishes
Pumpernickel with smashed avocado and faux lox; soba noodle salad with smoked tofu, toasted sesame seeds, peanuts, crispy kale, and Korean barbecue sauce; and maple-roasted squash with orange granola crumble and salted caramel ice cream.

What we say
As a vegetarian and vegan restaurant, Greens has already done more than its fair share for the environment, so let's also celebrate their championing of locally sourced craft ales such as Cheshire Brewhouse, the Liverpool Craft Beer Co., First Chop in Salford, and the Dunham Massey Brewery. And if it's cocktails you're after, they're loaded with both Didsbury Gin and Forest Gin, a local producer using product foraged from Macclesfield Forest – let's take what the forest doesn't need anymore and turn it into booze!

Hawksmoor

Manchester

What
British steak & seafood
restaurant & cocktail bar

Who
Will Beckett & Huw Gott,
founders

When
Lunch & dinner, daily

Address
184–186 Deansgate,
Manchester, M3 3WB,
plus other locations –
see website

+44 (0)16 1836 6980

thehawksmoor.com

Bookings
Phone, website, or
opentable.com

Price guide

What they say
"Hawksmoor's menus revolve around
the best ingredients we can find –
whether it be beef from grass-fed
native-breed cattle, sustainable
seafood from around the British coast,
seasonal fruits and vegetables, or great
British cheeses, combined with great
wines and interesting cocktails, all
served by people who love what they
do. All of our beef is grass-fed and
sourced from small British farms who
have the highest welfare standards.
We're actively reducing food waste,
combining great vegan and vegetarian
options in our menus, and currently
identifying single-use plastics used
in the restaurants and seeing where
alternatives could be used."

Signature dishes
Spring dumplings and fresh peas;
roasted hake with heritage tomatoes;
and bone-in prime rib steak.

What we say
In barely twelve years of business,
Hawksmoor has established itself
as the daddy of steakhouses.
Everywhere it opens, from Covent
Garden to Manchester, Hawksmoor
is swiftly recognized as one of the
best restaurants around. The vibe is
easygoing: it's about great cocktails,
cold beer, fat old red wines, big
steaks, great shanks of fat-dribbling
marrowbone, and lots and lots of chips.
Which is why their commitment to
animal welfare, waste management,
local communities, charity, best
practice on drinking water, and the rest
is so wonderful. This is sustainability
at its best.

225

England
North East

Battlesteads Hotel & Restaurant

Northumberland

What
One of the UK's leading sustainable tourism destinations

Who
Richard & Dee Slade, owners

When
Breakfast, lunch & dinner, daily

Address
Wark on Tyne, Hexham, Northumberland, NE48 3LS

+44 (0)14 3423 0209

battlesteads.com

Bookings
Phone

Price guide

What they say
"Since taking over the business thirteen years ago, we have taken the hotel on a green journey. It started with installing a biomass boiler for energy and now includes everything from growing our own fruit, vegetables, salads, and herbs in our kitchen garden and polytunnels, to supporting local food producers, to creating a wildlife pond, to producing our own book on bird watching, *Birds of Battlesteads*."

Signature dishes
Beetroots with semifreddo, pickled, yoghurt crisp, beetroot bloomer, and micro shoots; home-farmed shiitake and oyster mushrooms with tagliatelle, wild garlic pesto and Brinkburn cheese; and posh rhubarb and custard with house-grown forced rhubarb, cardamom custard panna cotta, rhubarb sorbet, and rhubarb pepper.

What we say
You might come here for the the eight-course tasting menu with its centrepiece of pink cutlet of local lamb with haggis shepherd's pie, but you'll stay for the breathless intimacy with nature afforded by five new, environmentally-friendly luxury timber lodges and the on-site observatory for post-prandial stargazing. The walled garden has been specially planted to encourage wildlife, with a bat box and an owl box plus bird feeders to encourage the many smaller species in the area. Badgers, foxes, herons, and red squirrels are frequently reported and a family of otters can be seen in the early morning on the river next to the bridge. Red squirrels! Otters! This place is a Beatrix Potter fantasy with lunch and dinner thrown in.

The Feathers Inn

Northumberland

What
A pub serving up tradition, innovation & sustainability in equal measure with flair & originality

Who
Rhian Cradock, owner/chef

When
Lunch & dinner, Wednesday to Sunday

Address
Hedley on the Hill, Stocksfield, Northumberland, NE43 7SW

+44 (0)16 6184 3607

thefeathers.net

Bookings
Phone or email
info@thefeathers.net

Price guide

What they say
"Quality and sustainability in equal measure. We work with very small suppliers, adapting to the needs of the produce that is available. We change our menu to suit the availability of produce not vice versa. We care about the wellbeing of the farmers, their families, and their livestock, and we utilize whole carcasses, teaching a new generation of staff about butchery, charcuterie, and the best way to use foraged and obscure plants."

Signature dishes
Black pudding with poached Wylam duck egg and devilled gravy; Hedley roe deer Wellington with St. George's mushrooms, roe liver parfait, sprouting broccoli, wild garlic, and hotpot potatoes; and burnt Northumbrian cream.

What others say
"If you eat at only one place in Northumberland, make it here."

jamie magazine

What we say
The fishermen they work with come from small fishing communities on the North East coast and they've been using lesser-known species of non-endangered fish for many years, such as gurnard, pollack, and razor clams. These benefit from plentiful stock levels, and by using these fish, they take pressure off the depleted stocks of endangered fish such as cod and haddock. Lobster and crabs are all sourced from dayboats in the North Sea landed at Sunderland and North Shields and delivered to the pub the next day. The lobsters are dispatched by cutting them in half down the middle, crab are killed prior to boiling by inserting a steel into their abdominal cavity.

Harissa Kitchen

Tyne and Wear

What
A restaurant and takeaway serving fresh & colourful food from all corners of the Mediterranean

Who
Nick Smith, manager

When
Lunch & dinner, Wednesday to Saturday, lunch Sunday

Address
31–35 Starbeck Avenue, Newcastle upon Tyne, Tyne and Wear, NE2 1RJ

+44 (0)19 1261 5501

harissakitchen.co.uk

Bookings
Phone or website

Price guide

What they say
"At Harissa we are passionate about making sure our food is absolutely delicious and stands out alongside all the other fantastic restaurants we have in the city. We love supporting the local economy by finding the best local businesses for our ingredients and, of course, looking after the environment with everything from supporting local litter pick-ups to choosing eco-friendly packaging. Creating a fair and happy working environment for our team full of training experiences, supporting the community through initiatives (such as our free Social Lunch Club), and tackling youth unemployment with trainee and apprenticeship programmes are amongst our passions as part of our community."

Signature dishes
Sautéed oyster mushrooms with roasted red onion, walnut salsa (mushrooms grown by their local YMCA through Urban Mushrooms enterprise, which employs young people and gives them transferrable skills for the future); Harissa vegetable kebab; and mezze sharing plates.

What we say
This beautiful little restaurant is not only committed to everything we hold dear but is bringing something entirely new – a sort of turbocharged Ottolenghi-style of Mediterranean cooking that is as gorgeous to behold as it is to eat – to a Newcastle restaurant scene that has picked up dramatically in recent years and now goes from strength to strength.

Longsands Fish Kitchen

Tyne and Wear

What
Seafood restaurant & award-winning fish & chip shop in the beautiful village of Tynemouth

Who
Simon Walsh, chef/owner

When
Lunch & dinner, Wednesday to Monday

Address
27 Front Street, Tynemouth, Tyne and Wear, NE30 4DZ

+44 (0)19 1272 8552

longsandsfishkitchen.com

Bookings
Phone or email contact@ longsandsfishkitchen.com

Price guide

What they say
"At Longsands we are passionate about sourcing the finest locally-caught seafood and shellfish and pairing it with seasonal ingredients. We build amazing relationships with all our suppliers to ensure the best sustainable and growing practices are carried out as we try to build a more sustainable business for years to come.

"We have worked tirelessly to change all our packaging to compostable and biodegradable to reduce plastic in our seas. We work closely with Surfers Against Sewage to promote Tynemouth as a plastic-free coastline. We were the second coastal community in the country to achieve this and, as an ambassador for it, we really do help and support other businesses in making changes, helping to protect – and reduce plastic in – our oceans."

Signature dishes
Fish and chips (line-caught and MSC-certified cod and haddock); Lindisfarne oysters, by the Sutherland family; and local halibut with Yorkshire asparagus.

What we say
We love the journey these guys have been on for the last three years, first opening a restaurant then gradually changing so many of their daily working practices towards sustainability and the environment, making themselves, in their words, "a far better business for it".

Yorkshire & the Humber

The Coach House at Middleton Lodge

North Yorkshire

What
A Georgian country estate with a relaxed restaurant

Who
James & Rebecca Allison, owners & Gareth Rayner, head chef

When
Breakfast, lunch, brunch & dinner, daily

Address
Kneeton Lane, Middleton Tyas, Richmond, North Yorkshire, DL10 6NJ

+44 (0)13 2537 7977

middletonlodge.co.uk

Bookings
Phone or email
info@middletonlodge.co.uk

Price guide

What they say
"We are always focused on seasonality and locality. We have just completed the restoration of our kitchen garden – a two-acre walled garden full of seasonal fruit, vegetables, and herbs that are picked daily for The Coach House menu. Gareth Rayner works closely with the estate's head gardener to produce niche English estate produce. We carefully manage our waste to be as environmentally friendly as possible, use borehole water, low use of single-use plastics, and celebrate imperfect fruit and veg."

Signature dishes
Garden salad (baked beetroot, goat's cheese, watercress, candied hazelnuts); eighteen-ounce T-bone from Country Valley; and soy-glazed duck breast with sweet potato, toasted seeds, and spring onion.

What others say?
"What comes across so strongly in Gareth's cooking is an unfaltering respect for ingredients."

Olive magazine

What we say
The Coach House was built for the carriages and horses of George Hartley, Esq., who commissioned the Georgian Palladian house to be built by John Carr. It fell into disrepair until recently being transformed into one of the loveliest hotels in the north of England. Its classical proportions are so easy on the eye, with arches, brick walls, beams, and huge feature windows on two sides. In summer, it's all about lunch in the courtyard, but inside the arched glass doors is a grand, vertiginous restaurant, a noisy bar, an open fire, and lounging spaces that spill out onto the terrace.

The Coach House at Middleton Lodge (p. 230)

Hansa's

West Yorkshire

What
Award-winning restaurant serving Indian vegetarian home cooking since 1986

Who
Mrs. Hansa Dabhi, founder

When
Dinner Monday to Saturday, lunch Sunday

Address
72-74 North Street, Leeds, West Yorkshire, LS2 7PN

+44 (0)11 3244 4408

hansasrestaurant.com

Bookings
Phone or quandoo.co.uk

Price guide

What they say
"Serving our customers with the very best in Indian vegetarian home cooking, specialities from the state of Gujarat on the west coast of India, with touches of East Africa, where the owner and chef, Hansa Dabhi, was brought up. 'I am very proud to say that over eighty per cent of our customers who come on a regular basis are non-vegetarians, which shows that I must be doing something right that people have supported me over all these years', says Hansa. 'I'm also very proud to have given women from ethnic minorities an opportunity to come and work with me in a safe environment, to come and practise working in a commercial kitchen and hone their culinary skills.'"

Signature dishes
Mixed platter; *bhagat mthiya*; and *chevti dal*.

What we say
Mrs. Dabhi is one of this country's true food heroes. A giant of the Indian vegetarian scene who has won every relevant award, most of them many times over. Not only does she serve wonderful food and write wonderful books, but she goes out and preaches the message about how properly sourced, lovingly prepared vegetarian food can change the world. She goes into primary schools to teach cooking, she takes her customers to India to educate them, she has launched a cookery school, and she raises money to support small schools in remote areas of India and Nepal. Hansa Dabhi, we bow down before you.

The Reliance

West Yorkshire

What
An informal bar & dining room serving seasonal food from our open-plan kitchen

Who
Joss Ainsworth & Becs Winlow, co-owners

When
Lunch & dinner, daily

Address
76-78 North Street, Leeds, West Yorkshire, LS2 7PN

+44 (0)11 3295 6060

the-reliance.co.uk

Bookings
Phone or email
bookings@the-reliance.co.uk

Price guide

What they say
"The simple things, done well, without pretension. Good seasonal food, well cooked. Local ales. Interesting wine. Friendly and knowledgeable staff who are passionate about what we sell and convey their enthusiasm to all of our customers. We serve a changing, seasonal menu to reflect the produce that's best, now. We also use good local suppliers whose products are great, for example Whiteley's veg (Pudsey), Taste Tradition butchers (Thirsk), and local breweries for our permanent ale lines: Roosters (Knaresborough), Acorn (Barnsley), and Magic Rock (Huddersfield). Our staff are incredibly important to us, and receive a high level of training; inevitably they stay for longer than the industry average and they leave with a stronger skill set than they started."

Signature dishes
Purple sprouting broccoli with feta, *za'atar* and preserved lemon (local purple sprouting broccoli from Whiteley's farm with a nod to the Middle East); wild garlic gnocchi with peas and goat's cheese (wild garlic foraged by the head chef and used in a simple seasonal dish); and pigeon with peas, lettuce and lardons (classic French cookery – using pigeon rough-shot locally).

What we say
Cellar cooling is run on the Geo Bar system, recycling the heat from the beer cellar to heat their hot water, food waste is low with daily deliveries, and then all scraps are collected by ReFood to go to renewable energy that gets pumped into the national grid rather than going to landfill. And the cooking is quite simply outstanding. Everyone's a winner.

235

England
East Midlands

Alchemilla

Nottinghamshire

What
Modern British food with an emphasis on seasonal ingredients, particularly vegetables

Who
Alex Bond, chef/proprietor

When
Dinner Tuesday, lunch & dinner, Wednesday to Saturday

Address
152 Derby Road, Nottingham, Nottinghamshire, NG7 1NF

+44 (0)11 5941 3515

alchemillarestaurant.uk

Bookings
Phone, website, or resdiary.com

Price guide

What they say
"The superb quality of our food is the focus and drive here at Alchemilla. We grow our own vegetables and herbs but the key consideration is quality and taste, so if that means going a bit further afield then we will. Sourcing from the UK is really important and we try to keep ninety-nine per cent of our ingredients from the UK. Johnny Pusztai is a farmer and butcher who breeds the best pork for miles around. The sheer love and focus that has gone into creating the perfect pig is evident in how the animals happily roam on his farm and the resulting taste – pure perfection."

Signature dishes
White asparagus, chamomile, and lemon (vegetable-based and the chamomile is foraged about two miles from the restaurant); pork jowl with kimchi and peanut; and yoghurt with pine and wood sorrel, using pine from Sherwood Forest.

What others say
"That was a great, great meal. I'm going back."

–Zeren Wilson, *Bitten & Written*

What we say
There are shades of Noma about this former Victorian coach house, unused for over a century, that has now been transformed into a super-modern restaurant space without losing those bucolic Midlands vibes. Bond cooked for a long time under local hero Sat Bains and the skill and range of the much-lauded tasting menu shows that influence thrillingly. An early summer visit found them serving their own fennel, allium, calendula, nasturtium, and woodruff. Very exciting.

John's House

Leicestershire

What
Modern British, set in a sixteenth-century farmhouse, on a family-run farm that supplies its produce

Who
John Duffin, owner

When
Lunch & dinner,
Tuesday to Saturday

Address
141 Loughborough Road,
Mountsorrel,
Leicestershire, LE12 7AR

+44 (0)15 0941 5569

johnshouse.co.uk

Bookings
Phone or website

Price guide

What they say
"We are fortunate that John's House restaurant is based on the family's working farm, where we grow our own produce, rear traditional breeds of livestock, have our own free-range hens, and forage for seasonal ingredients from the land's natural larder. We practise sustainable mixed farming. We graze our sheep and cattle on organic pasture. We grow our own cereals to feed the pigs and poultry and then the cycle continues, using composted manure from our livestock to maintain soil fertility. Much of our seasonal produce is foraged from the local hedgerows, meadows, and woodland by the kitchen staff."

Signature dishes
Raw scallops with oyster, cucumber, and elderflower; Stonehurst hogget with roast onions, St. George's mushrooms, and wild garlic; and strawberries with hay cream, and wild sorrel.

What we say
Most of the ingredients here involve less than one "food mile". Staff live on-site or in the local community. By picking produce daily and carrying it to the kitchen in a basket they are able to avoid the use of packaging altogether. No food is wasted. Any vegetable trim is either used as feed for livestock or composted and put back into the land. Every part of an animal carcass is utilized; for example the pigs' heads are turned into brawn and made into "crispy smoked pig's head" snacks and any cuts that aren't used by the restaurant are sold in the farm shop. If only all restaurants could be made this way.

The Cod's Scallops

Nottingham

What
A fine fish & chip restaurant and takeaway offering over twenty species of fish & shellfish daily

Who
John Molnar, owner/chef

When
Lunch & dinner,
Monday to Saturday

Address
311–313 Mansfield Road,
Nottingham, NG5 2DA,
plus other locations –
see website

+44 (0)11 5708 0251

codsscallops.com

Bookings
No bookings taken

Price guide

What they say
"We are passionate about sourcing quality sustainable fish and shellfish caught along our British coasts and showcasing underused species by displaying them on our impressive wet fish counter. We are passionate about our staff, investing in their development and wellbeing. We are passionate about delivering a quality well-loved product."

Signature dishes
MSC-certified cod with chips cooked in dripping, mushy peas, and homemade tartare sauce; dressed Norfolk crab with Jersey Royals, asparagus, lemon and herb butter, and salad of the day; and baked Scottish hake with lemon, herb and garlic butter, and chips cooked in dripping.

What we say
One of only seventy-five UK fish and chip shops to have this MSC certification, The Cod's Scallops does a huge amount to get the message out about using wild and sustainable fish wherever humanly possible. They hand out leaflets on sustainability to customers and encourage them to try underused species. They are also launching a children's colouring and activity sheet which will inform young diners on the importance of sustainability – because the sea's only hope is that the next generation of fish eaters is smarter than the last.

Hambleton Hall

Rutland

What
One of Britain's finest country house hotels with the longest-retained Michelin star in the UK

Who
Tim & Stefa Hart, owners & Aaron Patterson, chef

When
Breakfast, lunch, & dinner, daily

Address
Hambleton, Oakham, Rutland, LE15 8TH

+44 (0)15 7275 6991

hambletonhall.com

Bookings
Phone or website

Price guide
●●●●●

What they say
"What drives Head Chef Aaron Patterson every day is a desire for creativity in everything that he does and creates. After this, it is finding incredible local ingredients. We are really fortunate to be based in Rutland, as the location is bursting with incredible suppliers, farmers, artisans, poachers, foragers, and more. Aaron has a long history of living and working in this area, so he has the pleasure of knowing them all extremely well. Naturally this passion for ingredients is matched by the curious and informed guests. There's not a day goes by that the restaurant team doesn't receive a comment, a question, or a compliment on some aspect of the menu or ingredients."

Signature dishes
Short rib of beef cooked for thirty hours with horseradish and red wine sauce; seared tuna belly with shiitake, and lightly pickled vegetables; and salad of crab, yuzu, and granny smith apple.

What we say
Dining in a fairy tale Victorian hunting lodge overlooking a gigantic lake in the heart of hunting country would be a joy beyond measure even if you just ordered in pizza. But since opening as a country house hotel in 1979, Hambleton has been serving some of the best food in England. Aaron Patterson began here as a sixteen-year-old sous-chef and returned as head chef in 1993. That he holds Britain's longest-running continuous Michelin star is no surprise. That he does not hold two is a scandal.

Restaurant Sat Bains

Nottinghamshire

What
A restaurant with rooms in an old farmhouse & grounds

Who
Sat Bains, owner/chef & Amanda Bains, owner

When
Lunch & dinner,
Wednesday to Saturday

Address
Lenton Lane, Nottingham, Nottinghamshire, NG7 2SA

+44 (0)11 5986 6566

restaurantsatbains.com

Bookings
Phone

Price guide

What they say
"We aim for Sat Bains to encompass an absolute dining experience: blowing peoples' perceptions of modern British tasting menus. All produce is sustainable as much as it can be by working with ethical producers and farmers. We are trying to reduce plastic by having recyclable packaging programmes with a lot of our suppliers. We also changed our working conditions in 2015 to a four-day operation, allowing the team a full consecutive three days off, which has proven invaluable to morale, retention, and motivation."

Signature dishes
Monkfish XO with pickles, condiments, and lettuce; Anjou pigeon with tagine spices, black olive and dates (inspired by the artist Anna French); and The Rocky Road, which depicts and celebrates our strange location.

What we say
Quite simply one of the most progressive, adventurous, ambitious restaurants in the country. From the unique layout of his menu to the staggering things he can do with the simplest of ingredients, Sat Bains is in a league of his own. That it should all be happening down an unpromising track under pylons in a quiet corner of suburban Nottingham only makes it all the more extraordinary.

Bridges

What
Producing healthy, balanced food and fresh juices in Cambridge town centre for twenty years

Who
Meggy & Chan Yip, owners/chefs

When
Breakfast & lunch, daily

Address
20 Bridge Street, Cambridge, CB2 1UF

+44 (0)12 2330 0800

bridgescambridge.co.uk

Bookings
No bookings taken

Price guide

What they say
"We serve simple, healthy dishes that nourish the body as well as care for the environment. We are proud of our 'ugly' fruit and veg. We tell our customers that we trim the veg for their salad and the remaining can be used in their drinks by juicing. We promote via social media any other local suppliers or cafés (including our competitors) so we can help each other to support our local community."

Signature dishes
Vegetable soup made from scratch in winter (organic when possible); juicing of seasonal vegetables and fruits (organic when possible); and Oriental family-inspired dishes.

What we say
Meggy and Chan Yip were aghast when they saw how much sugar people were consuming when they first opened their little café. So they stripped everything back to the bare essentials of raw fruit and vegetables and built up from there, hoping to create a new generation that would be more conscious of the old adage that we are what we eat. It's all about hydration and nutrition starting from the best local, organic, zero waste principles. They made all the tables by recycling the scaffold boards that were used to build their own house and they are phasing out plastic as much as they can. A discount is given to customers who bring their own cups and flasks. They still believe simple is best.

Parker's Tavern (p. 246)

Parker's Tavern

Cambridge

What
A bar & restaurant in the centre of Cambridge serving eccentric British classics

Who
Tristan Welch, chef director

When
Breakfast, lunch & dinner, daily

Address
Regent Street,
Cambridge, CB2 1AD

+44 (0)12 2360 6266

parkerstavern.com

Bookings
Phone or email
enquiries@parkerstavern.com

Price guide

What they say
"Parker's Tavern is inspired by the area's great, yet often forgotten, culinary traditions. Being born and bred in East Anglia, Tristan's passion is for locally sourced ingredients, and using seasonal fare to recreate regional dishes with fun modern twists. His aim is to celebrate the area's producers and growers. Our staff are able to detail the provenance of every ingredient we serve. Knowing our suppliers personally gives us an edge on the best seasonal produce, so our seasonal menus are always a step ahead. Even the bar's house beer is brewed just half a mile away, and is – in true Cambridge style – delivered by bicycle."

Signature dishes
Chalk Stream smoked trout with a Grantchester cure (gently smoked trout cured to Welch's own recipe to give diners a true taste of the riverbank; Sansho pepper recalls the watercress growing wild on the banks of the Cam with notes of malt, hops, and beet molasses – all of which grow in the fields beside the river, subtly flavouring the water); the Huntingdon Fidget Pie; and the Duke of Cambridge Tart.

What we say
Local boy Tristan Welch has returned to Cambridge to turn this historic old coaching inn into one of the best restaurants for miles around. We still remember his mesmerizing cooking at Launceston Place and are delighted to find him going back to his roots.

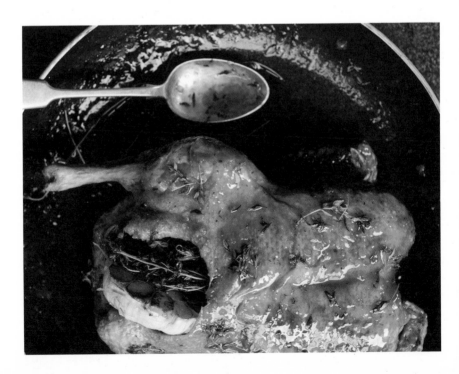

Hot Numbers Coffee

Cambridge

What
Combining great music, excellent coffee & delicious food since 2011

Who
Simon Fraser, owner

When
Breakfast & lunch, daily, dinner Thursday & Friday

Address
Unit 6 Dales Brewery, Gwydir Street, Cambridge, CB1 2LJ

+44 (0)12 2335 9966

hotnumberscoffee.co.uk

Bookings
No bookings taken

Price guide

What they say
"We work with a global community of passionate coffee experts to provide sustainably sourced speciality coffee which goes great with a dash of jazz and one of our gluten-free brownies. Our coffee production follows less-intensive methods that allow for soil improvement, reduction of pesticides, and modernization of processing, both increasing the quality of the crop and helping to protect the environment. In short, better coffee improves our experience as coffee lovers and helps to improve the lives of coffee farmers and their communities! Our chef, Adam, believes in a diverse and inclusive menu full of well-balanced flavours."

Signature dishes
Vegan French toast with aquafaba, roasted peaches, blackberries, and almond crumb; smashed avocado on toasted cornbread (gluten-free) with burnt lime, coriander, sesame, pickled carrot, pickled chilli, radish, a poached free-range egg, and sriracha; and lamb kofta with spiced chickpeas, yoghurt and lime dressing, and homemade foccacia.

What we say
Bright, lively, modern ethical food with some of the best coffee you'll find, in two supercool spaces – the other is on Trumpington Street, closer to the heart of old Cambridge – and with even cooler jazz. Swing into Hot Numbers Coffee for a drink, stay for the food.

The Linton Kitchen

Cambridge

What
Honest food, fantastic coffee, & down-to-earth cakes served around communal kitchen tables

Who
Gemma Whiting, owner

When
Breakfast & lunch, daily

Address
30 High Street, Linton, Cambridge, CB21 4HS

+44 (0)12 2389 4949

lintonkitchen.co.uk

Bookings
Email
gemma@lintonkitchen.co.uk

Price guide

What they say
"We are passionate about attention to detail and customer service. Our setting is informal, our food simple, honest, seasonal, and homemade. Our bakes are fresh and exciting. We like to offer urban-quality food and service in our informal, communal, and rural setting. We offer daily affordable luxuries – a flat white, a vegan muffin – but we serve this in a warm and nurturing environment, which suits the community around us."

Signature dishes
Brunch specials with local sourdough; rhubarb harvest dishes; and a "super-decent" sandwich with thick-cut ham, mature Cheddar, and homemade (rescued) banana and date chutney.

What we say
The Linton Kitchen has now established a separate micro-events company, which will see collaborations with many of their favourite super-ethical producers - this venture is launching at Fringe Events for the Eat Cambridge Food Festival 2018. It's an immersive production – a foraging workshop, on a punt, with an interesting tapas menu made. Keep an eye out for other events – pop-up suppers with local growers in awesome settings, local produce markets next to The Linton Kitchen, workshops aimed at engaging people in horticulture with horticulturalist Anna Taylor of Anna's Flower Farm (who supplies non-toxic flowers for their cakes, grown in compost from food waste) - teaching and encouraging guests to propagate unusual edibles no matter how little space they have. This little coffee shop has a lot going on behind the scenes. Inspirational!

Nanna Mexico

Cambridge

What
Local, independent, & proudly Mexican, serving humble Mexican street food

Who
Luis Navarro, founder/owner

When
Lunch & dinner, daily

Address
29 Petty Cury,
Cambridge, CB2 3NB

+44 (0)12 2366 5589

nannamexico.com

Bookings
Email
booking@nannamexico.com

Price guide

What they say
"At Nanna Mexico, we say that every great meal should be served with a great story and Luis' is surely one of the most inspiring: his beloved Nanna Margarita. In Mexico City, 1958, Margarita took her kitchen table out into the street and began to sell enchiladas. Her tasty fare was an instant hit and Margarita passed on to her grandson (Luis) both her secret recipes and her enterprising spirit. Luis is evangelical about food quality, shunning processed products in favour of fine locally sourced ingredients, with all dishes made from scratch. Our community is important to us – we run one-day workshops in prisons and teach in schools as well."

Signature dishes
Spicy chipotle sauce with succulent slow-cooked pork and melting cheese quesadillas; candy-pink frozen margaritas; and burritos.

What we say
We are especially impressed by Nanna's cooking school, which was launched to bring the tradition of making fresh, healthy food back to the local community. They decided to start in the classroom, partnering with schools and teachers to put fresh ingredients in the hands of children and teach them about cooking. This hands-on approach offers students a fun and new way to learn about food quality, nutrition, recipes, and preparation. There was never a more apt expression of truth, love, and (we assume) clean cutlery.

Pint Shop

Cambridge

What
Bar & dining room focusing on British beer & gin, with simple, seasonal, & British food

Who
Rich Holmes & Benny Peverelli, co-owners

When
Lunch & dinner, daily

Address
10 Peas Hill,
Cambridge, CB2 3PN

+44 (0)12 2335 2293

pintshop.co.uk

Bookings
Phone or website

Price guide

What they say
"We put equal focus on delivering in food, drink, service, and environment. In terms of small producers, they are absolutely key to what we do, from brewers and distillers to bakers and coffee roasters. Working with similar small businesses to us makes all our businesses stronger. We use local suppliers as much as possible. Our fishmonger and butcher are both family-owned businesses. Our bakers and coffee roasters are Cambridge based, we work with local brewers to brew 'collab' beers. We have our own gin, distilled four miles away by The Cambridge Distillery."

Signature dishes
Chicken Scotch duck egg; Blythburgh pork chop with cockles and samphire; and whole roasted bream with fennel and clementine salad.

What others say
"Lucky, lucky Cambridge."

–Lisa Markwell, *The Independent*

What we say
Rare to find anything half-decent to eat in central Cambridge that is not a chain or a disproportionately popular old place with a queue round the block. So hurrah for Rich and Benny, who converted this listed building in homage to the "Tom and Jerry" beer shops of the early nineteenth century. It has all those welcoming old vibes, plus dozens of local artisanal beers (and even more gins). Signs declare the three words of their philosophy: "meat, bread, beer" – one we also could live by. Especially if we were within reach of their counter groaning with pies, filled cobs, sausage rolls, and Scotch eggs.

Provenance Kitchen

Cambridge

What
Modern British food from an Airstream trailer for unique corporate events, weddings & pop-ups

Who
Greg Proud, chef/owner & Kate Holden, owner

When
Pop-ups

Address
Hill Farm Road, Whittlesford, Cambridge, CB22 4NB

+44 (0)77 7930 4833

provenancekitchen.com

Bookings
Email
ask@provenancekitchen.com

Price guide

What they say
"Our dream is to take food that one would usually expect to find in a high-end restaurant to wherever people wish it to be. Our converted original 1967 Airstream makes this possible and has been kitted out with wood-fired ovens and Japanese coal-fired grills. Our menus are updated monthly and we use the best seasonal ingredients. 'Modern British' best describes our food, with flavours from all over the world sitting beautifully alongside fish, meat, and vegetables that come from local suppliers and farms. We care passionately about sustainability and work with Cambridge Sustainable Food to ensure our business is doing all it can."

Signature dishes
Whole wood-fired plaice with seaweed butter, capers, grilled asparagus, and wood-fired potatoes; Hereford flank steak with wood-fired potatoes, land cress, and horseradish cream; and miso-baked hispi cabbage with freekah, pickled kohlrabi and harissa yoghurt.

What we say
God, we love these guys. Greg and Kate serve restaurant-quality, modern British food from their stunning, mint-condition Airstream and seasonal British tacos from their converted Rice trailer horsebox. They are based at a farm just outside of Cambridge and pop up in locations around the city, take over unique spaces throughout the week, and cater weddings all over the country and events at the weekend, letting their great local produce speak for itself in simple dishes based around a wood-fired oven. It's not just heaven. It's heaven on wheels.

Rainbow Café

Cambridge

What
Vegetarian, vegan & gluten free with attention to food allergies & religious requests

Who
Sharon Meijland, proprietor

When
Breakfast & lunch, Tuesday to Sunday, dinner Tuesday to Saturday

Address
Opposite King's College Gates, 9a King's Parade, Cambridge, CB2 1SJ

+44 (0)12 2332 1551

rainbowcafe.co.uk

Bookings
No bookings taken

Price guide

What they say
"Providing reliable and trustworthy food for customers with special requirements. It might be considered that excluding meat is something but excluding meat, dairy, gluten, added sugar, and fat is our joy. Our regular customers know that we always serve gluten free food in black dishes, and the sauce is coloured with turmeric, so there can be no errors. We have won all of the awards at gold level including Crème de la Crème at the FreeFrom Eating Out Awards for three years running. We also consider religious requirements, no garlic or onion for Jains (and others), and no nightshade or citrus for those with intolerance reasons. We have been marking the menu clearly for the last THIRTY years as Daoists require food in five colours. We try to keep cultural norms in, for example, Rastafarian food, which is vegan with no salt."

Signature dishes
Jamaican roti cups; artichoke filo parcel; and Kurdish pilaf (vegan and nightshade-free with no garlic or onion).

What we say
What an astonishing venture this is. Most restaurants make such a fuss about catering for the odd coeliac diner, the odd vegan, the occasional nut-dodger, and yet here is the Rainbow Café catering deliberately to every imaginable exclusion on the planet. With this level of commitment to the special needs of its customers, it is astonishing that they manage to cook anything at all. Hats off to you, Rainbow – we are not worthy.

The Tickell Arms

Cambridge

What
A cosy pub & restaurant serving seasonal modern British food

Who
Oliver Thain & Max Freeman, owners

When
Lunch & dinner, daily

Address
1 North Road, Whittlesford, Cambridge, CB22 4NZ

+44 (0)12 2383 3025

cambscuisine.com

Bookings
Website

Price guide

What they say
"We're serious about serving great quality food and local real ales with friendly service. We source local fresh produce and grow our own vegetables, herbs, and berries in the garden. In March 2018, we banned all plastic straws and stirrers. Our new policy is to reduce consumption by only giving a paper/PLA straw when requested. We used our excess plastic straws to create two rowing boats, Cambridge and Oxford, which we raced over The Tickell pond to draw awareness to the issue of single-use plastics. Our team is enthusiastic about making our business a more sustainable one, and about supporting local community causes."

Signature dishes
The Feather Bowl: quinoa, avocado, cucumber, cherry tomatoes, sunflower and pumpkin seeds, lemon and chilli dressing; whole lemon sole with crushed potatoes, kale, caper, and lemon butter; and sirloin steak with chips, chargrilled shallots, tomatoes, and sauce.

What we say
A lovely, bright, clean old pub five miles from Cambridge with plenty of local ales and excellent modern British food. The Tickell Arms has recently embarked on a pilot corporate partnership with Greener Growth, a community-interest company that helps neglected areas become food-producing and biodiversity-enhancing. Greener Growth helps keep the Tickell garden at its best year round, with a focus on edible produce, giving employees a chance to get out in the fresh air, while learning about nature, health, and wellbeing. Produce from the vegetable patch is used in the restaurant or shared with the community.

The Bell Inn

Bedfordshire

What
A pub focusing on simple pub food, creative wine list, spirits & beer selection

Who
Peter Creed & Thomas Noest, owners

When
Lunch & dinner, daily

Address
The Bell, Langford, Bedfordshire, GL7 3LF

+44 (0)13 6786 0249

thebelllangford.com

Bookings
Phone

Price guide

What they say
"We absolutely love our land (the Cotswolds) and revived The Bell Inn with a focus on the much-loved country pub-feel, showcasing a hearty, classic, British menu with the addition of wood-fired dishes and an extensive wine and beer list. We are very keen on having organic and biodynamic wines on our list and our coffee is fair trade. We use a number of small-scale food and beverage producers, such as Cacklebean eggs, Wood Brothers Distillery, Kelmscott Country Pork, and Rollright cheese."

Signature dishes
Burrata and Wye Valley asparagus with oregano, chilli, and lemon; garlic, parsley, and bone marrow flat bread; and wild boar meatballs with soft polenta, Parmesan, and sage.

What we say
Tom Noest is a genius of a cook and Peter Creed a genius of a host. What they have done with this pretty old pub is nothing short of divine. Putting in a proper pizza oven was brilliant, allowing them to serve pizza to locals who might come in (with kids) four times a week, but also allows the means to create a majestic garlic, parsley, and bone marrow flatbread, the bread crisp and chewy, running with buttery bone fat, and verdant with chopped parsley. So pure, so honest, so tear-jerkingly real and true. Roll in a slice of the roast dry-aged sirloin, spread it with fresh horseradish, and dip the whole thing into the gravy pot. Then write to us to say, "Thank you."

Church Street Tavern

Essex

What
Restaurant & bar

Who
Piers Baker, owner, & Ewan
Naylon, chef

When
Lunch & dinner, Wednesday
to Saturday, lunch Sunday

Address
3 Church Street, Colchester,
Essex, CO1 1NF

+44 (0)12 0656 4325

churchstreettavern.co.uk

Bookings
Website or resdiary.com

Price guide

What they say
"It is important to us to cook seasonally
because, in our view, produce tastes
better in its normal season and
doesn't require as much unnatural
assistance. It is important to us that
we obtain as much of our produce
locally as possible, as the shorter the
journey it has to travel, the better the
produce, especially vegetables, tastes.
It also keeps the money in the local
economy and our relationship with
suppliers closer.

"Our menu changes every four to six
weeks, in line with our seasons. We
buy our fish from inshore dayboats
that catch their fish seasonally. The
chefs forage for some produce at
different times of year, such as nettles,
crab apples, and damsons."

Signature dishes
Asparagus mousse with Norfolk crab.

What others say
"Now this is a pub to spend some
time in. A handsome, big-boned
townhouse just off the main shopping
drag which combines the warmth and
hospitality of the traditional tavern
with the serious cooking chops of the
Tavern 2.0."

–Tracey MacLeod, *The Independent*

What we say
An ambitious menu of big-hearted,
multifaceted dishes served in a
beautiful old Victorian savings bank
that is beautifully decorated, incredibly
comfy and bright, and full of artwork
that mirrors the beauty and range of
the cooking.

Grain Colchester

Essex

What
Global, seasonal, small-plate
restaurant

Who
Paul Wendholt & Jordan
Sidwell, chefs

When
Dinner Tuesday, lunch
& dinner, Wednesday to
Saturday

Address
11a North Hill, Colchester,
Essex, CO1 1DZ

+44 (0)12 0657 0005

grain-colchester.co.uk

Bookings
Phone

Price guide

What they say
"Grain is all about small plates and
big flavours. We work with seasonal
ingredients, food trends, and foraging
to create an ever-changing and
innovative menu. We like to use
some unusual combinations in our
cooking to enlighten our diners to
new flavour pairings. In the past,
foraging our own ingredients has
been a very sustainable method of
selecting ingredients. We use our
own sourdough starter to make our
bread, which reduces the use of raising
agents and creates a more natural and
sustainable product. Our concept as
a whole tends to reduce food waste
naturally – serving smaller portions
means fewer ingredients and the
chance or amount of waste reduced."

Signature dishes
Gnocchi with asparagus, mushroom,
and Parmesan; scorched mackerel with
courgette, watercress, and samphire; and
mango with IPA and grapefruit trifle.

What we say
Citing influences such as The Dairy in
Clapham, Lyle's, and The Clove Club,
these two young chefs, Wendholt
and Sidwell, launched a Kickstarter
campaign to raise money for a
small-plates-focused, modern, British
restaurant in Colchester and they have
taken the place by storm. The whole
hipster sharing thing was pretty new
to the town and they are eating it up.
The bread in particular gets huge raves
and although they admit they could
do more in the area of organic and
ethical meat sourcing, they are already
doing a lot of important things very
well indeed.

Market Bistro

Norfolk

What
Seasonal, sustainable
British food

Who
Lucy & Richard Golding,
owners

When
Dinner Tuesday, lunch
& dinner, Wednesday
to Saturday

Address
11 Saturday Market Place,
King's Lynn, Norfolk,
PE30 5DQ

+44 (0)15 5377 1483

marketbistro.co.uk

Bookings
Phone or website

Price guide

What they say
"Here at Market Bistro we are
absolutely passionate about our
customers, suppliers, the quality of
our produce, and our team. We have
a kitchen garden that is looked after
by our forager and enjoy the diversity
of only using seasonal produce in our
dishes. As much of our produce as
possible is sourced locally and, if not,
only from British farms. For example,
our cocktail made with local sea
buckthorn, fabulous Norfolk wines
(one award-winning), and locally
sourced sea vegetables such as sea
aster, samphire, and sea beet."

Signature dishes
Poached Norfolk quail breast with
confit leg, fermented pearl barley,
savoury custard, and pickled quail egg;
Dingley Dell pork belly, fermented
and barbecued cabbage, pickled and
poached shiitake mushrooms, charcoal
emulsion, black garlic; and sustainably
farmed Sterling White halibut with
purple sprouting broccoli, chicken
wing terrine, broccoli verde, and
broccoli purée.

What we say
This is an old, wonky, low-beamed
building in the heart of the tiny
marketplace, full of an ancient charm
you mightn't expect to go with such
a progressive approach to food and
cooking. Richard Golding was not
classically trained but has a technically
precise and very original style that
regulars adore. The staff are warm
and helpful, the atmosphere is cosy.
In short, it is everything people think
restaurants used to be, but never
really were.

Strattons Hotel

Norfolk

What
Boutique hotel, restaurant, & on-site café-deli offering cool, contemporary style with originality

Who
Les & Vanessa Scott, Hannah & Dominic Hughes, directors

When
Breakfast, lunch & dinner, daily

Address
4 Ash Close, Swaffham, Norfolk, PE37 7NH

+44 (0)17 6072 3845

strattonshotel.com

Bookings
Phone or email
enquiries@strattonshotel.com

Price guide

What they say
"In embracing local produce we are sometimes dealing with very small suppliers. These micro industries may only specialize in one or two different products or supply in extremely small quantities. To work with a supplier and the regionality of our foods, the kitchen has invested in and is constantly researching where we can source produce from and how we can use it on the menu. This leads to a greater respect and appreciation for the achievements of our farmers, dairies, fishermen, and microbreweries."

Signature dishes
Norfolk asparagus with soft-boiled quails' eggs, wild garlic aïoli, pickled mustard seeds, and caramelized almonds; Jacob rare-breed lamb rump with lamb neck and caper croquette, sautéed spring vegetables, salted anchovies, and wild garlic oil; and pan-fried sea trout with salt-baked new potatoes, griddled purple sprouting broccoli, and green sauce.

What we say
Since opening in 1990 they have put local sustainable sourcing at the heart of everything they do, as well as harvesting rainwater to make themselves more or less independent there and eschewing commercial waste collection to recycle almost everything. The whole business is used to showcase local skill and trade, with sculptures in the grounds made from recycled agricultural iron restating the environmental message and illustrating how waste can be used creatively. And get this: Director Vanessa Scott co-wrote *Norfolk's Own Cookbook: Everything Stops for Tea* to raise both the profile of Norfolk food and over £100,000 for Marie Curie Cancer Care. Inspirational.

The Sun Inn Dedham

Essex

What
A quintessential fifteenth-century coaching inn in the heart of Constable Country

Who
Piers Baker, owner & Jack Levine, chef

When
Lunch & dinner, daily

Address
High Street, Dedham, Colchester, Essex, CO7 6DF

+44 (0)12 0632 3351

thesuninndedham.com

Bookings
Website or resdiary.com

Price guide

What they say
"Keep warm by the fires, stay cool on the terrace, all year round there's somewhere to unwind. It is important to us to source produce as local to us as possible and to cut down on the journey from field to fork – because the produce is going to taste better. We buy baby vegetables from three miles up the road, keeping the money in the local economy and establishing long-lasting and great relationships with the growers."

Signature dishes
Wild sea bass with saffron sauce, clams, crab, samphire, and courgette; skirt steak with sour cream, blue cheese, asparagus, pickled shallot, and potato; and tagliatelle with brown shrimp, broad beans, peas, rocket, lemon, and crème fraîche.

What we say
A serious early-modern coaching inn with an elm bar, oak beams everywhere (mind your head), ancient meandering floors, open fires, and food sourced in what we now think of as the most modern, progressive way but which, you are reminded in this delicious temple to Old Suffolk, is the way some people have been doing it for a thousand years.

The Café in the Park

Hertfordshire

What
All-day casual dining with good ethics at the heart of all that they do

Who
Ian & Carly Trisk-Grove, co-founders

When
Breakfast & lunch, Monday to Friday

Address
The Aquadrome, Frogmoor Lane, Rickmansworth, Hertfordshire, WD3 1NB

+44 (0)19 2371 1131

thecafeinthepark.com

Bookings
No bookings taken

Price guide

What they say
"Our founding principle was to create a space which was accessible to our community. The focus has always been on sourcing with integrity – working alongside farmers and producers that treat the animals and people in their care with respect. Additionally, we feel that a happy team will encourage our customers to return again and again, and many of our team have worked with us for many years. We work alongside our team, as part of the team, and would never ask somebody to do a job that we weren't prepared to do ourselves. We want to be inclusive and have many volunteers who work two to eight hours a week; adults with varying degrees of learning difficulties."

Signature dishes
Park salad with British-grown quinoa, beetroot, cauliflower, harissa yoghurt, toasted seeds, dried tomatoes, and herb oil; The Café in the Park burger with brioche bun, piquillo mayo, cardamom-cured pickles, and twice-cooked chips; and rice bowl with wholemeal basmati, lentils, Lebanese tahini, and local yoghurt.

What we say
Not enough is being done by the industry to include people with learning disabilities in every aspect of restaurant life. The Café in the Park is setting an example that others really must follow, and follow soon, if we are to call ourselves a civilized twenty-first-century democracy. On top of that, it's serving delicious, creative food, crafted by a team of eight chefs. Plus, all baking is done in-house to ensure optimum freshness and quality.

Lussmanns

Hertfordshire

What
Five local-driven restaurants with a focus on making ethical & sustainable dining accessible

Who
Andrei Lussmann, owner

When
Lunch & dinner, daily

Address
Waxhouse Gate, St Albans, Hertfordshire, AL3 4EW, plus other locations – see website

+44 (0)17 2785 1941

lussmanns.com

Bookings
Website

Price guide

What they say
"Our menus have been a celebration of provenance since before it became the restaurant marketing buzz word du jour and sustainability is at the heart of everything we do. From sourcing to controlling our impact on the environment – since 2012, Lussmanns has recycled all waste so that nothing goes to landfill. Strict on traceability, unwavering on a commitment to sustainability, and truly vocal about local, Lussmanns offers a menu with nothing to hide and absolutely everything to deliver."

Signature dishes
MSC house fishcake with baby spinach and caper and parsley butter sauce; hunter's linguine with wild rabbit, free-range pancetta, oyster mushrooms, and garlic; and oven-baked paella with chargrilled market vegetables and local halloumi.

What we say
We were impressed with Lussmanns from the moment it first opened in St Albans in 2011. We had walked in on a whim and found a three-tier steel and glass building with a lot of light and a sensible fish and grill-based menu, doing good business for a Monday lunch. So we sat and ate and were impressed. Then we saw notes about its very progressive approach to everything from recycling to stock ordering, which involved trying to throw no fish away at all. "What's the point of buying sustainable fish", the manager said to us, "if you end up throwing it away at the end of the night?" We have been huge fans ever since and very much enjoyed watching the brand expand.

Back to the Garden

Norfolk

What
Farmshop, butcher, deli & restaurant

Who
Delaval Astley, owner

When
Breakfast & lunch, daily

Address
Fakenham Road, Letheringsett, Norfolk, NR25 7JJ

+44 (0)12 6371 5996

back-to-the-garden.co.uk

Bookings
Phone

Price guide

What they say
"Much of the meat and vegetables are sourced from our own organic farm. You can eat under the ceiling of a massive eighteenth-century oak, or, if it's warm, amongst the flowers in our garden, a place of serenity and calm that's good for the soul. Our menu is full of the kind of food we all want year in, year out. Our specials and our Sunday menu are a constantly changing, seasonally-focused celebration of the best of the week or day."

Signature dishes
Full English breakfast with house-made sausages and black pudding, organic eggs, homemade hash browns, mushrooms, and tomatoes; butcher's selection (changes daily depending on butcher recommendations); and *shakshuka*.

What we say
People visiting this breathtaking part of Norfolk, close to the wild and beautiful coast, often stop by Back to the Garden to pick up supplies and stay for a bite of lunch, and then keep coming back forever for the peace, serenity, proximity to nature, and terrific, simple cooking.

The Crown and Castle

Suffolk

What
A village restaurant with twenty-one en suite bedrooms

Who
Tim Sunderland, general manager

When
Lunch & dinner, daily

Address
Market Hill, Orford, Suffolk, IP12 2LJ

+44 (0)13 9445 0205

crownandcastle.co.uk

Bookings
Phone, website, or email
info@crownandcastle.co.uk

Price guide

What they say
"Good food is at the heart of our operation – food that customers like to eat and that respects the seasons and locality. Food that is not just a reflection of the chef's ego but is honest, authentic, and toothsome. The Crown and Castle is a welcoming place which offers thoughtful service and food that is bought, prepared, and served with integrity."

Signature dishes
Kerr's Farm asparagus with herbed ricotta *gnudi* and Parmesan; locally landed cod with *vignarola* (spring stew of violet artichokes, peas, broad beans, and mint); and loganberry jam and frangipane tart with toasted almond ice cream.

What we say
Tim Sunderland voices a concern common to many of our entrants when he says: "Although we do use all leftovers for staff lunches and to make stocks, it would be easier to reduce food waste if local authorities provided any means of properly disposing of it. We struggle to get general rubbish removed, never mind food. We wish the notion of pig swill could be re-introduced, particularly these days when we have to segregate raw and cooked foods anyway". So come on, local authorities: sort out your waste collection. And central government, let's get some movement on bringing food waste back into swill!

Wyken Vineyards

Suffolk

What
A vineyard restaurant with most ingredients & game from within a ten-mile radius of the estate

Who
Carla Carlisle, owner

When
Lunch daily, dinner Friday & Saturday

Address
Wyken Road, Stanton, Bury St Edmunds, Suffolk, P31 2DW

+44 (0)13 5925 0287

wykenvineyards.co.uk

Bookings
Phone or website

Price guide

What they say
"We try hard to keep to our ten-mile radius rule, with wild game from the estate, hogget from our flock of Shetland lambs, salads from our garden, onions, potatoes, and asparagus from the farm, and, of course, wines from our vineyard. Being a community, everyone and everything from staff, farm, garden, shop, restaurant, farmers' market, to our special customers matter deeply to us. We grow what we can and we source from local growers. We started the weekly farmers' market on the farm, which also benefits the restaurant, and we benefit from our ancient woodlands, which supply wild venison year-round and pheasant and partridge in season."

Signature dishes
Asparagus: picked just before service, served either with olive oil and Parmesan or hen's egg and hollandaise; wild venison lightly pan-smoked over Wyken vine prunings and Cromer crab; and wild garlic risotto (wild garlic from local woods).

What we say
Matching wonderful British food to marvellous British booze for longer than anyone can remember, they are committed not just to the Slow Food movement here but to a slow mood movement, too. They don't take tables larger than eight because it disrupts the feeling of the restaurant, nor do they do weddings or corporate events... they are faithful to a loyal clientele that, in return, is faithful to them.

259

Scotland

21212

Edinburgh

What
Edinburgh's only Michelin-star restaurant with rooms

Who
Paul Kitching, chef

When
Lunch & dinner,
Tuesday to Saturday

Address
3 Royal Terrace,
Edinburgh, EH7 5AB

+44 (0)34 5222 1212

21212restaurant.co.uk

Bookings
Phone or email
reservations@21212restaurant.
co.uk

Price guide

What they say
"At 21212 our menu is always evolving, with new dishes coming and going every week. We challenge ourselves to learn something new and experiment with different foods every week, which gives us our dynamic menu. We also make sure we have virtually no food waste, with every part of our ingredients being used in some way (we even use the skin from garlic cloves for stock). Our team is fundamental to the running of 21212, and everybody supports and respects one another. Ultimately, however, our passion lies in our guests' experience. We strive to make sure that from the moment they walk through the door into our microcosm, every detail is perfect in order to make their 21212 experience unforgettable."

What others say
"Some of the most highly characterised, beautifully realised, best-value cooking in the UK."

–Matthew Fort, *The Guardian*

What we say
There is nothing like eating in a grand Edinburgh town house like this, sprawling over many floors, with a magnificent ground-floor dining room, beautiful first-floor lounge with vertiginous ceilings and then four bedrooms to boot. Paul used to run Altrincham's Juniper, one of the great North Western restaurants of the 1990s and early 2000s, and his loyal following here proves that he is still performing at his peak.

bia bistrot

Edinburgh

What
Serving fresh, seasonal, local, sustainable, & homemade food

Who
Roisin & Matthias Llorente, chefs/owners

When
Lunch & dinner,
Tuesday to Saturday

Address
19 Colinton Road,
Edinburgh, EH10 5DP

+44 (0)13 1452 8453

biabistrot.co.uk

Bookings
Phone or website

Price guide

What they say
"We pride ourselves on providing seasonal, sustainable, and homemade food. We are part of the Slow Food Chefs' Alliance, which connects us with producers from the Ark of Taste (created to promote produce that is disappearing and to try and safeguard these unique flavours, e.g. Shetland lamb from Richard Briggs and peasemeal from Golspie Mill).

"We are also part of the 'real wine' movement, a term embracing wines that are made organically, biodynamically, and naturally. By no means precise nor prescriptive, it serves chiefly to highlight growers who work with minimal mediation, ideally to obtain the purest articulation of terroir, fruit, and vintage."

Signature dishes
Confit Borders wild rabbit salad with prunes and fava beans; roasted lamb rump with kale, layered potato cake, and mint jus; and meringue with rhubarb jelly and stewed rhubarb.

What we say
Locals rave about this traditional restaurant with its distressed wooden floors, reclaimed wooden tables, the occasional pew, shiny glassware, quirky art choices, and down-home blackboard specials. The food is affordable and hearty, the service is incredibly friendly, the vibe is relaxed, and their wine game is very strong indeed, with all waiting staff having finished or currently training for their WSET (Wine and Spirit Education Trust) level two.

Cafe St Honoré

What
Cafe St Honoré serves the best Scottish ingredients in an authentically Parisian interior

Who
Neil Forbes, chef director & Joe Simpson, head chef

When
Lunch & dinner, daily

Address
34 Thistle Street North West Lane, Edinburgh, EH2 1EA

+44 (0)13 1226 2211

cafesthonore.com

Bookings
Website or bookatable.co.uk

Price guide

What they say
"Apart from our brilliant and enthusiastic team at Cafe St Honoré, I am most passionate about the producers. Those crazy people who get up so early to feed animals and till the land in all weathers regardless of whether it is blisteringly hot or there is two feet of snow on the ground. It staggers me what hardships these artisans go through for a love of growing and breeding. It is inspiring to see their pride as they deliver, say, dirty root veg with a ruddy-cheeked complexion and look of an outside grafter. The farmer, forager, or monger is essential for Cafe St Honoré to operate."

Signature dishes
Wild garlic croquettes with Katy Rodgers crowdie, pickled organic beetroot, and radish; Belhaven trout with purple sprouting broccoli, capers, preserved lemon, and crushed pink fir heritage potatoes; and Montezuma's organic dark chocolate, either a nemesis or a fondant, served simply with Katy Rodgers crème fraîche, and a dusting of sweet and nutty praline.

What others say
"Honesty, integrity and a passion for his craft."

–Richard Bath, *The Scotsman*

What we say
One of the first fifteen members of the SRA, Cafe St Honoré has placed sustainability at the heart of its operation from the outset and annually scores a rating from them of ninety per cent or better. It is an extraordinary fusing of the virtues of French cooking with all that is best about Scottish produce and hospitality. A rare and exotic jewel.

Cafe St Honoré (p. 261)

Fhior

Edinburgh

What
Fhior – meaning true – is a modern restaurant serving fresh, focused & clean cooking

Who
Laura & Scott Smith, chef patrons

When
Dinner Wednesday & Thursday, lunch & dinner, Friday & Saturday

Address
36 Broughton Street, Edinburgh, EH1 3SB

+44 (0)13 1477 5000

fhior.com

Bookings
Phone or website

Price guide

What they say
"We're fiercely focused on Scottish sustainable sourcing, whatever the season. Menus are ultra-seasonal, adapting to peak availability, freshness, and flavour. Seasonal produce gluts are traditionally preserved (fermented, pickled, salted) and brought back on later menus to add interest. We support small producers specializing in traditional techniques or ancient/rare produce, such as our Orcadian beremeal bread and Shetland black potato. Local wild food foraging is a standard part of each week. Our wine list follows a similar ethos in that it is natural, showcasing independent producers with strong sustainability and low-intervention credentials."

Signature dishes
East Neuk lobster with salted rhubarb and charred cucumber; braised bay gem with smoked hogget and peas; and strawberry with woodruff, rapeseed oil, and seeds.

What we say
We love the energy, passion and even, yes, anger behind this brand new restaurant only just starting up as we go to press. The concept was designed with the reduction of food waste at its heart. They plan to serve a set menu to reduce food waste by limiting the amount of stock needed to support an à la carte menu. Where they do provide an à la carte menu, this will be dictated by what is being served on the set menu. They plan to utilize trimmings and scraps in stocks and sauces or preserve them for future use. And they actively look forward to using less fortunate-looking fruit and vegetables as taste and freshness is paramount.

David Bann

Edinburgh

What
Long-established vegetarian restaurant serving food with an international influence

Who
David Bann

When
Lunch & dinner, daily

Address
56–58 St. Mary's Street, Edinburgh, EH1 1SX

+64 (0)13 1556 5888

davidbann.co.uk

Bookings
Phone or email
info@davidbann.co.uk

Price guide

What they say
"Here at David Bann, we've been perfecting the art of good food and service since 2002. We work with the seasons and our local suppliers as and when possible, highlighting the beauty of vegetarian produce. Although it is not always possible to only use local produce, we strive to whenever in season (from Greencity cooperative in Glasgow), and always prefer to use British artisan cheese."

Signature dishes
Parsnip and blue cheese pudding with pea sauce; spiced quinoa, spinach, hazelnut and walnut courgette wrap; and whisky panna cotta with pear and caramel sauce.

What we say
Still Scotland's leading vegetarian restaurant after more than fifteen years in this excellent Old Town spot just a few steps from the Royal Mile. Its modern, slick interior was in stark contrast to the hippy-dippy look preferred by most vegetarian restaurants when it first opened and perhaps that has kept it feeling so relevant. They have always recycled responsibly and place their commitment to the life vegetarian at the heart of their eco-conscious philosophy.

Gardener's Cottage

Edinburgh

What
A charming Georgian cottage serving dishes made from locally-ourced produce

Who
Dale Mailley, chef proprietor

When
Lunch & dinner, daily, weekend brunch

Address
1 Royal Terrace Gardens, London Road, Edinburgh, EH7 5DX

+44 (0)13 1677 0244

thegardenerscottage.co

Bookings
resdiary.com

Price guide

What they say
"We only use ethically sourced ingredients from local farmers and producers. I'm proud of the mutually beneficial relationships I have built over the past six years with all our suppliers, from small dayboats fishing for mackerel in Dunbar to our organic farmer in East Lothian. My job, as a chef, is to take the best produce I can source and handle it with care and respect to give the diner a true sense of place."

Signature dishes
Dunbar dayboat mackerel tartare with Gullane pepper dulse and fennel cracker with green gooseberries; Grierson's organic mutton loin with asparagus, cucumber, pink fir apple potatoes, yoghurt, and groats; and smoked hay with chocolate and rye teacake.

What we say
A restaurant that is both quirky and outstanding. A haven of good practice and a destination of pilgrimage for foodies across the country, most of them drooling over the famous mutton loin, which they use here for its more intense flavour and better marbling than the younger, more popular lamb. The whole carcass is delivered from an organic farm in Perthshire, then butchered in-house so the entire animal can be used. Preserving the skill of whole-animal butchery is extremely important here. The meat is cooked over charcoal, and served with freshly-dug pink fir apple potatoes from East Lothian, cooked in the embers. A simple garnish of new-season cucumbers, slightly salted, adds freshness, and homemade yoghurt introduces sharpness. One of the great platefuls of the world.

Hendersons

Edinburgh

What
Founded in 1962, Britain's longest-running vegetarian restaurant

Who
Barrie Henderson, general manager

When
Breakfast, lunch & dinner, daily

Address
94 Hanover Street, Edinburgh, EH2 1DR

+44 (0)13 1225 2131

hendersonsofedinburgh.co.uk

Bookings
Website or email
mail@hendersonsofedinburgh.co.uk

Price guide

What they say
"We are passionate about providing fresh and delicious vegetarian and vegan food. We use a variety of organic Scottish ingredients in all our dishes and we also serve organic coffee and use organic milk. Hendersons is a relaxed place with a history of association with the local art and music scene in Edinburgh. In the past we have held art exhibitions for homeless people to display their work, or provided free space for young local artists. Through the decades we have built up a large following who come for the healthy vegetarian and vegan food and for the atmosphere."

Signature dishes
Jerusalem artichoke and kale barley risotto; Hendersons vegetarian haggis with root mash, red wine gravy, wilted spinach, and fresh herbs; and raw blueberry cheesecake made with coconut, hazelnuts, cashews, and maple syrup.

What we say
Founded in 1962, Hendersons is Britain's longest-running vegetarian restaurant and is still striding into the future with some of the boldest environmental initiatives around. All their packaging is compostable and comes from the local Edinburgh company Vegware. They sell many of their organic wines by the carafe to reduce packaging by up to eighty per cent and they upcycle packaging and waste materials for decoration. For example, they use all their pallet wood for cladding walls and building shelves and other decorations. They also recently decorated a wall with the silver bags from their bag-in-box wine – giving a whole new meaning to the phrase "getting plastered".

The Kitchin

Edinburgh

What
Michelin-starred restaurant in Edinburgh

Who
Tom & Michaela Kitchin, owners

When
Lunch & dinner, Tuesday to Saturday

Address
78 Commercial Quay, Edinburgh, EH6 6LX

+44 (0)13 1555 1755

thekitchin.com

Bookings
Email info@thekitchin.com

Price guide

What they say
"I am fanatical about sourcing the best and freshest produce available. I love it when we get produce delivered straight to the restaurant. We often have freshly-caught lobsters from the fisherman's boat, or game which has just been shot that day and brought in by the gamekeeper straight to our doorstep! Sustainability and the sustainability of produce is very important to me. We work closely with the seasons and only use ingredients that are in season. Sometimes the season for certain produce is very short, however you have to embrace the moment and appreciate it while it lasts!"

Signature dishes
Rockpool: local seafood with sea vegetables, ginger, and a Newhaven shellfish consommé; grouse from the Borders with Perthshire girolles, wild lingonberries, and bread sauce; and gooseberry crumble soufflé with vanilla ice cream.

What others say
"Kitchin's 'philosophy', as expressed in his book *From Nature to Plate*, is to take the finest local ingredients and cook them with the classical French technique learnt under his mentor Pierre Koffmann; but to refrain from every trace of pretension. His dishes are complex – and look exquisite – but each ingredient is there to complement and draw out the others rather than to allow him to showboat."

–Matthew Norman, *The Daily Telegraph*

What we say
Tom Kitchin is probably the most famous chef in Scotland – and for all the right reasons.

Wedgwood

Edinburgh

What
Intimate, unique restaurant with a creative approach to Scottish wild food

Who
Paul & Lisa Wedgwood, chef patrons

When
Lunch & dinner, daily

Address
267 Canongate,
Edinburgh, EH8 8BQ

+44 (0)13 1558 8737

wedgwoodtherestaurant.co.uk

Bookings
Phone, website, or resdiary.com

Price guide

What they say
"From the outset, our ethos was placing food first and encapsulating our vision of a perfect night out. We use every part of the ingredient where possible, from making haggis using every part of the animal, whether it be rabbit, pigeon, or venison, to our top-to-tail leek dish which began with tempura root and finished with a risotto of the greens. This minimizes our food waste and ensures we are always being creative with our cooking."

Signature dishes
Lobster thermidor crème brûlée with smoked pepper dulse, bloody Mary sorbet, Parmesan shortbread, and caviar; Scotch beef tartare, with kombu, soy, shaved egg, scurvy grass, and bone marrow crumb; and loin of Perthshire venison with its own haggis, cocoa carrots, and pickled cabbage.

What others say
"Come for the bone marrow popcorn and stay for the parsnip crème brûlée with thyme ice-cream."

–Linda Macdonald, *The Telegraph*

What we say
At one end you have a deep-rooted belief in local and sustainable produce and practice (foraging here is not just for show, but an integral part of what they do) with Paul Wedgwood also very active in food education in schools, taking classes of city children out into the local countryside to give them an introduction to wild food and make salad less scary, and at the other end you have a wonderfully chic, fun restaurant in a glitzy part of town. Sheer class.

Timberyard

Edinburgh

What
The very best of seasonal and foraged Scottish ingredients with spectacular natural wines

Who
Radford family, owners

When
Lunch & dinner, Tuesday to Saturday, lunch Sunday

Address
10 Lady Lawson Street, Edinburgh, EH3 9DS

+44 (0)13 1221 1222

timberyard.co

Bookings
Phone, website, or email eat@timberyard.co

Price guide

What they say
"Family members Ben, Jo, Abi, Lisa, and Andrew, along with a fabulous team, are the faces behind Timberyard, an authentic brick warehouse with a south-facing yard for sunny days and a wood-burning stove for colder nights. Ingredients are carefully sourced from local artisan growers, breeders, producers, suppliers, and foragers. To name a few: St Brides Poultry, Sea Magee, Shaws Butchers, Fish Brothers, Ken Holland, Forage & Funghi, Ochil Foods, Burnside, Greencity Wholefoods, Clarks, and Phantassie Organics. We pour only natural wine from small producers and growers from across Europe. Our garden of raised beds supplies fresh herbs and edible flowers to the kitchen and bar."

Signature dishes
Hen's egg with asparagus, goat's butter, truffle, and hemp; bass qith celery, wild leek, apple, clams, and potato; and sea buckthorn with pumpkin and buttermilk.

What others say
"Revolutionary, game changing, paradigm shifting... "

–Joanna Blythman, *Sunday Herald*

What we say
Famed for The Atrium and Blue, the Radford family have installed their son Ben in a restaurant that owes more to Noma and the Nordic kitchen than it does to the whims and distractions south of the border. After all, Scandinavia is no further away than Hoxton, so why not? This was a neglected eighteenth-century building when they found it, bricked up and wet, walls bowing. They renovated it with local builders and tradesmen, preserving the beams and the raw brick, dragging all that was strong and old and local into the modern world with love and commitment – just like the cooking.

Bakehouse Café

Forres

What
Ethically run café & organic bakery promoting local, seasonal slow food & regional artisan producers

Who
David Hoyle, owner

When
Breakfast & lunch, daily, dinner Friday & Saturday

Address
91–92 Findhorn Road, Forres, IV36 3YG

+44 (0)13 0969 1826

facebook.com

Bookings
Phone

Price guide

What they say
"Our wish is to offer food that is healthy and enjoyable to eat, ecologically sustainable, and good for the local economy. We use local seasonal produce from small independent growers and producers for the vast majority of our dishes, and also sell seasonal fruit, vegetables, eggs, and honey, alongside bread from our adjacent organic bakery. We recycle everything that we possibly can, with our food waste going to a biodiesel programme. Being a member of the Bakehouse team is like being in a big, loving family. Many of the people who leave for other adventures find themselves coming back, often time and time again!"

Signature dishes
Taste of India: a vegetarian or vegan *dal*; Cullen skink; and French toast.

What we say
A delightful little café offering good, simple staples with their heart and soul rooted in the slow-food movement and all that is best in ethical eating. They supply their excellent bread all around the area, try to oven-bake (rather than fry) as much they can for the sake of their customers' health, aim to provide as much vegan and vegetarian food as they can, and treat staff and guests alike as part of the family. It doesn't get better than that.

The Flodigarry Hotel

Isle of Skye

What
Hotel with local-produce menu of the best produce that can be sourced from the Isle of Skye

Who
Paul & Bette Temming, owners

When
Breakfast, lunch & dinner, daily

Address
Staffin, Isle of Skye, IV51 9Hz

+44 (0)14 7055 2203

hotelintheskye.co.uk

Bookings
Phone, website, or email
info@flodigarry.co.uk

Price guide

What they say
"Our location is enchanting: we're in the middle of nowhere, the most northerly point on the Isle of Skye. Living and working here in this breathtaking landscape has changed us, not only as a chefs but as people. Our love for food goes so much further than just the taste and the smell. We deeply appreciate the fresh vegetables from the greenhouse, and can see art in the colour of a thirty-five-day-matured piece of beef. Our staff and producers are our heroes. The fisherman, the farmers, our butcher and our grocer, and all those others. We feel we are the best hidden gem of the island if not Scotland; perhaps hard to find but definitely worth the long drive!"

Signature dishes
Isle of Skye-reared twenty-eight-day-hung Highland beef; monkfish served with langoustine and squid ink; and Kilmuir lamb.

What we say
Sometimes you have to go to the end of nowhere to find the beginning of something beautiful. Beautiful like the Old Man of Storr, the Kilt Rock, and the sombre ruins of Duntulm Castle. Or beautiful like the dinosaur footprints and the ribs of twenty-eight-day-hung Highland beef from animals only slightly smaller.

The Three Chimneys

Isle of Skye

What
A world-renowned, five-star restaurant with rooms in the Isle of Skye, Scotland

Who
Shirley & Eddie Spear, owners & Scott Davies, head chef

When
Breakfast, lunch & dinner, daily

Address
Colbost, Dunvegan, Isle of Skye, IV55 8ZT

+44 (0)14 7051 1258

threechimneys.co.uk

Bookings
Phone or website

Price guide

What they say
"From working with a local Skye sea salt producer, to nipping over to Dunvegan Pier to collect creel-caught brown crab, lobsters, and langoustines straight from the fishing boats, we are committed to using the finest local produce and minimizing food miles. Oysters and mussels are raft and rope-grown in Skye sea lochs. King scallops are hand-dived in Loch Sligachan. We use dozens of local suppliers to the business, including buying all our Highland beef, Soay lamb, rare-breed pork, and local wild venison from Orbost Farm, just five miles from the restaurant."

Signature dishes
Dunvegan crab and langoustines; head-to-tail Orbost beef; and Edinbane blueberries with almonds, honey, and lemon curd.

What we say
Critics and guests alike fall over themselves to lavish praise on this extraordinary restaurant with rooms that has made a single virtue of its apparent greatest weakness – its remote location. A recent refurbishment has brushed away the cobwebs that come with thirty-three years of solid service, but the restaurant still retains its modest, croft character, with small rooms, stone walls, and low ceilings. New chef Scott Davies has settled in well, using local ingredients with verve and vigour. Savour drinks after dinner in the lounge of The House Over-By just across the courtyard – with the wood-burning stove, books, and Lewis-men chessboard, occasionally reaching for the binoculars for a spot of bird, seal, and star-watching – this is surely the standout experience.

The Whitehouse Restaurant

near Oban

What
Vibrant and ingredient-led modern Scottish cooking in Lochaline

Who
Jane Stuart-Smith & Sarah Jones, owners

When
Lunch Tuesday to Saturday

Address
Lochaline, Morvern, near Oban, PA80 5XT

+44 (0)19 6742 1777

thewhitehouserestaurant. co.uk

Bookings
Email info@ thewhitehouserestaurant. co.uk

Price guide

What they say
"At The Whitehouse, we absolutely love serving the best local food with heart and innovation. We've created a relaxed and welcoming place for all to feast on our local produce. In 2017, we radically redesigned our menu to cut food waste to an absolute minimum (our chickens eat all non-protein waste and everything that can be composted is). We grow most of our herbs and salad leaves, keep our own chickens, and support local allotment surplus when we can."

Signature dishes
Pressed oak-smoked Mull hough with Mike's pickles, Lochaline lochside wild garlic, and piccalilli; sea water-poached Gigha halibut with wormwood and beach fennel pollen; and Frozen Ardtornish raspberry Bellini with Botanist's gin, house-made raspberry sorbet, champers, and raspberry foam.

What we say
Lochaline is a very remote community consisting of about 180 residents. The Whitehouse is twenty-five miles down a single-track road on the coast overlooking the Isle of Mull. As well as serving incredible dishes, the restaurant works closely with the community, only employing local staff and providing training to encourage confidence and ensure customers are provided with the ultimate experience. They have also worked with the local high school and provided practical work experience for young staff on hospitality courses. For delicious, fresh and exciting fare that aids the community and does its bit to help the environment, a visit to The Whitehouse hits the spot.

The Captain's Galley

Scrabster

What
The beating heart of Scrabster, gateway port to Scandinavia and the North

Who
Jim Cowie, chef/owner & Mary Cowie, front of house/owner

When
Dinner Wednesday to Saturday

Address
The Harbour, Scrabster, KW14 7UJ

+44 (0)18 4789 4999

captainsgalley.co.uk

Bookings
Phone, website, or resdiary.com

Price guide

What they say
"We built Captain's Galley not just on sustainability, but on five pillars: simplicity, integrity, traceability, seasonality, and sustainability. As a chef, I make no distinction regarding imperfections, whether a carrot is bullet straight or bent, it's a carrot, therefore perfect. Having spent all my life in the fishing industry, my love and passion are mostly in sourcing the finest seafood in the world, direct from the local fishermen who just happen to be amongst my closest friends, and who look after me well. So, for me, going out for supplies is mostly a catch up with a true friend."

Signature dishes
Crab risotto; bouillabaisse; and smoked lythe.

What we say
At the height of the recent refugee crisis when displaced people were pouring out of war-torn Syria and landing mostly on the Greek island of Lesbos, a woman called Melinda McRostie, who happened to run a restaurant there called The Captain's Table, took it upon herself to provide shelter, blankets, and food for them. Learning of this, Jim Cowie started fundraising events to support her at The Captain's Galley in Scrabster. He contacted every restaurant in the world named "Captain's Table" or "Captain's Galley" (of which there are over 100) encouraging them to get involved and organize fundraising events in support of their namesake restaurant in Lesbos. Astonishing work.

Killiehuntly

Kingussie

What
A reinvention of the traditional Scottish Highland retreat

Who
Anne Pedersen, owner & Jenny Hutchison, chef

When
Hours change seasonally

Address
Kingussie, PH21 1NZ

+44 (0)15 4066 1619

killiehuntly.scot

Bookings
Email hello@killiehuntly.scot

Price guide

What they say
"We invite you to feel at home, to stop and be still, to take off your shoes, to relax, to sit and laugh in the beautifully designed kitchen, to eat from the garden and the surrounding area. We share dinner at our table, which has a lot of history. We are passionate about design, wildlife, and health. It's about nurture, not service. The dishes I create are packed with flavour from raw vegetables, grains, and foraged items. The ingredients we choose with care, not so for the unblemished carrot, but to know that that carrot has come from care. Following the seasons cements you in a time and place. We take care to ensure the dishes suit the weather and the guests, and the ingredients come from Scotland."

Signature dishes
Smoke-roast Glenfeshie venison with garden salad, pickles, and artichoke purée; dark chocolate and Spey whisky mousse with spruce tip syrup oats; and salted char with crisp skin, seaweed mayo, sorrel, and sea purslane.

What others say
"Think of it as 'hygge in the Highlands'; like staying in the weekend home of a Danish dignitary."

–Lucy Gillmore, *The Independent*

What we say
A unique and breathtaking experience. We love seeing the Nordic influence filtering into Scotland and being redefined as something so specifically theirs. A chance for Scotland to grasp the Scandi nettle (or thistle?) and begin to do things with food and culture that her more populous southern neighbour never can.

Frankie's Fish and Chips

Shetland

What
Purpose-built, offering local & sustainable seafood, low food miles, & premium-quality fresh produce

Who
Valerie Johnson, founder/director

When
Lunch, & dinner, daily, breakfast Monday to Saturday

Address
Brae, Shetland, ZE2 9QJ

+44 (0)18 0652 2700

frankiesfishandchips.com

Bookings
Phone or website

Price guide

What they say
"Frankie's is dedicated to sourcing and serving local and sustainable produce. We offer a large selection of seafood produce which is caught and landed at local markets in Shetland and processed locally. Ninety-eight per cent of these are MSC-certified, and all come from the incredibly rich waters around Shetland, meaning that they are not only sustainably caught or harvested, but that they are very low in food miles. We pride ourselves on our staff training and our staff's extensive knowledge of the products that we offer."

Signature dishes
North Sea haddock and smoked haddock homemade fishcakes; Shetland honey and chilli Blueshell mussels; and local king scallops in garlic and Shetland butter.

What we say
There is definitely something special about being the most northerly fish and chip shop in Britain, but there is something even more special about being the Best Fish and Chip Shop in Britain, which Frankie's was named in the 2015 Seafish National Fish and Chip Awards. Paul Williams of Seafish said at the time, "The competition gets fiercer each year. This year was no exception... but Frankie's Fish and Chips stood out throughout the judging process. Their passion and determination has to be admired." Well, we do. We admire it a lot.

The Bay Fish & Chips

Stonehaven

What
Fish & chip shop located on the seafront in the rural Aberdeenshire town of Stonehaven

Who
Calum Richardson, owner/founder

When
Lunch & dinner, daily

Address
Beach Road, Stonehaven, AB39 2RD

+44 (0)15 6976 2000

thebayfishandchips.co.uk

Bookings
No bookings taken

Price guide

What they say
"Our beautiful Stonehaven surroundings remind us of our responsibility for the environment, and whether the sun is out or the rain is coming in sideways, we want to make sure that our business is efficient, sustainable, and environmentally friendly. Our founder, Calum Richardson, is also dedicated to raising the profile of the fish and chip industry and sustainable businesses in Europe and beyond, disproving stereotypes and promoting fish-frying as a career."

Signature dishes
Classic fish supper; seafood platter; and "The Bay" fishcakes.

What others say
Winner, Independent Takeaway Fish and Chip Shop of the Year. Seafish National Fish & Chip Awards 2013.

What we say
The classic fish supper is a perfect example of their food philosophy and approach to sustainability. Sustainably caught MSC-certified fish is brought in by suppliers (they work so closely together they know the number of the boat it came in from), coated in their homemade, sustainably portioned batter, and then one of their award-winning fryers cooks it in front of you and serves it with chips made from locally grown potatoes and a side of homegrown herby tartare sauce. They also bake and griddle their fish – staying true to their belief that everyone should be able to enjoy a fish supper, regardless of dietary requirements.

277

Wales

The Whitebrook

What
A Michelin-starred restaurant in the Wye Valley where every dish features foraged ingredients

Who
Chris Harrod, chef/owner & Kirsty Harrod, owner

When
Lunch & dinner, Wednesday to Sunday

Address
Whitebrook, Monmouthshire, NP25 4TX

+44 (0)16 0086 0254

thewhitebrook.co.uk

Bookings
Phone or website

Price guide

What they say
"Nestled in the Wye Valley, our location is stunning – you're not likely to stumble upon us! One of the draws is that, thanks to the amazing produce we have on the doorstep, there's a sense that The Whitebrook could exist nowhere else – a gastronomic rural retreat in the peaceful countryside. Our menu has been described as 'the Wye Valley on a plate' because our vegetables are either grown in our kitchen garden, sourced from amazing suppliers just down the road, or foraged from the countryside that surrounds us. I've scouted out producers within a very small radius and have curated a little black book which provides me with the freshest and best quality ingredients from fruit and vegetables to native meat."

Signature dishes
Wye Valley asparagus with hogweed, maritime pine, and hedgerow pickings, Tintern mead; Huntsham Farm suckling pig with caramelized celeriac, pear, and lamb's sorrel; and Cornish cod with clams, radish, kohlrabi, rainbow chard and buttermilk.

What others say
"Had a delicious meal at the one star Michelin @TheWhitebrook. A young chef who once worked five years with me @lemanoir. Bravo Chris. Proud of you."

–Raymond Blanc, @raymond_blanc

What we say
A post-Nordic kitchen commitment to crystallizing time and place on each plate by micromanaged local sourcing and foraging, with a warmth and love for the end product that is more Raymond Blanc than René Redzepi. A wonderful example to us all and an honour to have them in the book.

The Potted Pig

Cardiff

What
Located in a former bank vault beneath the city, with a passion for good food

Who
A collective of talented chefs

When
Lunch & dinner, Monday to Saturday, lunch Sunday

Address
27 High Street,
Cardiff, CF10 1PU

+44 (0)29 2022 4817

thepottedpig.com

Bookings
Website or email
info@thepottedpig.com

Price guide

What they say
"Our aim is to educate our diners through food and drink. Both our food and wine menus are innovative and different, while always conscious to complement the other. In regard to our food menu, we will only use what's in season and of the highest quality and, of course, local. This allows our menu to be ever-changing and exciting. We source our wines from independent suppliers, ensuring there is an exclusivity to our list. Cardiff has some fantastic wild produce to offer that's ours for the picking, particularly rhubarb and wild garlic!"

Signature dishes
Pork, cooked more than half a dozen different ways, including confit pork shoulder and belly (which takes four days to make); whole ham hock; and whole suckling pig that will feed a group.

What others say
"The Potted Pig, located in reconditioned, brick-lined bank vaults, is a jewel. They describe their food as British, with an occasional nod to French classics in one direction and New York grills in the other, and that just about does it. It is solid, gutsy food without dogma and with quite a lot of pig."

–Jay Rayner, *The Guardian*

What we say
Great effort is made at this wonderful place to keep staff fully on top of all there is to know about the food and drink on offer, which includes the little known (by us) fact that gin pairs beautifully with pork. So they stock thirty-six different kinds (and were doing so long before the recent gin boom) including five small-batch Welsh gins. Love it.

Treehouse

Ceredigion

What
Organic food shop
& restaurant

Who
Adam Williams, owner

When
Breakfast & lunch,
Monday to Saturday

Address
Victoria House, 14 Baker Street, Aberystwyth, Ceredigion, SY23 2BJ

+44 (0)19 7061 5791

treehousewales.co.uk

Bookings
Phone or email
info@treehousewales.co.uk

Price guide

What they say
"Good, honest food using the best, freshest organic and locally sourced ingredients at a price that is genuinely affordable to everyone. Using and showcasing local produce is what the Treehouse is about – everyday we create a truly local dish, the criteria being that every ingredient (with the exception of a few herbs and spices – we're not into bland food!) has to have been grown, farmed, produced, or picked in Wales. It can be challenging during the 'hungry gap' when we have swede, meat, eggs, and dairy (and laver bread, of course!), but it proves that a truly national cuisine needn't be just stews and cheese on toast."

Signature dishes
Roast tofu and sweet potato goulash with roast aubergine, apricot, and pistachio couscous; tomato and butternut squash soup with wild garlic pesto; and roast Llwyn Teifi pork shoulder with Ceredigion new potatoes, honey roast carrots, Swiss chard, and Welsh cider gravy.

What we say
What a heart-filling attitude these guys have. It's not just the daily Welsh food challenge, the whole business is based on minimizing waste: produce that is looking a bit tired in the shop is turned into soup, if someone comes in with a glut of courgettes, then courgettes go onto the specials menu. Every aspect of the business comes under environmental scrutiny, from gas and electricity use to van mileage to composting to packaging. Being good is a struggle, and Treehouse is winning.

Enochs Fish & Chips

Conwy

What
Ethical, sustainable fish & chips with a conscience

Who
Danny & Donna White-Meir, owners

When
Lunch & dinner, daily

Address
146 Conwy Road, Llandudno Junction, Conwy, LL31 9DU, plus other locations – see website

+44 (0)14 9258 1145

enochs.co.uk

Bookings
No bookings taken

Price guide

What they say
"We are passionate about sustainability – the whole shebang. The product, place, and people are all important to us. We think that this reflects in our approach to delivering great fish and chips, value, and service. We like to use our local fish when it is at its best and when it's in season, for example lobster caught off the Great Orme's Head, just three miles away."

Signature dishes
Homemade Thai fishcakes; MSC cod and chips (sustainably caught and coated in a house recipe batter with crisp golden chips, and mushy peas); and MSC pesto-crusted haddock (green pesto and golden crumb topping).

What we say
The use of exclusively sustainable local fish at more and more of Britain's fish and chip shops is one of the happiest eco food stories of recent times. But at Enochs they go even further in their commitment to the cause. Nearly all their takeaway packaging is biodegradable, compostable, or recyclable. They have moved to reduce chemicals in all their washing up and their oven cleaner is made from the natural solvents in orange peel. And, after years searching for a healthier frying medium they came upon a "heart healthy" high-oleic sunflower oil to cook their fish and chips, the health benefits of which far outweigh the traditional palm oils and are, of course, much less catastrophic for the environment.

Grub Kitchen

Pembrokeshire

What
The UK's first full-time edible insect restaurant

Who
Andy Holcroft, chef/owner

When
Hours change seasonally

Address
Lower Harglodd Farm, St Davids, Pembrokeshire, SA62 6BX

+44 (0)79 8669 8169

grubkitchen.co.uk

Bookings
Phone or email info@grubkitchen.co.uk

Price guide

What they say
"We are most passionate about innovative, sustainable, and thought-provoking food that not only challenges our preconceptions surrounding entomophagy, but which also tastes great! Turning edible insects from novelty to normalcy and helping to kick-start this exciting new industry is paramount to the future of the innovative food sector. We love rising to a challenge and changing society's perception of insects as food and is one we are winning one meal at a time!"

Signature dishes
Grub Kitchen's gourmet bug burger: VEXo™ (textured insect and plant-based protein) with extra meal worms, crickets, and grasshoppers in a brioche bun with black ant mayonnaise, cheese, coleslaw, gherkins, chips, and salad; conservation-grade Welsh black beef with pulled beef skirt, slow-roast short-rib, ribeye steak, roasted shallots, salsa verde, confit tomatoes, and roast Trecenny Farm new potatoes; and cricket-powder crepes with Lochmeyler Pembrokeshire honey ice cream, bug brittle, and strawberry coulis.

What we say
Coming at you right out of the left field... these guys have heard what we've all heard about the future of animal protein and they are giving it a go. You may laugh now, you may make a little sickly face, but for your children and your children's children it may be the only option. You owe it to them to give it a go!

CAT Cafe

Powys

What
A fantastic café at the Centre for Alternative Technology serving delicious, sustainable, local food

Who
The Centre for Alternative Technology (CAT)

When
Breakfast & lunch, daily

Address
Llwyngwern Quarry,
Machynlleth,
Powys, SY20 9AZ

+44 (0)16 5470 5950

visit.cat.org.uk

Bookings
No bookings taken

Price guide

What they say
"The CAT Cafe is fully vegetarian and offers a wide variety of imaginative vegan dishes, salads, and cakes. We strive to ensure all our ingredients are sustainably sourced, and we use produce grown and foraged on the CAT site in a great number of our dishes. Our café perfectly caters for our visitors, accommodation guests, and the local community and is always very good value for money. Sustainability is at the core of everything we do. The Centre for Alternative Technology (CAT) is a world-renowned environmental education centre that researches and supports greener ways of living. We love experimenting with growing unusual crops and heritage varieties that people might not come across elsewhere."

Signature dishes
Sweet Malaysian curry; vegetable frittatas; and a wide range of delicious salad dishes.

What we say
A really kind, nurturing space offering well thought-out and nutritious vegetarian and vegan food to visitors, from a charity at the front line of the environmental effort.

The Felin Fach Griffin

Powys

What
A dining pub with rooms near the book town of Hay-on-Wye

Who
Charles & Edmund Inkin, owners, & Julie Bell, general manager

When
Lunch & dinner, daily

Address
Felin Fach, Brecon,
Powys, LD3 0UB

+44 (0)18 7462 0111

felinfachgriffin.co.uk

Bookings
Phone, website, or resdiary.com

Price guide

What they say
"The Welsh Borders is home to farmers producing great ingredients. Welsh beef and lamb, game from local estates, cheeses from world-renowned dairies. And, like so many things, food is best kept simple. Menus change daily and seasonally. In winter, you might have venison from the nearby Welsh Venison Centre or, in summer, Welsh lamb with peas picked that morning from our own kitchen garden. Our garden team takes the concept beyond what we could have hoped for, turning our food miles into food paces. The best strawberries we've tasted. Red, white, and blackcurrants, raspberries, apples, pears, and medlars. And sticks of pink rhubarb. Peas, broad beans, and salads. Leeks, onions, red and white cabbages, and rows of garlic. And the ingredients for the piccalilli and chutneys that we sell in our little shop."

Signature dishes
Tempura garden broccoli with Stilton, garlic, and salted almonds; pork belly with Glamorgan sausage, peas, and spring onions; and buttermilk jelly with Hereford strawberries, shortbread, elderflower, and chervil.

What others say
"Exceptional anywhere in Europe – in Wales, it was as damn near miraculous as the Angel of Mons."

–A. A. Gill, *The Sunday Times*

What we say
Nestled in some of the most beautiful countryside in Britain, this place offers a welcome return to a time when life was lived a little slower, with all the respect for nature's bounty that entails. A pub restaurant of true spiritual beauty. God's own food in God's own country.

Ynyshir Restaurant & Rooms

Powys

What
Destination restaurant between the mountains of Snowdonia & the beaches of the west coast

Who
Gareth Ward, chef/owner

When
Lunch & dinner, Wednesday to Saturday

Address
Eglwys Fach, Machynlleth, Powys, SY20 8TA

+44 (0)16 5478 1209

ynyshir.co.uk

Bookings
Phone, website, or email info@ynyshir.co.uk

Price guide

What they say
"Our place, our location, and our approach – using the best-quality ingredients from the UK and our local area and making them taste amazing. It is no-bullshit dining with the most flavour we can get out of our dishes. We serve what Chef Gareth Ward calls, 'alternative British snap'.

"Our philosophy is translated into every small dish taking you on a journey of flavours, textures, and ingredients. There is everything to be learned from the people who grow, raise, and catch the food we prepare – the whole animal is used, the whole plant, the milk, and the buttermilk. It is the utmost respect for the ingredients. The suppliers are just as important as the chefs."

Signature dishes
Not French onion soup; wild garlic prawn; and Welsh Wagyu sirloin.

What we say
Their chefs forage for wild garlic, sea vegetables from the beach one mile away, birch sap from trees in their grounds, elderflowers and berries as well as brambles, which are all used both fresh and preserved. This kind of ancient local Welsh practice is married to an openness to new ideas that has seen them develop a relationship with the Wagyu herd of farmer Ifor Humphreys (thirty miles away), whose family has been farming cattle there for generations but knew a good new thing when they saw it. Gareth Ward's use of Japanese techniques and ingredients helps him keep the dishes light but flavourful.

Ynyshir Restaurant & Rooms (p. 283)

Northern Ireland

Mourne Seafood Bar

Belfast

What
Irish seafood in a casual setting in the centre of Belfast

Who
Andy Rea, Bob McCoubrey, Joanne McCoubrey & Sean Fitzpatrick, directors & Gerard Lynott, head chef

When
Lunch & dinner, daily

Address
34 Bank Street,
Belfast, BT1 1HL

+44 (0)28 9024 8544

mourneseafood.com

Bookings
Phone, website, or email
belfast@mourneseafood.com

Price guide

What they say
"As a fish restaurant, we take our responsibility for sourcing seriously. We work alongside Seafish UK to promote the benefits of eating seafood in our restaurant and cookery school. Our mussels and oysters are direct from local shellfish farmers, and our lobsters directly from two boats who practise V-notching. Our menu is determined by what is landed weekly at our local port of Kilkeel and changes daily."

Signature dishes
Carlingford oysters; Mourne seafood casserole, mixed seafood with fresh tomato sauce, potatoes, fennel, thyme, and garlic, served with grilled focaccia; and fillet of hake with saffron risotto cake, samphire, and sauce *vierge*.

What we say
Conveniently located next to the Kelly's Cellars pub, Mourne offers up its excellent and sustainable seafood in traditional style or with a continental or Asian twist. Their very unpompous aim is to serve fresh local seafood at an affordable price and they do it with charm, vigour, and great commitment.

Our Good Things

More Good People
Doing Good Things

The restaurants in this guide support the following farmers' markets, and hero producers, farmers, fishers, bakers, brewers, growers, dairies, and social enterprises as nominated by the restaurants. Because we're all in this together.

Hero Producers

ENGLAND

Greater London

Alliance Wine
alliancewine.co.uk

Androuet
androuet.com

Belu
belu.org

Bibendum Wine
Bibendum-wine.co.uk

Black Hand Food
blackhandfood.com

Bread Ahead
Borough Market
breadahead.com

Bread Factory, The
breadltd.co.uk

Brick Brewery
brickbrewery.co.uk

Brickhouse Bakery, The
brickhousebread.com

Café Direct
cafedirect.co.uk

Cannon and Cannon
cannonandcannon.com

Caravan Coffee Roasters
caravancoffeeroasters.co.uk

Cheese Merchant, The
cheesemerchant.co.uk

Cobble Lane
cobblelanecured.com

Coffee by Tate
tate.org.uk

Columbian Coffee
Company, The
thecolombiancoffeeco.org

Dusty Knuckle, The
thedustyknuckle.com

Dynamic Vines
dynamicvines.com

E5 Bakehouse
e5bakehouse.com

East London Liquor Company
eastlondonliquorcompany.com

Ellis Wines
elliswines.co.uk

England Preserves
englandpreserves.co.uk

Exmouth Coffee Company,
The
exmouthcoffee.co.uk

Fields, Morris & Verdin
fmv.co.uk

Forty Hall Farm
fortyhallfarm.org.uk

Good and Proper Tea
goodandpropertea.com

Gringa Dairy
gringadairy.com

Ham and Cheese Company,
The
thehamandcheeseco.com

Hamish Johnstone Fine
Cheeses
hamishjohnstone.com

Hawkes Brewing Company
wearehawkes.com

HG Walter
hgwalter.com

Indie Ecology
indieecology.com

James Knight of Mayfair
james-knight.com

Jing Tea
jingtea.com

Kernel Brewery, The
thekernelbrewery.com

La Latteria
lalatteria.co.uk

Lea & Sandeman
leaandsandeman.co.uk

Liberty Wines
libertywines.co.uk

London Beer Factory, The
thelondonbeerfactory.com

London Bio Packaging
londonbiopackaging.com

Maisons Marques et
Domaines
mmdltd.com

Mash Purveyors
mashpurveyors.com

Minicrops
minicrops.com

Moxon's Fishmongers
moxonsfreshfish.com

Natoora
natoora.co.uk

Natural Born Wine
naturalbornwine.com

Neals Yard Dairy
nealsyarddairy.co.uk

Newcomer Wines
newcomerwines.com

Newton & Pot
newtonandpott.co.uk

OrganicLea
organiclea.org.uk

Porchetta & Grill
porchettaandgrill.com

Premier Fruits
premierfruits.com

Red Church Brewery
redchurch.beer

Red Squirrel Wine
redsquirrelwine.com

Rubies in the Rubble
rubiesinthrrubble.com

Secret Smokehouse
secretsmokehouse.co.uk

Soap Co., The
thesoapco.org

Southbank Fresh Fish
southbankfreshfish.co.uk

St Mary's Brewery
stmarysbrewery.co.uk

Twickenham Fine Ales
Twickenham-fine-ales.co.uk

Upper Scale, The
Billingsgate Market
theupperscale.co.uk

Vino Beano, The
thevinobeano.com

Whiteheath Farm
whiteheathfarm.weeby.com

Wholegood
wholegood.co.uk

Wildes Cheese
wildescheese.co.uk

Woods Food Service
woodsfoodservice.co.uk

SOUTH EAST

Brighton

Bird & Blend Tea
birdandblendtea.com

Brighton and Newhaven
Fish Sales
brighton-fish-sales.co.uk

Fin and Farm
finandfarm.co.uk

Infinity Foods
infinityfoodswholesale.coop

Red Roaster Coffee
redroaster.co.uk

Saddlescombe Farm
camillaandroly.co.uk

Berkshire
Copas Farm
copasfarms.co.uk

Vicar's Game
vicarsgame.co.uk

Buckinghamshire
Chapel Down Brewery
chapeldown.com

Chart Farm
chartfarm.com

Chegworth Valley
chegworthvalley.com

Kingsdown Water
kingsdownwater.co.uk

M&J Seafood
mjseafood.com

Michael's Wholefoods
michaelswholefoods.co.uk

Simpson's Wine
simpsonswine.com

Timpson's Small Holding
timpsonssmallholding.com

Vale Brewery
valebrewery.co.uk

Watt's Farms
wattsfarms.co.uk

Wild Bread
wildbread.org

Hampshire
Chalkstream Farms
chalkstreamfoods.co.uk

Fluffets Farm
fluffetsfarm.co.uk

Hattingley Valley Wines
hattingleyvalley.co.uk

Kelmscott Country Pork
kelmscottcountrypork.co.uk

Laverstoke Park Farm
laverstokepark.co.uk

Naked Jam
naked-jam.co.uk

Parsonage Farm
parsonage-farm.co.uk

Raimes
raimes.co.uk

Vintage Roots Ltd
vintageroots.co.uk

Violife Foods
vegancheese.co.uk

Hertfordshire
Chiltern Fish & Game
chilternfishandgame.co.uk

Kent
Forager Ltd.
forager.org.uk

Hush Heath Estate
and Winery
hushheath.com

Micro Roastery
microroastery.co.uk

Walmestone Growers
walmestonegrowers.co.uk

Oxfordshire
King Stone Dairy
rollrightcheese.com

Mr Finn's
mrfinns.co.uk

Oxford Wine Company
oxfordwine.co.uk

Paddock Farm
paddock.fm

Windrush Valley Goat Dairy
windrushvalleygoatdiary.
wordpress.com

Wood Brothers Distillery
woodbrosdistilling.com

Surrey
Ham and Cheese Company,
The
thehamandcheeseco.com

Hogs Back Brewery
hogsback.co.uk

Imbham Farms
imbhamfarmgranary.com

Les Caves de Pyrene UK
lescaves.co.uk

One Gin
thespiritofone.com

Thames Side Brewery
thamessidebrewery.co.uk

Sussex
Clayton Organic Farm
claytonorganicfarm.com

Court Garden Vineyard
courtgarden.com

Davenport Vineyards
davenportvineyards.co.uk

Goodwood Home Farm
goodwood.com

Hammerpot Brewery
hammerpot-brewery.co.uk

Judges Bakery
judgesbakery.com

Maynard's Farm
maynardsfarm.co.uk

NamaYasi Japanese Farm
namayasi.co.uk

Nutbourne Vineyards
nutbournevineyards.com

Rookery Farm
rookeryfarm.com

Stopham Vineyard
stophamvineyard.co.uk

SOUTH WEST

Bristol
Arthur David
arthurdavid.co.uk

Bristol Beer Factory
bristolbeerfactory.com

Bristol Cheesemaker, The
Bristol-cheese.co.uk

Bristol Dry Gin
bristoldrygin.com

Community Farm, The
thecommunityfarm.co.uk

Essential Trading
Co-operative
essential-trading.co.uk

Extract Coffee Roasters
extractcoffee.co.uk

Frank Water
frankwater.com

Homewood Cheeses
homewoodcheeses.co.uk

Lye Cross Farm
lyecrossfarm.co.uk

Roasted Rituals Coffee
roastedritualscoffee.com

RS Wines
rswines.co.uk

Severn Project
thesevernproject.org

Vine Trail
vinetrail.co.uk

Wogan Coffee
wogancoffee.com

Xisto Wines
xistowines.com

Cornwall
Bosavern Community Farm
bosaverncommunityfarm.
org.uk

Cornish Bunch, The
thecornishbunch.co.uk

Cornish Crown Brewery
cornishcrown.co.uk

Cornish Duck Company
cornishduck.com

Curgurrell Farm
curgurrellfarmshop.co.uk

Fal Oysters
faloyster.co.uk

Flying Fish Seafood
flyingfishseafoods.co.uk

Good Earth Growers
goodearthgrowers.org

Hanson Fine Foods
hansonfinefoods.co.uk

Harbour Brewing Company
Ltd
harbourbrewing.com

Harvey Bros
stivesmeat.co.uk

Matthew Stevens
matthewstevens-cornishfish.
co.uk

Murt's Shellfish
murtsshellfish.co.uk

Newlina Eco Gardens
newlinaeco-gardens.co.uk

Origin Coffee Roasters
origincoffee.co.uk

Padstow Brewing Company
padstowbrewing.co.uk

Padstow Kitchen Garden
padstowkitchengarden.co.uk

Philip Warren Butchers
philipwarrenbutchers.co.uk

Portscatho Fish
portscathofish.co.uk

Primrose Herd
primroseherd.co.uk

Slight Hill Farm
slighthill.weebly.com

Splattenridden Farm
splattenridden.co.uk

St Ewe Farm
stewe.co.uk

St Ives Cider
stivescider.co.uk

Trevibban Mill
trevibbanmill.com

Trink Dairy
trinkdairy.co.uk

Warrens Bakery
warrensbakery.co.uk

Wild Harbour
wildharbour.co.uk

Wild Smoked
wildsmoked.co.nz

Williams Dairy
williamsdairy.co.uk

Wrecking Coast Distillery
thewreckingcoastdistillery.
com

Yallah Coffee
yallahcoffee.co.uk

Cotswolds
Bottlegreen Drinks
bottlegreendrinks.com

Burkes Beers
burkesbeers.co.uk

Cotswold Gold
cotswoldgold.co.uk

SaltPig Curing Company Ltd.
saltpigcuring.co.uk

Devon
Ashridge Cider
ashridgecider.co.uk

Bake House Salcombe, The
bakehousesalcombe.co.uk

Barnaby's Brewhouse
barnabysbrewhouse.com

Britannia of Beesands
britanniashellfish.co.uk

Cabrito Goat
cabrito.co.uk

Creedy Carver
creedycarver.co.uk

Devil's Choice Seafood
devilschoice.co.uk

Devon Rose Farm
devonrose.com

Favis of Salcombe
favis-os.com

Forest Produce
forestproduce.com

GR Fine Foods
grfinefoods.co.uk

Haye Farm
hayefarmdevon.co.uk

Henderson Seafood
hendersonseafood.co.uk

Heron Valley
heronvalley.co.uk

Higher Hacknell Farm
higherhacknell.co.uk

Husbandry School, The
husbandry.co.uk

Kingfisher Brixham
kingfisherbrixham.co.uk

Langridge Organic
langridgeorganic.com.uk

Luscombe Drinks
luscombe.co.uk

Lyme Bay Winery
lymebaywinery.co.uk

Modern Salad Grower, The
themodernsaladgrower.co.uk

Piper's Farm
pipersfarm.co.uk

Riverford
riverford.co.uk

Salcombe Brewery
salcombebrewery.com

Salcombe Dairy
slacombedairy.co.uk

Sharpham
sharpham.com

Sladesdown Farm
sladesdownmeat.co.uk

Sole of Discretion
soleofdiscretion.co.uk

Trill Farm
trillfarm.co.uk

Dorset
La Chasse
lachasselimited.co.uk

Portland Shellfish
portlandshellfish.co.uk

Wessex Conservation Grazing
wessexconservationgrazing.
co.uk

Wrights Dairies
wrights-dairies.co.uk

Gloucestershire
Bibury Trout Farm
biburytroutfarm.co.uk

Butt's Farm Rare Breeds
buttsfarmrarebreeds.co.uk

Cerney Cheese
cerneycheese.co.uk

Coln Valley Smokery
colnvalley.co.uk

Cotswold Brew Company
cotswoldbrewco.co.uk

Cotswold Curer, The
thecotswoldcurer.co.uk

Cotswold Distillery
cotswolddistillery.com

Cotswold Kids Meat
cotswoldkidsmeat.com

Cotteswold Dairy
cotteswold-dairy.co.uk

Court Farm Shop
courfarmshop.co.uk

Donnington Brewery
Donnington-brewery.com

Eastleach Downs Organic
Farm
eastleachdowns.co.uk

Ethical Addictions
eacoffee.co.uk

Just Kidding
cotswoldkidmeat.com

Local Yolks
localyolks.co.uk

New Wave Seafood
new-wave.co.uk

North Cotswold Brewery
northcotswoldbrewery.co.uk

Portway Farm Shop
portwayfarmshop.co.uk

R Oil
r-oil.co.uk

Severn and Wye Smokery
severnandwye.co.uk

Shipton Mill
shipton-mill.com

Sibling Distillery
siblingdistillery.com

Stroud Brewery
stroudbrewery.co.uk

Three Choirs Vineyard
three-choirs-vineyard.co.uk

Todenham Manor Farm
todenhammanorfarm.co.uk

Vin Est Wines
vin-est.com

Winstones Ice Cream
winstonesicecream.co.uk

Somerset
Somerset Cider Brandy
somersetciderbrandy.com

Strode Valley Organics
strodevalleyorganics.org

Walter Rose & Son
walterroseandson.co.uk

Westcombe Dairy
westcombedairy.com

Westcountry Foods
westcountryfoods.com

Wooley Park Farm
wooleyparkfarm.co.uk

Yeo Valley
yeovalley.co.uk

Wiltshire
Andrew Barclay
andrewbarclaybutcher.com

Bath Harvest Oils
bathharvestoils.co.uk

Bradley's Juice
bradleysjuice.co.uk

Buttle Farm
buttlefarm.co.uk

Castle Farm Organics
castlefarmorganics.co.uk

Castlemead Poultry
castlemeadpoultry.co.uk

De Luca Mozzarella
delucamozzarella.com

Easy Jose Coffee
easyjosecoffee.co.uk

Godminster Cheese
godminster.com

Harry's Cider Company
harryscidercompany.co.uk

Honey and Daughter Cider
honeyscider.co.uk

Hurdlebrook Farm
hurdlebrook.co.uk

Ivy House Dairy
ivyhousefarmdairy.co.uk

Kensons Farm
kensonsfarm.wordpress.com

Lievito Bakery
lievito.co.uk

Lovejoys Wholesale
lovejoyswholesale.com

Montgomery Cheese
montgomerycheese.co.uk

Pilton Cider
piltoncider.com

WEST MIDLANDS

Herefordshire
Huntsham Court Farm
huntsham.com

Sixteen Ridges Vineyard
sixteenridges.co.uk

Shropshire
Augernik Fruit Farm
augernikfruitfarm.weebly.com

B. Fresh Juices
b-fresh.co.uk

Warwickshire
Aubrey Allen
aubreyallen.co.uk

Barry the Butcher
barrythebutcher.co.uk

NORTH WEST

Cheshire
Cheshire Brewhouse, The
cheshirebrewhouse.co.uk

Forest Gin
forestgin.com

Walk Mill
walkmillflour.co.uk

Cumbria
Cartmel Valley Game Supplies
cartmelvalleygamesupplies.
com

Caterite Food Service
caterite.co.uk

Higginson's of Grange
higginsonsofgrange.co.uk

Lake District Farmers
lakedistrictfarmers.co.uk

Low Sizergh Barn
lowsizerghbarn.co.uk

McClures
wmcclure.co.uk

Slack House Farm
slackhousefarm.co.uk

Thornby Moor Diary
thornbymoordairy.co.uk

Udale Specialty Foods
udale.com

Lancashire
Courtyard Dairy, The
thecourtyarddairy.co.uk

Leagram Organic Dairy
cheese-experience.com

Pugh's Piglets
pughspiglets.co.uk

Real Lancashire Black
Pudding Co
reallancashireblackpuddings.
co.uk

Wellocks
wellocks.co.uk

Manchester
Black Cat Cakery, The
theblackcatcakery.com

Cowherds
cowherds.org.uk

Didsbury Gin
didsburygin.com

Dunham Massey Brewing
Company
dunhammasseybrewing.co.uk

First Chop Brewing
firstchop.co.uk

Heart and Graft Coffee
heartandgraft.co.uk

Ice Shack
iceshack.co.uk

Manchester Veg People
vegpeople.org.uk

R Noone & Son Ltd
rnooneandson.co.uk

NORTH EAST

Newcastle
Beckleberrys
beckleberrys.co.uk

Charlotte's Butchery
charlottesbutchery.com

Deli-fresh
delifreshltd.co.uk

Gilchester's Organics Ltd.
gilchesters.com

Muddy Fingers Pottery
muddyfingerspottery.com

YMCA Newcastle/Urban
Mushrooms
ymcanewcastle.com
/urban-mushrooms

County Durham
Hodgson Fish
hodgsonfish.co.uk

Medomsley Bangers
medomsleybangers.wixsite.
com

Liverpool
Adam's & Russell
adamsandrussell.co.uk

Liverpool Craft Beer Co.
liverpoolcraftbeer.com

Northumberland
Borderfields
borderfields.co.uk

Carroll's Heritage Potatoes
heritage-potatoes.co.uk

Chain Bridge Honey Farm
chainbridgehoney.com

Doddington Dairy
doddingtondairy.co.uk

Lindisfarne Oysters
lindisfarneoysters.co.uk

Northumberland Pedigree
Milk and Cream
northumbrianpedigree.com

Northumberland Sausage
Company
northumbriansausagecom-
pany.co.uk

Rothbury Bakery
rothburybakery.com

Sunny Hill Free Range Eggs
sunnyhilleggs.com

Tyne and Wear
Hop Garden, The
thehopgarden.toucansurf.com

Ravensworth Grange Farm
ravensworthgrangefarm.co.uk

YORKSHIRE &
THE HUMBER

Acorn Brewery
acorn-brewery.co.uk

Farmison & Co.
farmison.com

Ginger Pig, The
thegingerpig.co.uk

Magic Rock Brewing
magicrockbrewing.com

Northumbrian Pedegree
northumbrianpedegree.co.uk

Smales Fishmongers
smales.co.uk

Suma Wholefoods
sumawholesale.com

Swaledale Foods
swaledalefoods.co.uk

Taste Tradition
tastetradition.co.uk

Vinceremos Organic Wines
& Spirits
vinceremos.co.uk

Whiteley's Farm
whiteleysfarm.blogspot.com

EAST MIDLANDS

Dutch Eel Company
detcheel.com

Johnny Pusztai
johnnypusztai.com

Kitsch Hen, The
the-kitsch-hen.co.uk

Launde Farm Foods
laundefarmfoods.co.uk

Lincoln Russet
lincolnrusset.co.uk

EAST

Cambridge
Bacchanalia Wine Merchants
winegod.co.uk

Cambridge Distillery, The
cambridgedistillery.co.uk

Cambridge Organic Food
Company
cofco.co.uk

Cambridge Wine Merchants
cambridgewine.com

Essex
Fisher & Woods
fisherandwoods.co.uk

Kandula Tea
kandulatea.com

Rare Breed Meat Company,
The
therarebreedmeatcompany.
co.uk

Sarah Greens Organics
sarahgreensorganics.co.uk

Select Butchery
selectbutchery.co.uk

Thunderley Hall Farm
thunderleyhallfarm.com

Wicks Manor Farm
wicksmanor.com

Hertfordshire

Cambridge Juice Company
cambridgejuicecompany.com

Duchess Farms
duchessoil.co.uk

Fern Verrow
fernverrow.com

Mad Squirrel Brewery
madsquirrel.uk

Marrfish
marrfish.co.uk

Stickleback Fish
sticklebackfish.co.uk

Wobbly Bottom Farm
wobblybottomfarm.co.uk

Norfolk

Bonallack Great Granola
greatgranola.co.uk

Bray's Cottage Pork Pies
perfectpie.co.uk

Leigh's Bees
leighsbees.co.uk

Mrs Temple's Cheese
waisingham.co

Norfolk Quail
norfolkquail.co.uk

Savory & Savory Eggs
norfolkquail.co.uk

Suffolk

Crystal Waters Ltd
onlinefish.co.uk

Dingley Dell
dingleydell.com

E. W. Revett & Son
revett.co.uk

Frank & Earnest Coffee
Roasters
fandecoffee.co.uk

Hodmedod
hodmedods.co.uk

James White Drinks
jameswhite.co.uk

K. W. Clarke Family Butchers
kwclarke.co.uk

Maple Farm, The
maplefarmkelsale.co.uk

Marybelle Dairy
Marybelle.co.uk

Nethergate Brewery
nethergate.co.uk

Pinney's of Orford
pinneysoforford.co.uk

Pump Street Bakery
pumpstreetbakery.com

Salter & King Butchers
salterandking.co.uk

Smashing Wines
smashingwines.co.uk

Sutton Hoo Chicken
suttonhoochicken.co.uk

SCOTLAND

Edinburgh

Armstrong's of Stockbridge
armstrongsofstockbridge.
co.uk

Secret Herb Garden
secretherbgarden.co.uk

Vegware
vegware.com

Highlands

Ardgay Game
ardgaygame.co.uk

Black Isle Dairy
blackisledairy.co.uk

Coast & Glen
coastandglen.com

Golspie Mill
golspiemill.co.uk

Highland Fine Cheeses
hf-cheeses.com

Highlands Wholefoods
Workers Cooperative
highlandswholefoods.co.uk

McLeod Organics
mcleodorganics.co.uk

Really Garlicky Company, The
reallygarlicky.co.uk

Wester Ross Fisheries, Nairn
wrs.co.uk

Rest of Scotland

Blackface Meat Company
Scotland, blackface.co.uk

Briggs Shetland Lamb
briggs-shetlandlamb.co.uk

Burnside Farm Foods
burnsidefarmfoods.co.uk

Gigha Halibut
gighahalibut.co.uk

Greencity Wholefoods
greencity.coop

MacDuff Beef, Wishaw
macduffbeef.co.uk

Mossgiel Farm
mossgielfarm.co.uk

Teeny Weeny Farm, The
flowersfromthefarm.co.uk

Westfield Farms
westfieldspelt.co.uk

WALES

Acre Hill Estates
acrehillestates.co.uk

Coates and Seeley
coatesandseeley.com

Daphne's Original Welsh
Lamb
daphnesoriginalwelshlamb.
co.uk

Dyfi Distillery
dyfidistillery.com

Farmer Tom Jones
farmertomjones.com

Felin Ganol Watermill
felinganol.co.uk

Forest Coal Pit Farm
forestcoalpitfarm.co.uk

Go Fishguard Bay
gofishguard.co.uk

Ifor's Welsh Wagyu
iforswelshwagyu.co.uk

Loka Polly
lokapolly.co.uk

Nantclyd Organic Farm
nantclydfarm.co.uk

Rhug Estate
rhug.co.uk

Skyborry Cider
skyborrycider.co.uk

Trealy Farm
trealyfarm.com

Trehill Farm
trehillfarm.co.uk

Wild Horse Brewing Company
wildhorsebrewing.co.uk

NORTHERN IRELAND

Broighter Gold
broightergold.co.uk

Carlington Oyster Company
carlingfordoystercompany.ie

Glenarm Organic Salmon
glenarmorganicsalmon.com

Hannan Meat
hannanmeats.com

Social Enterprises

Action Against Hunger
actionagainsthunger.org

Ali Forney Centre, The
aliforneycentre.org

Alzheimer's Research UK
alzheimersresearchuk.org

Amantani
Amantani.org.uk

Ambitious about Autism
ambitiousaboutautism.org.uk

Baby Quest Foundation
babyquestfoundation.com

British Hen Welfare Trust
bhwt.org.uk

Camel Valley Vineyard
camelvalley.com

Children's Society, The
childrenssociety.org.uk

Citadel, The
citadel.org.uk

Clarity Enterprises
clarity.org.uk

Clink, The
theclinkcharity.org

Crisis
crisis.org.uk

Electric Umbrella
electricumbrella.co.uk

Fareshare
fareshare.org.uk

Felix Project, The
thefelixproject.com

Fisherman's Mission
fishermansmission.org.uk

Food Made Good
foodmadegood.org

Food Newcastle
foodnewcastle.org

Fortune Centre of Riding
Therapy, The
fortunecentre.org

Grocery Aid
groceryaid.org.uk

Hands Up Foundation
handsupfoundation.org

Honey Pot Children's
Charity, The
honeypot.org.uk

Hospitality Action
hospitalityaction.org.uk

House of St Barnabas, The
hosb.org.uk

Keats Community Organics
London

Key4Life
key4life.org.uk

Kitchen Social
mayorsfundforlondon.org.uk/
kitchen-social-great-things-
to-eat-and-do/

Made in Hackney
madeinhackney.org

Magic Breakfast
magicbreakfast.com

National Lobster Hatchery
nationallobsterhatchery.co.uk

No Kid Hungry
nokidhungry.com

Not Just Soup
notjustsoupkitchen.co.uk

Novus
novus.ac.uk

Pink Plates
breastcancercare.org.uk

Project Waterfall
projectwaterfall.org

Refugee Community Kitchen
refugeecommunitykitchen.
com

Roman River Festival
romanrivermusic.org.uk

Rucksack Appeal, The
rucksackproject.org

Scan Appeal
scannappeal.org.uk

Sick Children's Trust, The
sickchildrenstrust.org

Soil Association
soilassociation.org

Southampton Hospital
Charity
southamptonhospitalcharity.
org

Spartens Community Football
Academy
spartenscfa.com

Spires
spires.org.uk

Spitalfields Crypt Trust
sct.org.uk

Springboard Charity, The
charity.springboard.uk.net

Square Food Foundation
squarefoodfoundation.co.uk

Switchback
switchback.org.uk

Teenage Cancer Trust
teenagecancertrust.org

Happy Hippie Foundation,
The
happyhippies.org

Thornage Hall Camphill
community
thornagehall.co.uk

Wallace & Gromit's
Children's Charity
wallaceandgromitcharity.org

WaterAid
wateraid.org/uk

Wood Street Mission
woodstreetmission.org.uk

Working Well Trust
working-well.co.uk

Our Good Thing

The Sustainable Restaurant Association

We believe in celebrating restaurants that serve food which both tastes good and does good. Restaurants that don't just lovingly prepare their dishes, but thoughtfully source their produce as well. Restaurants that take extra measures to ensure their food doesn't harm the land or ocean from which it comes.

That's why ten per cent of the publisher's revenue from sales of every copy of *Truth, Love & Clean Cutlery: A Guide to the Truly Good Restaurants and Food Experiences of the UK* will go to the Sustainable Restaurant Association (SRA), to help food-service businesses work towards sustainability and guide customers towards more sustainable choices.

Founded in 2010, the SRA is a not-for-profit member organisation that accelerates change towards a more sustainable food system. With a mission to make sustainability a part of the DNA of every restaurant, big and small, it's helping thousands of restaurants and the people who work for them become more sustainable. It's also making it easier for customers seeking dining experiences that match their values to find what they're looking for. "Our customers not only want to enjoy high quality food, but also want to know that the restaurants they eat in are managing their business responsibly", explains president of the SRA, Raymond Blanc OBE.

Following a framework that focuses on sourcing, society and the environment, the SRA's sustainability rating and membership programme promotes best practice and healthy competition by awarding restaurants stars if they score a certain percentage or higher. Other initiatives, like One Planet Plate, a campaign that helps diners choose the most sustainable item on more than 1,500 restaurants' menus, and Unwrapping Plastics, the first sector-specific guide to help food-service businesses find alternatives to single-use plastic, steer the future of the food industry on a more positive, planet-friendly path.

The SRA's purpose is to help restaurants be a positive force for change and combat the increasingly urgent problems facing our food system. We were thrilled to work with them in creating the *Truth, Love & Clean Cutlery* restaurant survey, and are proud to support them in any way possible.

thesra.org

The Editors

Giles Coren
Editor

Giles Coren is a London-based columnist and award-winning restaurant critic for *The Times* newspaper. He is author of the bestselling *How To Eat Out*, presenter of two current hit BBC TV series, *Back In Time For Dinner* and *Amazing Hotels*, and is editor-at-large of *Esquire UK*.

Jules Mercer
Associate Editor

Jules Mercer is a food editor at *Time Inc.* (UK). She was an editor for *The Great South African Cookbook* and a contributor to South Africa's *The Sunday Times Cookbook*.

Andrew Stephen
CEO, Sustainable Restaurant Association

Andrew Stephen is the CEO of the Sustainable Restaurant Association, a not-for-profit membership organisation based in the UK, which aids food-service businesses to work towards sustainability in their sector and guides customers towards more sustainable choices.

Index

By location

Index

Acknowledgements

We are grateful to everyone who contributed to the making of *Truth, Love & Clean Cutlery*. We would especially like to thank the respective editors: Jill Dupleix, who came on board from the very beginning and adopted the entire project as fairy godmother; Giles Coren who buoyed us throughout with his brilliant writing and generous humour; Jules Mercer for her unfailing commitment and grace which supported us through many a stressful moment; Alice Waters whose integrity and kindness guided us throughout; Gabriella Gershenson who graciously gathered together the US writing team, and Katrina Power, whose indomitable powers of persuasion spanned forty writers in forty-five countries. To them, we are profoundly grateful.

To the contributing regional writers and editors whose words so beautifully captured the restaurants contained here: Amanda Bahl, Carolyn Bánfalvi, Anna Berghe, Vee Bougani, Nelson Carvalheiro, Javier Sánchez Castro, Larissa Dubecki, Lara Dunston, Jody Eddy, Osayi Endolyn, Wolfgang Fassbender, Devra Ferst, Paula Forbes, Mindy Fox, Nicholas Gilman, Daniel Gray, Dara Moskowitz Grumdahl, Adrian Hale, Nigel Hopkins, Lauraine Jacobs, Bethany Kehdy, Lee Tran Lam, Janice Leung-Hayes, Alexander Lobrano, Joy Manning, Josimar Melo, Natashca Mirosch, Martin Morales, Rebecca Flint Marx, Erin Byers Murray, Rachel Tepper Paley, Lara Rabinovitch, Lara Shunk, Chandra Ram, Hanna Raskin, Carlos Reyes, Leonardo Romanelli, Marjorie Ross, Vir Sanghvi, Laura Shunk, Pietro Sorba, Osavi Endolyn, Tara Stevens, Robbie Swinnerton, Mikko Takala, Aylin Oney Tan, Ole Troelsø, Mac van Dinther, Femke Vandevelde, Max Veenhuyzen, Ronit Vered and Samantha Wood. Thank you, these books would not exist without you.

A very special thank you to Dan Barber, Phil Bingley, Liam Fox, Irene Hamburger, Varun Mehra, Cristina Mueller, Andrea Muhlhausen, and Claire Sullivan, for their kind and generous assistance. Thank you also to Andrew Stephen and the team at the Sustainable Restaurant Association.

Words cannot express how grateful we are to be able to work alongside our generous colleagues at Blackwell & Ruth: Cameron Gibb, Stefanie Lim, Elizabeth Blackwell, Nikki Addison, Olivia Hopkinson and Kate Raven; and our wonderful *Truth, Love & Clean Cutlery* team: Karin Reinink, Shelley White, Jane Curtain and Rose Fooks. We couldn't have done any of it without you.

And finally, to the restaurants and food experiences who agreed to be part of *Truth, Love & Clean Cutlery* – thank you. Your passion and care inspired us to create this project and we are truly thankful for your generosity. We hope this book helps celebrate your outstanding efforts to make the world a better place, plate by plate.

Ruth Hobday and Geoff Blackwell
Blackwell & Ruth

B&R.

Blackwell & Ruth
Suite 405 IronBank
150 Karangahape Road
Auckland 1010, New Zealand
blackwellandruth.com

Visit us at:
Web: truthloveandcleancutlery.com
Facebook: Truth Love and Clean Cutlery
Instagram: @truthloveandcleancutlery
Twitter: @truthloveandCC

Publisher: Geoff Blackwell
Editor in Chief: Ruth Hobday
Design Director: Cameron Gibb
Designer & Production Coordinator: Olivia Hopkinson
Publishing Manager: Nikki Addison
Digital Publishing Manager: Elizabeth Blackwell
Truth, Love & Clean Cutlery Membership Manager: Karin Reinink
Truth, Love & Clean Cutlery website developer: Phil Bingley

ISBN: 978-0-473-43225-6
A catalogue record for this book is available from the National Library of New Zealand.
Printed and bound in China by 1010 Printing Ltd
10 9 8 7 6 5 4 3 2 1

Distributed by Thames & Hudson Ltd, 181a High Holborn, London WC1V 7QX,
thamesandhudson.com

This book is made with FSC®-certified paper products and is printed with soy
vegetable inks. The Forest Stewardship Council® (FSC®) is a global, not-for-profit
organization dedicated to the promotion of responsible forest management worldwide
to meet the social, ecological, and economic rights and needs of the present generation
without compromising those of future generations.